ON THE MODERATION OF REASON IN RELIGIOUS MATTERS

EARLY MODERN CATHOLIC SOURCES

Volume 11

EDITORIAL BOARD

Ulrich L. Lehner
University of Notre Dame
Series Editor

Trent Pomplun
University of Notre Dame
Series Editor

Paul Richard Blum
Loyola University Maryland

Susannah Monta
University of Notre Dame

Jorge Cañizares-Esguerra
University of Texas at Austin

Felipe Pereda
Harvard University

Wim DeCock
KU Leuven

Jean-Louis Quantin
École Pratique des Hautes Études
(PSL)—Sorbonne

Simon Ditchfield
University of York

Erin Rowe
Johns Hopkins University

Carlos Eire
Yale University

Jacob Schmutz
Université Catholique de Louvain

Marco Forlivesi
D'Annunzio University of
Chieti-Pescara

Jean-Luc Solère
Boston College

LUDOVICO ANTONIO MURATORI

ON THE MODERATION OF REASON IN RELIGIOUS MATTERS

Translated by ULRICH L. LEHNER

THE CATHOLIC UNIVERSITY
OF AMERICA PRESS
Washington, D.C.

Copyright © 2024

The Catholic University of America Press

All rights reserved

The paper used in this publication meets the minimum requirements of American National Standards for Information Science—Permanence of Paper for Printed Library Materials, ANSI Z39.48-1992.

∞

Cataloging-in-Publication Data is available from the Library of Congress

ISBN: 978-0-8132-3844-9 (cloth)
ISBN: 978-0-8132-3845-6 (ebook)

CONTENTS

Introduction   1
The Biography of Ludovico Muratori   2
The Muratorian Heritage   9
    De Ingeniorum Moderatione in Religionis Negotio (1714)   10
        Book I   14
        Book II   26
        Book III   29
About This Edition   32

Bibliography   33

Preface   41

Chapter 1: On Knowledge and Truth   51
Which Truths Are Necessary to Know?   51
About the Outstanding Nature of Truth and Goodness   51
Each Truth Can Be Pursued and Acquired   52
Objections against This Opinion Are Refuted with the Help of St. Augustine   55
There Are Two Realms of Truth, Namely Knowledge and Persuasion   57
There Is an Order among Truths   60
Especially the Truths of Religion Must Be Pursued   61

Chapter 2: On Prudent and Imprudent Doubt   63
Is It Necessary to Begin the Search for the True Religion with Doubt?   63
The Necessity of Doubt for the Avoidance of Error and the Danger of Losing the Truth by Doubt   64
The Praise of Prudent Doubt and the Rejection of Imprudent Doubt   67

Chapter 3: On Doubt in Religion   69

Doubt in Religion   69

Not Everybody Is Allowed to Doubt One's Religion   70

Reason and Authority in Religious Questions as Well as Their Importance   71

How to Determine Which Religion Is True   71

Pagans, Jews, and Muslims Must Reasonably Doubt Their Religion   73

The Rational Basis for Their Doubts   74

Chapter 4: On Doubt in the Christian Faith   79

Whether a Christian Can and Should Doubt His Faith?   79

It Seems Licit That a Christian Can Doubt, but It Is Connected with Grave Dangers   80

A Christian Can Doubt, but How Should He Do This and Not Endanger the Gift of Faith?   80

The Truth of the Christian Religion Is Based on Reason and Authority   82

Why Christians Could Reasonably Forgo Doubt and Just Embrace Their Religion in Tranquility   83

In the Catholic Church, Scholarly Research of Religion Is Mainly Done by the Clergy   84

Chapter 5: On Faith and Its Reasons   86

Is Authority or Reason the Beginning of the Acceptance of the True Religion?   86

Phereponus Has Attributed an Absurd Opinion to St. Augustine   87

The Boastful Manicheans Are Refuted   88

Extrinsic Reasons of Faith [*motiva credibilitatis*] Precede Faith: For the Acceptance of Dogmas, One Cannot Demand Demonstrative Proofs   90

The Custom of the Catholic Church Is Praised, Which Does Not Demand Anyone to Believe without Reason   92

The Difference between Knowledge and Faith   94

Miracles Are Extrinsic Reasons   99

Phereponus's Other Opinion That Catholics Demand Belief without Reason   100

Chapter 6: On the Weakness of Reason and Judgment — 110

The Weakness of the Human Mind and of Human Reason 110

How Easily Humans Fail—And the Reasons for That: Negligence of Scientific Education and Lethargy in the Search for Truth 111

Bodily Weakness, Lack of Aids to Find the Truth, and the Abuse of Such Aids 112

Weakness of Memory and Untamed Imagination, Especially When the Mind Is Moved by the Passions 114

The Perversity of the Will 117

Narrowness of Human Judgment, Ignorance, and Obliviousness 118

Choosing the False Principles for Judgment 119

Chapter 7: On the Weakness of Reason and the Acceptance of Authority — 124

The Weakness of Human Reason according to Common Experience 124

Humility Is Necessary for Our Reason to Recognize the True Religion: Wisdom and Strength Must be Asked from God 127

What Is Knowledge, What Is Belief, and What Is Reasonable Faith? 130

The First Principles for the Guidance of Reason and Wisdom in Their Search for True Religion 130

Reason and Authority Prove That Christianity Is the Only True Religion 131

Chapter 8: On Recognizing Christianity as the Only True Faith — 135

The Recognition of the True Religion of Christ among a Multitude of Sects 135

Scripture as the First Repository of Truth 136

The Difficulty of Recognizing True Doctrine through Human Powers 137

The Need for a Divinely Appointed, Visible Interpreter of the True Religion 140

The Catholic Church as the Only True and Infallible Church 142

Chapter 9: On the Necessity of an Infallible Church — 144

Heretics Unjustly Deny the Catholic Church the Gift of Infallibility 144

The Truth of the Matter 145

The Audacity of the Protestant Method and How It Leads to a Myriad of Heresies 146

Praise of the Catholic Method 147

The Inadequacy of Reason for the Interpretation of Scripture
and the Doctrines of Faith 148

God's Commandment to Listen to the True Voice of the Church 150

Chapter 10: On the Plausibility of an Infallible Church 154

Justification of the Authority of the Catholic Church in Matters of
Doctrine against the Objections of Phereponus 154

Believing the Church with Reasons 156

The Protestant Assumption of an Unreliable Authority 157

Their Uncertain Way to Truth 158

The Age of Christian Doctrine and the Number of Believers as
Evidence for the Truth 161

Novelty and a Small Number of Believers as a Sign of Error
Outside the Church 163

Refutation of the Objections of Phereponus 166

Chapter 11: On Reason, Tradition, and Authority 168

The Pernicious Heresies of Socinianism 168

If God Teaches Us, We Must Believe What He Teaches Even if It
Transcends Reason 170

The Punishable Presumptuousness of Reason 172

The Sources from Which the Truth of Christian Doctrine Is Drawn 173

The Authority of Tradition and Its Necessity in the Church of God 174

The Principles of Tradition and Authority 177

Praise of Dogmatic Theology and of Petavius, Whom Phereponus
Should Have Held in Higher Esteem 181

Chapter 12: On the Freedom of Thought 183

The Desire for Freedom of Thought 183

The Threefold Structure of Christian Doctrine 184

One Must Always Ask Whether a Doctrine Has Been Revealed by God 185

The Existence of a Dogma, Its Meaning, and Its Evidence Must Be
Distinguished 187

What Is Allowed to the Human Mind and What Is Not 189

Contents

Chapter 13: On the Limits of Freedom in Theology — 192

The Danger of Writing about Authority 192

The Consequences of Unreasonable Zeal, and the Usefulness of Moderation 193

The Infallibility of the Church in the Proclamation of a Dogma— under Two Conditions 196

Which Dogmas for Contemplation Can or Cannot Require Actions, and Which Can Be Freely Explained? 198

Whether the Question of the Angels as Corporeal or Incorporeal Beings Has Been Decided by the Councils 203

Some but Not All Proofs for Dogmas Always Belong to the Faith 204

On the Freedom of the Human Mind 208

Chapter 22: On the Exegesis of Scripture and the Copernican System — 212

Whether the View of the Astronomers about the Daily Movement of the Earth Contradicts Holy Scripture 212

Holy Scripture Makes Use of Popular Sayings and Images to Express a Certain Truth 214

What Do Expressions Like "the Whole World," "the Ends of the Heavens," "the Sun Becomes Warm" as Well as Other Expressions about the Heavens, the Stars, and the Sun Mean? 215

When Must We Accept the Proper, Literal Sense in Holy Scripture and When Are We Allowed to Use Another Way of Interpretation? 224

Index — 231

ON THE MODERATION OF REASON IN RELIGIOUS MATTERS

Introduction

On the Moderation of Reason in Religious Matters

ULRICH L. LEHNER

Ludovico[1] Antonio Muratori was the Enlightenment's Erasmus. Like the scholar from Rotterdam, he excelled in countless fields of academic discourse—be it the interpretation of poetry, aesthetics, epistemology, historiography, or theology. He fought fervently against all forms of superstition, campaigned for a Christocentric Catholic piety, and maneuvered between ideological factions as a man of tactful moderation.[2] Moreover, he was arguably the most important proponent of

---

1. The editor preferred the modern writing to the ancient form "Lodovico."
2. Cf. Muratori, *De ingeniorum moderatione*, bk. 1, ch. 9, [81]: "Thus, they are convinced they cannot be mistaken in relying on the authority of the Catholic Church, an authority in which reason finds both support and restraint. A support, so that reason may walk along that middle road on which truth is found; a restraint so that reason may be kept from going astray." On the middle road between extreme doubt and credulity, see also ibid., bk. 1, ch. 2, [15]. The imagery of holding a middle and thus moderate course between Scylla and Charybdis is also found in Erasmus of Rotterdam, *The Enchiridion of Erasmus*, trans. Raymond Himelick (Bloomington: Indiana University Press 1963), 46. The Enlightener Benito Feijoo wrote: "The sacred virtue of Religion, conveyed by the Ship of the Church, sails between two opposing shoals: one is impiety and the other superstition. Should it smash into either one, it will suffer a most disastrous shipwreck. Thus, it is necessary to guide Religion through a middle course equidistant from either side. But to maintain this just conduct, it is necessary to keep in mind a warning of utmost importance: the Religion of the common folk is in little

Catholic Enlightenment. Yet, while his writings on Italian history are still widely cited, his theological ideas have long been sidelined as examples of eighteenth-century "liberalism" and found appreciation only in the last decades. This translation contributes to the growing interest in Muratori by making a large section of his influential book *On the Moderation of Reason in Religious Matters* available in English for the first time.

The Biography of Ludovico Muratori

Muratori was born in 1672 in Vignola, in the Italian province of Modena. His parents were artisans belonging to the higher middle class and were thus able to send their gifted son to the Jesuit high school and lyceum in Modena. Ancient Greek, however, he learned from his private tutor, Benedetto Bacchini (1651–1721), only after his graduation. This teacher also inspired his student to study ecclesiastical history. Yet, the young man was not content following merely in the footsteps of established Italian historiography. Instead, he aspired to merge in his works a French emphasis on diligent archival research, exemplified by the monks of St. Maur,[3] a German obsession with philological acuity, and an Anglo-Italian openness to empirical studies into a program for his academic career. After his ordination to the priesthood in 1695, Muratori indeed became a scholar and after a period in the Ambrosiana Library in Milan, found employment as archivist and librarian of the d'Este family in Modena. Over the next decades he published dozens of volumes based on meticulous archival research, both text

---

or no danger from the first shoal; and on the contrary, it is in very great danger from the second. The People, instructed from infancy in what they should believe, never go astray on their own in the direction of impiety. At least, this risk is very remote. I say on their own; this does not mean that they cannot be persuaded by the intimation of impious teachers. Thus, it is sufficient to keep them away from such masters to avoid that danger. On the contrary, the shoal of superstition is so treacherous that to avoid smashing into it, extreme vigilance is required on the part of those who steer the ship." Feijoo, "The Problem of Miracles," in *The Catholic Enlightenment: A Global Anthology* (Washington, DC: The Catholic University of America Press, 2021), ed. Ulrich Lehner and Shaun Blanchard, 85.

3. See Thomas Wallnig, *Critical Monks: The German Benedictines, 1680–1740* (Leiden: Brill, 2018).

editions as well as studies. Yet, his work as a historian formed only a part of his scholarly life.

His first book was in fact a literary study, *On Perfect Italian Poetry* (1706),[4] which was followed by two extremely successful volumes, *Reflections on Good Taste in the Arts and Sciences* in 1708 and 1715.[5] Here he not only presented himself successfully as a polymath who could juggle literature, philosophy, theology, the natural sciences, and the arts, but developed a normative vision of what a well-rounded scholar should look like. Such a "genius" must, he insisted, first and foremost be shaped by the goodness and beauty found in ethics, art, and poetry. Both intellect and will have to aspire to honesty, goodness, and truth, and not honor or profit. The search for truth, however, is often impeded by prejudice and blind faith, which he identified not just with religious credulity but also with philosophical and theological narrowness. After all, the fondness for a particular thinker such as Aristotle easily blinds a scholar for thoroughly assessing contradicting truth claims.[6] "Good taste" in the arts and sciences was therefore not just prudence and aesthetics but a rather holistic program that included the personal commitment of the researcher.[7] He lays out a similarly holistic vision in his *Moral Philosophy* (1735).[8]

4. For the sake of readability, I decided to translate Muratori's book titles in this Introduction even if the books themselves were never translated into English.

5. Ann Caesar and Michael Caesar, *Modern Italian Literature* (Cambridge: Polity Press, 2007), 24–25. Karl-Heinz Braun, "Das Reformprogramm des katholischen Aufklärers Lodovico Muratori," in *Religion und Aufklärung*, ed. Albrecht Beutel and Martha Nooke (Göttingen: Mohr Siebeck, 2016), 707–17.

6. It is not surprising that Muratori identified this mentality with the scholastic style of the time, which he chastised for being too speculative. Consequently, he ridiculed Scotus and only grudgingly acknowledged the value of Aquinas's writings. Cf. also Muratori, *De ingeniorum*, bk. 1, ch. 6, [54]. Benito Feijoo argues similarly, when he dismisses the attempt to use the authority of Aristotle for a defense of misogyny: "Let us now leave aside these proofs, which are derived from Aristotelian doctrines that are either untrue or uncertain, and are of use to women only in arguing with closed-minded devotees of Aristotle who believe whatever their master said," see Benito Jerónimo Feijoo, "In Defence of Women," in *In Defence of Women*, ed. Joanne Barker (Cambridge: Modern Humanities Research Association, 2018), 30–81, at 58).

7. Ludovico Muratori, *Riflesioni sopra il buon gusto . . .* vol. 1 (Venice: 1708), chapter 5, 66–90; vol. 2 (Cologne: 1715), ch. 10 on the problems in theological discourse.

8. Paola Vismara, "Ludovico Antonio Muratori (1672–1740): Enlightenment in

His profound knowledge of different disciplines made him a true "polymath" and the quintessential personification of the *Republic of Letters*.[9] Yet, his academic engagement was not disconnected from his commitment as a Catholic priest and a citizen. His work also aimed at contributing to the common good of church and society. This can be seen most clearly in his books on *The Defects of Jurisprudence* (1742) and especially in his influential small volume *On Public Happiness* (1749). In the latter, he develops a model for the "enlightened" leader of a commonwealth, reminding politicians to serve the welfare of *all* citizens. Moreover, in such a commonwealth government is not disconnected from religion, as the support of the Church is seen as a necessary element of societal peace, contentment, and order.

Among ecclesiastics, theologians, and philosophers he achieved fame with his writings on religion. His vivid style differed substantially from the rather dry, scholastic tone of his contemporaries. He had a clear distaste for ostentatious religious practices associated with Early Modern Catholicism. Instead, he preferred a simpler vision of Christian spirituality and theology, inspired by the late medieval *devotio moderna* and the *Catholic Reform*. Among the theological writers most regularly cited one finds therefore Jean Gerson (1363–1429) and Thomas à Kempis (1380–1471).

Muratori brought a new culture into Catholicism that called for a humbler intellectualism and thus a Christian philosophy that echoed Erasmus of Rotterdam (1466–1536). Theology and Church doctrine should avoid extremes and find their way back to moderation, the virtuous middle between extremes. After all, he witnessed such extremes on a daily basis: the Jansenist crisis was in full swing. While the supporters of Cornelius Jansen (1585–1638) advocated a rigid Augustinianism, the Jesuits seemed to embrace the contrary extreme of laxism.[10] In philosophical circles another extreme had taken root—

---

a Tridentine Mode," in *Enlightenment and Catholicism in Europe: A Transnational History*, ed. Ulrich L. Lehner and Jeffrey Burson (Notre Dame, IN: University of Notre Dame Press, 2014), 249–68.

9. Cf. Paola Gambarota, *Irresistible Signs: the Genius of Language and Italian National Identity* (Toronto: University of Toronto Press: 2010), 74–98.

10. The complex history of Jansenism is reconstructed diligently in Shaun

namely, skepticism. Renewed by Descartes, who used it to establish unshakeable knowledge, it found many followers also among theologians and bishops. Perhaps its most famous defender was the French bishop Pierre-Daniel Huet (1630–1721). Although Huet was a critic of Cartesianism, he acknowledged—very much like Muratori—that its skepticism correctly pointed out the weakness of the human mind, which some contemporaries seemed to forget.[11] Although they agreed that such a stance taught the human person humility,[12] they differed on what human reason unaided by faith could achieve. While Huet embraced fideist apologetics,[13] Muratori considered such a path too extreme. For him, a faith without criteria for its truth claims was irrational like the ancient pagan religions but had nothing in common with the faith of Christians.[14] He was convinced that the best solution was to be found in a moderate in-between position that avoided fideism and rationalism, and he consequently defended such a view for the next three and a half decades.[15]

Blanchard, *The Synod of Pistoia: Jansenism and the Struggle for Catholic Reform* (Oxford: Oxford University Press, 2020).

11. Muratori, *De ingeniorum*, bk. 1, ch. 6. Nevertheless, Huet's full treatise on the weakness of the human mind, *Traité philosophique de la foiblesse de l'esprit humain*, did not appear until 1723. Earlier parts, however, were already printed in 1690 under the title *Alnetanae Quaestiones*.

12. Thomas M. Lennon, "Pierre-Daniel Huet: Skeptic Critic of Cartesianism and Defender of Religion," in *Oxford Handbook of Descartes and Cartesianism*, ed. Steven Nadler et al. (Oxford: Oxford University Press, 2019), 780–91; Sebastien Charles, "On the Uses of Skepticism against a Certain Philosophical Arrogance: Huet as a Critic of Cartesian Logic and Metaphysics," *Science et Esprit* 65 (2013): 299–309; April Shelford, "Thinking Geometrically in Pierre-Daniel Huet's *Demonstratio Evangelica* (1679)," *Journal of the History of Ideas* 63 (2002): 599–617.

13. Thomas M. Lennon, "Pierre-Daniel Huet," in *The Plain Truth: Descartes, Huet and Skepticism* (Leiden: Brill, 2008), ch. 1.

14. Dario Antiseri, *Ragioni della razionalità. Interpretazioni storiografiche*, vol. 2 (Rubbettino: Soveria Mannelli, 2005), 1–53, at 29.

15. The last extensive critique of Huet's views is found in his late works on human imagination: see Ludovico Muratori, *Della Forza della Fantasia Umana* (Venice: 1745); see also his smaller volume *Delle forze dell'intendimento umano, o sia il Pirronismo confutato* (Venice: 1745). On Huet see Elena Rapetti, "A Man Who Sticks Only to His Own Sentiments: Pierre-Daniel Huet's *Traite philosophique de la foiblesse de l'esprit humain*," in *The Skeptical Enlightenment: Doubt and Certainty in the Age of Reason*, ed. Jeffrey

Thus, it was only consequential that he contended in his writings also with all kinds of extremisms. Among Catholics, for example, he found one in the rejection of scientific progress, such as the Copernican worldview, because it relied on Protestant authors. Why, he asked, should a Catholic not read or cite Protestant books that contained important truths? Likewise, he wondered why Catholics should cling to a Ptolemean explanation of Holy Scripture if the Copernican view did neither undermine nor contradict faith or morals?[16] Moreover, as a historian he was aware of change over time and therefore reminded theologians that historical knowledge was necessary for the understanding of Church tradition. After all, the timeless truths that God had revealed were expressed and explained in timebound vocabulary and imagery. His diligent requests for a reform within the Church were therefore grounded in the vision of a Catholicism that was intellectually flexible, and moderate in its practices—a Catholicism that was able to patiently answer the challenges of the eighteenth century. Nowhere in his works does he articulate this vision clearer than in *On the Moderation of Reason in Religious Matters* (1714) and *On the Regulated Devotion of Christians* (1747). The first had catapulted him to the center of Catholic renewal for the entire eighteenth century. At a time when radical Enlighteners either championed the rejection of ecclesiastical authority for the sake of human autonomy or ridiculed the truth claims of the Christian revelation, he called for a moderate, virtuous use of human freedom founded on the religion he considered to be the only true one—Catholicism.[17] Far from sanctioning and downplaying problems of intellectual honesty and moral decay within the Church, he also demanded that Catholics should regain the

---

Burson et al. (Liverpool: Voltaire Foundation and Liverpool University Press, 2019), 45–68.

16. See Muratori, *De Ingeniorum Moderatione*, bk. 1, ch. 22, also in this volume.

17. For the differentiation of radical/secular and moderate (often religious) Enlightenment, see Martin Mulsow and Jonathan Israel, eds., *Radikalaufklärung* (Berlin: Suhrkamp, 2014); Jonathan Israel, *Radical Enlightenment: Philosophy and the Making of Modernity 1650–1750* (Oxford: Oxford University Press, 2001); Margaret Jacob, *The Secular Enlightenment* (Princeton, NJ: Princeton University Press, 2019); David Sorkin, *Religious Enlightenment: Protestants, Jews, and Catholics from London to Vienna* (Princeton, NJ: Princeton University Press, 2008).

freedom to prudently doubt and think. If the Church wanted to be taken seriously in the Republic of Letters, its philosophers and theologians had to climb out of the "trench warfare" between Scotism, Thomism, Suarezianism, and Augustinianism. Instead of petrifying the opinions of their schools of thought, he desired free discourse about them in an atmosphere of moderation and mutual respect. Many shared his views, including a number of erudite cardinals in Rome, especially his close friend Prospero Lambertini (1675–1758), who in 1740 assumed the throne of St. Peter under the name Benedict XIV and reigned until 1758.

His *On the Regulated Devotion of Christians* (1747) verbalized the widespread frustration of many clergymen about liturgical excesses and abuses.[18] Among the first, the disproportionate veneration of the saints especially bothered Muratori, because it seemed to obfuscate the centrality of Christ. He also did not shy away from naming certain prayers and rituals as outright superstitious. Yet, what fired up his critics was his call for a curtailing of Marian devotions. They saw in it an attack on the Mother of God herself. Nevertheless, despite the harsh criticism, within a few years the book spread his ideas about focusing on the centrality of Christ in the liturgy all over Europe. Muratori was now read in several European languages, and *On Regulated Devotion* had become a bestseller that was reprinted for decades to come.[19]

As already mentioned, Muratori had suggested in *On Regulated Devotion* that some Catholics exaggerated the veneration of Mary. Yet, he went even further and questioned several "pious theological opinions" about her, which were not part of the deposit of faith, but widely accepted. For example, he outright rejected the idea that the veneration of the Blessed Virgin Mary was necessary for gaining salvation. This did not come as a surprise to his enemies, since already seven years earlier, in 1740, he had called the oath Catholic university students took to defend the *Immaculate Conception* up to death "superstitious."

---

18. Ludovico Muratori, *Della regolata divozion de' cristiani* (Venice: 1747). From the second edition (1748) onwards the title was slightly altered, and *divozion* changed to *divozione*.

19. See Shaun Blanchard, "Liturgical Renewal and the Fight against Superstition," in *The Catholic Enlightenment: A Global Anthology*, ed. Ulrich L. Lehner and Shaun Blanchard (Washington, DC: The Catholic University of America Press, 2021), 21–36.

For Jesuits and other intransigent forces, he had become the most hated Catholic theologian. Certainly, the *Immaculate Conception* or the teaching that Mary was from the very first moment of her existence without the stain of original sin was not yet a defined dogma, but her feast was in the liturgical books. Thus, there was an established practice to venerate her this way, and a widespread consensus among theologians that this teaching was accepted, even if not defined by a council. Muratori, however, relativized it further. In his view, the teaching of the *Immaculate Conception* should not be counted among doctrines received by the faithful, but rather as a theological "opinion," namely of Duns Scotus, which could be freely discussed and consequently also rejected. As a pious and honorable opinion, but strictly speaking not a truth *de fide*, no Catholic would be obliged to embrace it, he reasoned. In the eyes of critics, however, this time he had gone too far. They denounced him as a freemason simply because his last name meant "mason" in Latin![20] In a letter to the rector of the University of Salzburg, which had publicly denounced the book that sparked the affair, *On the Avoidance of Superstition* (1740),[21] he wrote: "You will have to prove to me that it is licit to risk our lives for a mere opinion or you must prove to me that this opinion is a truth of faith. If you can do neither, say outright whether it is not always absurd and most imprudent (*minime ferendum*) to equate human opinions with dogmas of faith?"[22]

Also, within the Roman Curia he had created powerful enemies with this claim and only avoided censorship due to the protection

20. See Ulrich L. Lehner, *Enlightened Monks: The German Benedictines, 1740–1803* (Oxford: Oxford University Press, 2011), 175–203.

21. Ludovico Muratori, *De superstitione vitanda, sive censura voti sanguinarii in honorem immaculatae conceptionis deiparae emissi, a Lamindo Pritanio, antea oppugnati, atque a Candido Partenotimo Theologo Siculo, incassum vindicate* (Mediolani: 1740). About the affair, which rocked the Benedictine University of Salzburg, see also Giovanni B. de Gaspari, *Vindiciae adversus sycophantas juvanienses* (Cologne [i.e. Venice]: 1741). On the oath to defend the Immaculate Conception, which Muratori called "superstitious," see now Felice Santi Fiasconaro, *Il Pensiero Immacolista Di Ignazio Como (1774) Nella Controversia Con L.a. Muratori Sul "Voto Sanguinario"* (Palermo: Officina di studi medievali, 2004).

22. At Anonymous, *Benediktinermuseum: Heft Zwei* (Tegernsee: 1791), 233. *De Superstitione Vitanda* had been the answer to a series of vitriolic attacks on him for publishing his stance in Muratori, *De Ingeniorum Moderatione*, bk. 2, ch. 6.

of Pope Benedict XIV. Exhausted from defending himself constantly against the most tactless and insidious accusations, Ludovico Muratori died in 1750.

The Muratorian Heritage

Muratori's groundbreaking historical works contributed to the Italian unification process of the nineteenth century. Yet, outside Italy his name began fading away in theological circles from the 1860s and remained in relative obscurity until the early twentieth century. After all, since the early 1800s the time of Catholic Enlightenment was over. The space for a dialogue with modern philosophies, and especially Protestant ones, increasingly shrank and almost dissipated by the 1860s.[23] Now the celebrated hero of Catholic Enlighteners was at best seen as a benevolent "liberal," at worst as a heterodox enemy of the Church, but in both cases as somebody at the fringes of the Church.[24] Many of Muratori's ideas, such as calling Protestants "separated brethren," his Christocentrism, his liturgical reforms, his understanding of revelation as an encounter with the triune God rather than a set of propositions, the importance of historical scholarship for biblical exegesis, and much more, *only* became fully acceptable in Catholic circles after 1965, a full two hundred years after his death. He was truly ahead of his time![25] Eugenio Pacelli, later Pius XII, knew and appreciated "il grande Muratori"[26] as a historian, but since most of his writings were never translated, a broad international reception of the theologian and philosopher Muratori has yet to occur. The time is ripe for that since his name echoes vividly through the works of contemporary

---

23. Cf. Lehner, *Catholic Enlightenment*, 206–19.

24. Ulrich L. Lehner, "De Moderatione in Sacra Theologia: Über die Grenzen theologischer Rede bei Ludovico Muratori (1672–1750)," in *Der dreifaltige Gott. Christlicher Glaube im säkularen Zeitalter*, ed. George Augustin et al. (Freiburg: Herder, 2017), 349–64.

25. Shaun Blanchard, "Proto-Ecumenical Catholic Reform in the Eighteenth Century: Ludovico Muratori as Forerunner of Vatican II," *Pro Ecclesia* 25 (2018): 71–89.

26. Eugenio Pacelli on letterhead of the Secretariat of State of 8 July 1938, Nr. 170175, auctioned off in 2016 and since then in a private collection; https://www.auction.fr/_en/lot/pius-xii-1876-1958-pope-of-the-roman-catholic-church-1939-58-t-l-s-e-card-9742473.

historians. They have realized that the librarian of Modena truly deserves to be called "the great Muratori."[27]

De Ingeniorum Moderatione in Religionis Negotio (1714)

Although finished in 1708,[28] the book was not published in Paris until 1714.[29] Muratori's treatise went through at least sixteen editions until 1870, but was only twice translated, both times into German in 1770 and 1837, respectively. Throughout the volume, which was an apology for the Catholic method of reasoning, he carefully avoided attributing to the pope the charism of infallibility while at the same time not questioning its attribution to the entire Church. This was not uncommon at the time, since papal infallibility was not yet dogmatically defined. Moreover, his stance probably also showed the profound disappointment about his treatment by the Holy See since 1711. Employed by the d'Este family, he had dared to criticize the political claims of the papacy to the city of Comacchio, based on a careful analysis of historical documents. The answer of his critics, however, mixed spiritual and political arguments, disregarded historical evidence, and painted him as an enemy of the papacy, a likely schismatic or even heretic, and a disloyal son of the Church. Such personal attacks wounded him deeply, and from this time on, he understandably asserted his own position more forcefully in the fight against the political abuse of theology, or superstition.[30]

27. For a recent assessment and overview, see Mario Rosa, ed., *Lodovico Antonio Muratori: Religione e politica nel Settecento* (Florence: Olschki, 2018).

28. Corrado Viola, "Le 'Osservazioni critiche' di Giusto Fontanini al 'De ingeniorum moderatione' di Lodovico Muratori," *Studi sul Settecento e l'Ottocento* 15 (2020): 103–21.

29. The Parisian editors added a few sentences to make the text sound more Gallican, as the author claimed in 1716. See also Vismara, "Immoderato," 318.

30. Manuela Bragagnolo, "Droit et histoire: Muratori et la critique de la papauté à travers ses sources inédites du xvie siècle," in *Droits antiromains xvie–xxie siècles: Juridictionnalisme catholique et romanité ecclésiale*, ed. Bernard Hours and Sylvio De Franceschi (Paris: Larhra, 2020), 129–47; Matteo Al Kalak, "La Provvidenza deciderà: Comacchio, Paolo Segneri e i dilemmi di Muratori," *Rivista di storia del cristianesimo* 11 (2014): 115–40. For an assessment of Muratori's unpublished piece "Della fallibilità dei pontifici nel dominio temporale" (1708), see for example Stephen J. Barnett,

Despite his reservations about papal infallibility and his irenic way of speaking about Protestant authors, he nevertheless stuck to the standard view of granting toleration to non-Catholics only under duress. Likewise, he did not waver calling out the doctrinal mistakes he identified in the writings of Lutherans and Calvinists, a few of whom answered with printed attacks.[31] This, however, does not mean that Muratori was a "hardliner"—far from it. After all, he had to defend himself against the accusation of being too cozy with Protestant writers, whom he often cited approvingly. Yet the librarian appreciated truth and good scholarship wherever he found it, regardless of confessional affiliation. In fact, his deemphasis on doctrines contested by Protestants could made him appear, as fellow historian Giusto Fontanini (1666–1736) stated, as a deist or as a dangerous "concordantist," who could sacrifice Catholic doctrine for concord with the Protestant churches.[32]

The main occasion for the book was the edition of Augustine's writings by the nominally Arminian Jean Leclerc (1657–1736), who was most likely a Socinian and thus an anti-Trinitarian.[33] His commentaries portrayed the Church Father as embracing an unintelligible religion, calling for credulity and subjugation to ecclesiastical arbitrariness. He contrasted the "darkness" of Catholicism with the light of reason that reigned in the Remonstrant[34] circles of his church.[35] The

---

"The Temporal Imperative. Criticism and Defence of Eighteenth-Century Roman Theocracy," *History of Political Thought* 22 (2001): 472–93.

31. See for example Martin Chladenius, *Disputatio theologica posterior adversus Lamindum Pritanium excutiens ac refellens methodum pontificiorum* (Wittenberg: 1717); Chladenius, *Dissertatio theologica ... adversus Lamindum Pritanium vindicans methodum euangelicorum in inquirenda veritate coelesti quam ...* (Wittenberg: 1717).

32. At Viola, "Le osservazioni," 113. As examples for such attempts, he cites Giorgio Vicchio, Philip Melanchthon, da Giorgio Cassandro, da Teofilo Milettiere, and Marco Antonio De Dominis.

33. Sarah Mortimer, "Early Socinianism and Unitarianism," in *Oxford Handbook of Early Modern Theology, 1600–1800*, ed. Ulrich L. Lehner et al. (Oxford: Oxford University Press, 2016), 361–72.

34. Th. Marius van Leeuwen et al., eds., *Arminius, Arminianism and Europe: Jacobus Arminius (1550/60–1609)* (Boston: Brill, 2009); Freya Sierhuis, *The Literature of the Arminian Controversy: Religion, Politics and the Stage in the Dutch Republic* (Oxford: Oxford University Press, 2015).

35. Cf. Mark W. Elliott, "Jean Leclerc," in *Handbuch der Bibelhermeneutiken:*

incomparable Pierre Bayle (1647–1706) wrote of him: "Mr. Leclerc distinguishes himself daily by his boldness in publishing heretical opinions, and in condemning the authors who do not please him."[36] Bayle, who philosophically shared much of Leclerc's freethinking, describes him as an easily irritable, unforgiving, and rash person, whom one better not cross in any way.[37]

Muratori could not sit idle seeing one of the greatest ecclesiastical writers of all times being so grossly and viciously misinterpreted. He rose to Augustine's defense, and at that occasion also offered a full-blown defense of intellectual pursuits in the Catholic faith. Although there was nothing new in his claim that faith was based on reasonable grounds (*motiva credibilitatis*), he did not stick to the standard blueprint of apologetic handbooks and neither allowed Leclerc's attacks to shape his response. Richard Simon (1638–1712) had committed the latter mistake, and it made his rebuttal to the Dutch theologian an extremely cumbersome reading.[38] Instead, Muratori addressed the main issues raised in Leclerc's interpretation, but decided to use the opportunity to give in books one and two a comprehensive appraisal of the powers of human reason and how these are used in and through the faith. Thereby he refuted Leclerc's methodology by indirectly demonstrating its inadequacy. After all, Leclerc's criticism rested on two odd pillars; namely, the exaggerated powers of reason and the skepticism toward anything received by tradition or authority. Therefore, Muratori did not choose mind (*mens*) or soul (*anima*) for his book title but "ingeniorum" (genitive plural of *ingenium*), meaning the holistic genius,

---

Von Origenes bis zur Gegenwart, ed. Oda Wischmeyer et al. (Berlin: DeGruyter 2016), 463–74; Jean Leclerc, *Variorum exercitationes in S. Augustini opera* in: *Patrologia Latina*, ed. Migne 47 (Paris: 1877), 197–570. One of the better studies on Leclerc is Walther Ludwig, "Humanistische Erforschung und Anerkennung nicht-christlicher Kultur und Religion—Schritte auf dem Weg zur Toleranz," in *Wechselseitige Wahrnehmung der Religionen im Spätmittelalter und der Neuzeit*, vol. 2, ed. Ludger Grennzmann et al. (Boston: De Gruyter, 2012), 7–58.

36. Gustave Masson, *The French Oratorians: I: Richard Simon* (London: 1866), 14.
37. Masson, *The French*, 15.
38. Leclerc had also attacked the famous Oratorian and exegete Richard Simon, who responded in *Réponse au livre intitulé Sentimens de quelques theologiens de Hollande sur l'Histoire critique du Vieux Testament* (Rotterdam: 1686).

intelligence, and talent of the human person—and thus it is only moderately well rendered into English with the noun "reason." This human genius is for him not a free spirit like for Leclerc but finds its limits in religion and the virtues that the natural law places upon it. It finds through moderation true fulfillment and happiness.[39]

Nevertheless, the librarian of Modena hesitated to publish his book, because it also argued for a freer discussion of research within the Church. Muratori was convinced that if there was more freedom to pursue the truth, the faith would again flourish. Acknowledging the value of prudent reasoning for faith and life would, he believed, profit the whole of society.[40] Thus, he expressed to a friend on March 25, 1707: "Catholics as well as heretics need such a treatise."[41] Fearing that Italian typesetters could disfigure the Greek and Hebrew letters in the text, Muratori decided to publish his book in Paris. This move, however, also allowed him to circumvent papal censorship that could have stopped the publication. After all, in France one could openly support Copernicus and Galileo without fear of being reprimanded. The librarian dedicated his work to one of the great intellectuals at the court of Louis XIV, Jean Paul Bignon, but did initially prefer a pseudonym instead of his own name on the title page. He hid behind *Lamindus Pritanus*, although the identity of the author was quickly discovered.

De Ingeniorum is divided into three books. Book one is comprised of twenty-four chapters, book two of fourteen, and book three, which deals mainly with questions about the writings of Augustine, of seventeen chapters.[42] Neither book has a clearly identifiable single topic, but rather treats a variety of seemingly disparate problems. Nevertheless, one could say that book one lays out to some degree his methodology, which is then applied to case studies thereafter.

---

39. This is also the vision of modern Thomistic virtue ethics. See William C. Mattison, *Introducing Moral Theology. True Happiness and the Virtues* (Grand Rapids, MI: Brazos, 2008).

40. Vismara, "Immoderato," 331.

41. Vismara, "Immoderato," 316.

42. The number after the chapter is the original pagination, not the page number in the new edition. In the text it is set in [brackets].

Book I   Already in the first chapter, Muratori (bk. 1, ch. 1) outlines that the search for truth can never be illicit and should never be censored. Especially the search for the true religion must be a priority for every human being. The human intellect undertakes this search and thereby gains a deeper understanding of the faith. Reason and faith are therefore never opposed but in perfect harmony with each other. Thus, the appropriate use of reason can never pose a danger to the Church, society, or the individual. It is rather the misguided use of reason, perverted through sinfulness and a fallen human nature, which disfigures intellect and will (ch.1, 6). Thus, the human person has to diligently care for these faculties so that they lead to integrity and wisdom and not to decay and vice (ch. 1, 9).

Doubt has its value, argues Muratori, even in the search for the true religion (bk. 1, ch. 2) but when one has found it, such doubt has to come to an end. After all, while doubt helps to avoid the errors of credulity and intellectual pride, its unlimited use leads to skepticism, which is a fruitless enterprise. Limited doubt follows certain criteria that guarantee its prudential use. Among the most important ranks the prohibition to doubt the highest, self-evident principles. Within the true religion, Catholic Christianity, prudent doubt must be used methodologically so that it does not lead the believer away from the divine revelation. It is used therefore only to gain deeper insight into the truth of the faith. For example, a theologian uses "doubt" like a thought experiment in order to inquire about the accuracy of his terminology. He looks to gain more insight but does not take doubt as a realistic option. The use of doubt as part of a theological method is only safe in the hands of trained experts. Among the inexperienced or untrained, Muratori thinks, it could easily lead to skepticism or superstition.

In the third chapter, Muratori deepens these reflections: Only those who "effortlessly admit that their religion is based on throughout certain principles and foundations may refrain from doubting" their faith (bk. 1, ch. 3, [18]), since the authority of their religion is intelligible. Authority in and of itself is fallible and should only be trusted if it fulfills the criteria of trustworthiness. Criticism and the sciences offer these criteria and establish which human witnesses can be trusted. Once one has found out whom to trust, doubt "can rest":

First, one must ask whether the religion one professes, contradicts proper reasoning [*rectae rationi*]. If it does, then one must not only doubt its truth, but immediately reject it [*in ipsam protinus dicenda sententia*]. Yet, if it does not contradict reason in any way, then one must examine *secondly*, whether it originates in God or humans. This means that one must ask whether this religion has been introduced [*inducta*] by a divine or a human authority. If it originates in human authority, then one must doubt its truth; if it originates in God, then any doubt about its truth must be excluded, for the divine authority has power over reason [*supra rationem*] and is free from any suspicion of deception. But even then, it remains to be examined, and *thirdly* must be doubted, whether that which we rightly believe to be revealed [*an quae Deum tradidisse*] by God is also correctly understood and interpreted by us. Once we have done this by means of reason or by more reliable means—if God has offered them—it is prudent [21] to rest [*prudentis erit conquiescere*], so that we do not put ourselves in greater danger by imprudent doubt [*inconsulta dubitatione*] (bk 1, ch. 3, [20–21]).

Since Muratori argues for Catholic Christianity as the perfect "conspiration" of reason and authority, members of all other religions must doubt their creeds—he mentions pagans, Jews, and Muslims—and uses for this section the arguments from the classical treatise *demonstratio christiana* developed by apologetic theologians.[43]

In chapter 4, Muratori offers a defense of his view on doubt. After all, he anticipated strong disapproval for his defense of doubt among Christians (bk. 1, ch. 4). His critics probably fear, he explained, that such doubt would destroy the certainty of faith through skepticism. Muratori, however, counters that he in no way encourages *universal* doubt like Descartes, and especially not in religious affairs. Nevertheless, he points to the value of *prudent* doubt, which helps the baptized to get a deeper understanding of their faith, but also acknowledges its dangers if used improperly. Moreover, Catholics could calm

---

43. See for example Stephen G. Burnett, "Western Theologies and Judaism in the Early Modern World," in *Oxford Handbook of Early Modern Theology, 1600–1800*, ed. Ulrich L. Lehner et al. (Oxford: Oxford University Press 2016), 469–81, and Emanuele Colombo, "Western Theologies and Islam in the Early Modern World," *Oxford Handbook*, 482–98. On the development of this treatise see Gerhard Heinz, *Divinam christianae religionis originem probare: Untersuchung zur Entstehung des fundamentaltheologischen Offenbarungstraktates der katholischen Schultheologie* (Mainz: Grünewald, 1984).

their inquisitive minds by trusting the Church since she is founded on reason *and* authority.

Although faith is a divine gift, its acceptance can be prepared in the mind by reasons for the faith, which are also called motives for faith (*motiva credibilitatis*) (bk. 1, ch. 5). These are, however, not logical demonstrations but rather *extrinsic* reasons for the faith, arguments that show the credibility of the Church's witnesses as well as the intelligibility of her doctrines and miracles. Having such reasons, however, elevates belief beyond the "blind faith" that Jean Leclerc attributes to Catholicism, and in particular to Augustine. Moreover, the Arminian charges the bishop of Hippo with demanding belief without reasons and to blindly trust Church authorities. Muratori convincingly shows that Leclerc not only misunderstands the Church Father but deliberately misinterprets him. After all, what Augustine stresses is that a candidate for baptism cannot require logical proofs for truths of faith, but he certainly can demand good reasons for why he should trust the Christian message and the priests (*motiva credibilitatis*).

In chapter 6, Muratori tackles the weakness of the human mind. The latter is easily deceived or deceives others. He urges the reader to become aware of factors that influence the human mind in order to set up protective boundaries. At the beginning of this inoculation against error must be the acknowledgement of the weakness of reason itself. "We must not expect any progress toward the true knowledge and love of God, unless we have first arrived at the insight of our own weakness" (bk. 1, ch. 6, [49]). Such humility protects from pride, which often leads the mind into error. The humble mind finds help in the liberal arts, which provide tools to discern truth from falsehood. Nevertheless, even these tools can be abused for evil purposes, and often weak memory and an untamed imagination likewise impede the proper working of the mind. After all, if a person allows the passions to engage limitlessly with an object of research, the soul's ability to rationally investigate it dissipates (bk. 1, ch. 6, [53]). Likewise, the "perversity of the will" can cause the mind to err, because it draws reason into the pursuit of false goods, ignorance, and oblivion (bk. 1, ch. 6, [55]).

For example, if the image of Plato, of Epicurus, of Aristotle has taken hold of our minds, and if their views and philosophies have become known to us, if their image is accompanied in us by admiration, love and reverence, then the soul is so taken and dominated by this image that it now only appreciates the views of Plato, of Epicurus, of Aristotle and despises all others. The opposite occurs when, instead of love and admiration, we are taken by hatred and contempt for a writer and a certain view. As long, however, as such vivid images rule over imagination and memory without any restraint, and as long as the inner affects dominate with their arbitrariness, the soul will remain subject to error (bk. 1, ch. 6, [54–55]).

The weakness of reason points the mind to the need for divine revelation (bk. 1, ch.7). Left to its own powers, reason is incapable of finding the one true God. Yet, if paired with humility, it lays the foundation for finding faith:

Yet, one must not assume that God has hidden the truth of his religion so much that human reason could never reach it. On the contrary, one must assume that he has made the arrangement that we, if we make the right use of his assistance and the natural powers of reason, can reach this truth with certainty. He invites those who are endowed with reason and wants that they come to Him through His grace, but not entirely without the use of reason. Even if the powers of the human mind are weak, if divine assistance is available, they are very capable, and through them become able to recognize the true, revealed religion and to distinguish it from false and invented ones. Thus, the mind must be kept away from excessive disregard of itself as well as from excessive presumption; for on both sides there is danger that one either does not believe in any revelation or in a false one. About the powers of human reason and how to use them properly, reason itself will give us information (bk. 1, ch. 7, [65]).

Finding the true religion can happen through *intrinsic* reasons based on syllogisms or through *extrinsic* reasons. For the latter, the person trusts the witness and the arguments of people. Such extrinsic reasons must conform to certain principles. The highest of these is the conviction that there is a good God, and the second the principle of testimony;[44] namely, that one must believe the witness of others if there is no evidence that they were deceived or want to deceive (bk. 1, ch. 7, [66]).

---

44. Muratori does not call it a principle of testimony, but contemporary philosophers of religion. For a version of this principle see Richard Swinburne, *The Existence of God* (Oxford: Oxford University Press, 1979), 273–92.

The search for the true religion leads the seeker to the puzzling realization that several Christian churches claim to be the true foundation of Christ. Before joining a church that might be a false one, the person has to carefully inquire, "on which side there is light and truth, and on which side there is darkness and error" (bk. 1, ch. 8, [70]). Nevertheless, what guidelines or principles should a person follow in this process of choosing? Muratori excludes Holy Scripture as insufficiently clear (bk. 1, ch. 8, [71]) and instead embraces the idea of a divinely appointed interpreter of God's revelation as a more reliable guide, which he identifies with the Catholic Church: "We can and must, according to the dictates of reason, enter her [the Church, U.L.], reject all other Christian churches as false, and firmly and reliably believe all that she teaches, even if it is disputed by heretics" (bk. 1, ch. 8, [73]). This Church is not only infallible in teaching true doctrine but must also prevent error from entering into the deposit of faith. "If one replied to this that it is up to human reason to judge whether the Church has erred or not, and whether she has properly interpreted Scripture or not, one appeals to the weakest possible judge or at least a completely unqualified one" (bk. 1, ch. 8, [74]). If Protestants, Muratori reasons, nevertheless invoke Scripture as the *only* rule of faith and reason as its interpreter, such a move opens the door not only to the privatization of the biblical text but also to a myriad of heresies (bk. 1, ch. 9, [77–78]):

Protestants determine the meaning of the divine word and the doctrines of faith according to each one's private opinion [*privato ingenio*], according to that person's convictions. Thus, in such an important matter, as witnessed by daily experience and amply demonstrated by the many disputes still existing among them, they accept a weak and unreliable counselor and arbiter. Catholics, on the other hand, examine and determine the meaning of Holy Scripture according to their own reason as well as according to the judgment of the Church (bk. 1, ch. 9, [80]).

Thus, according to Muratori, the "Catholic method," which relies, as he already earlier pointed out, not on reason alone but also on authority, overcomes the endless doubt private interpretation produces and leads with certainty to the true meaning of Scripture.

Leclerc, however, argues that before one submits to the Church's authority, her claim to such authority has to be proven. In his rebuttal,

Muratori shows that the believer cannot expect a mathematical demonstration of her teachings (bk. 1, ch. 10), but concedes that she can and must give reasons for her assertions. Thus, Catholics do not believe blindly, as Leclerc insinuates, but rather trust the Church for *good reasons*. Protestants, however, who only accept Holy Scripture as a rule of faith, must rely on rather undependable authorities such as exegetes and nonhierarchical leaders, who have neither been promised nor claim guidance by the Holy Spirit. Besides, the teachings of the Catholic Church reach back to antiquity and thus back her claims to authoritatively interpret the revelation of God. Most interesting is perhaps a negative argument: no Christian "sect," as he calls non-Catholic churches sometimes, can prove to be the true church of Christ, be they Lutheran, Reformed, or Socinian. While these confessions sometimes doubt whether the members of their competitor churches are saved, no one doubts that in principle one can find salvation within the Catholic Church (bk. 1, ch. 10, [88]). Consequently, a church that no other church denies the possibility of salvation must be the place where one can certainly encounter the authentic Christian message. In chapter 11 he singles out Socinianism (bk. 1, ch. 11) as the best example for the prideful exaltation of the powers of reason. Especially its rejection of tradition is shown to be contradictory and convinces its adherents to interpret Scripture according to their own liking and not according to the intention of God (bk. 1, ch. 11, [105]).

In chapter 12, Muratori reflects about *praiseworthy* (*expetita*) freedom in religion, which holds the middle between minimalistic freedom, which leads to superstition, and excessive freedom, which leads to heresy. Such praiseworthy liberty finds its limitation through the three hierarchies of truths. The first contains the definitive, revealed teachings of the Church (*documenta*) on faith, morals, or discipline. This is the realm of truths that God has entrusted to the Church and in which he keeps her infallible. The second comprises propositions that are not revealed but relate to the faith. Also, this realm belongs to the realm of the Church's authority, but to a lesser degree. About the third hierarchy, truths of worldly sciences, the Church cannot have any competent authority. Following this classification, a theologian has therefore the freedom to speculate on subjects and areas in which the Church neither makes a doctrinal claim nor has proclaimed a definitive decision (*in utriusqua magna est ingeniis libertas*; bk. 1, ch. 12, [109]), and thus in the second or third hierarchy. He also identifies three dimensions within the first hierarchy in which the theologian can find freedom of research and expression: although the theologian is not allowed to withhold assent to the existence of a teaching (*existentia dogmatis*), there is considerable freedom in how he explains doctrines (*modus explicandi*), or how he proves them (*rationes*). As an example, Muratori cites the dogma that the condemned suffer in hell. While their suffering is held as a truth of faith, the *modus explicandi* of *how* such suffering is to be understood is not defined and thus open for different interpretations. However, the theologian enjoys the greatest freedom when he conceives proofs or arguments (*rationes*) for a dogma. Often, they are taken from Scripture or tradition, but sometimes also from philosophy. Some of these may be irrefutable, while others might be weak or even useless. "From this side a wide field opens for the freedom of the human mind," Muratori explains.[45]

Within this chapter, he also reminds the reader of a careful hermeneutic of authoritative texts. After all, one cannot simply cite the text of a council or a Church Father as a proof for a dogma or a theological opinion if the text did not intend such a meaning. For example, within the conciliar documents, things are sometimes mentioned *incidentally* and cannot therefore be cited as sources of dogmatic authority (bk 1, c. 13, [122]).[46] This was for Muratori of the utmost importance since he experienced how theologians indiscriminately declared utterances of councils or Church Fathers as definitive Catholic teaching. He explained that things the councils and Church Fathers only discussed *incidentally* (*obiter dicta*) and did not reject as outright heretical, could be freely discussed, criticized, and consequently also rejected. These comments are embedded in a discussion about the "immoderate" expansion of ecclesiastical teaching authority (*immoderata ... extollatur*).

---

45. Muratori, *De Ingeniorum*, bk. 1, ch. 12, 113: "Quapropter late patet ex hac parte Ingeniorum libertas."

46. This point was also emphasized by François Véron, *Regle générale de la foi catholique* (Paris: 1649) and Henry Holden, *Divinae fidei analysis* (Paris: 1652), and Beda Mayr, *Vertheidigung der Katholischen Religion* (Augsburg: 1789).

This was a rather bold term, because it suggested that the Church had either done just that in the past or was in danger of doing it. Either way, Muratori reminded Catholics that the Church cannot claim authority in areas over which she has no authority, particularly the realms of history and natural sciences (bk. 1, c. 13, [115]). Nonetheless, in the eighteenth century, theologians who uttered such a gentle reminder were often reprimanded or suspected of heresy. Having suffered such accusations himself, Muratori argues passionately against a culture of denunciation and suspicion. The people who spread rumors about others are, as he testifies, most often driven by exaggerated zeal (*zelum exuberantem*). It fuels their excessive authoritarianism, but also their hatred. Unable to discern the sources and levels of authority, these zealots are fed by "superstition" and have abandoned the sobriety of reason (bk. 1, c. 13, [115]). Their rash enthusiasm (*inconsultus ardor*) is deaf to arguments. By eradicating the borders of Church authority, these self-appointed guardians of "Zion," as Muratori calls them, try to prove their dedication to the Church, but in reality expose her to ridicule. After all, why would the Church rule in questions that are not about faith or morals, or that eliminate all freedom?[47] While the intention and will of such fanatics might be good, they lack *scientia* and *prudentia*. Their inflationary expansion of Church authority turns the Church into a tyrannical authoritarian institution: "Whoever commands things to be believed that are not to be believed at all will be thought a tyrant, and whoever scatters lies among the truth will be thought a teacher of error and falsehood" (bk. 1, c. 13, [116]).

Ultimately, then, the preachers of such zeal are nothing but pious flatterers (*pios assentatores*), whose godliness is dangerous to the mission and life of the Church. Accordingly, Church authorities should flee them and put their hope in honest and courageous (*cordati*) Catholics.[48]

Chapter 14 establishes that the Church has the authority to define

---

47. For a nineteenth-century example of such an extreme position see Ulrich L. Lehner, "Päpstlicher als der Papst: Georg Kaiser's (1801–1872) Papalismus," in *Glaube und Kirche in Zeiten des Umbruchs. Festschrift für Josef Kreiml*, ed. Sigmund Bonk et al. (Regensburg: Pustet Verlag, 2019), 577–95.

48. Muratori, *De Ingeniorum*, bk. 1, ch. 13, 116: "Pietatem sapit horum facinus, sed perniciosam pietatem."

and promulgate revealed teachings. Chapter 15 deals with the difference between doctrine and discipline. Like most Church historians of his time, Muratori acknowledges that discipline changes, but not doctrine, and that the Church has the authority to require certain disciplinary actions on pain of sin (bk. 1, ch. 14, [151]).[49] Acknowledging that over time many abuses of her discipline occurred, Muratori emphasizes also here her limitations in setting up new or changing old disciplines (bk. 1, ch. 14, [151]).

Chapter 16 deals with the theological dimension of Church history. While the revelatory and inspired part of Church history must be accepted by all, Church history in the narrow sense must not, because it is based on fallible human witness and interpretation (bk. 1, ch. 16). Only teachings that Christ himself revealed or which prophets and apostles have written down or handed on orally can demand supernatural faith (bk. 1, ch. 16, [157]). The Church's infallibility only pertains to their interpretation. Consequently, all non-revealed teachings and decisions cannot demand supernatural faith. Muratori included in this latter category not only the canonization of the saints but also *facta dogmatica*; that is, logical conclusions from an already existing dogma. For example, the proposition "*x* is the legitimate Pope" or the teaching about the *Immaculate Conception* could be deduced from doctrines about the primacy of St. Peter or about the sinlessness of Jesus (bk. 1, ch. 17). Although decisions of the papal court or of councils about faith and morals are for Muratori "free from error" (bk. 1, ch. 18), the thinking Christian must differentiate between the content of the teaching, the person, and the words through which the teaching is expressed (bk. 1, ch. 19). This leads him to the establishment of a hermeneutic of Church documents that *rejects* blind obedience. Such a hermeneutic also leads him to the realization that the Church cannot judge infallibly whether an author has said this or that. This was also an argument used by the Jansenists to defend their cause and to reject the censoring of their authors. Consequently (bk. 1, ch. 20), the condemnation of books and propositions are not part of the Church's infallible teaching charism but nevertheless have to be accepted in obedience.

49. For example, fasting on days of abstention or the obligation to participate in the Eucharist on Sundays.

Against extremist views that demanded more censorship, Muratori insists that the right to academic freedom is so precious that the Church can only restrict it if opinions violate the faith or somehow undermine the dignity of Holy Scripture. Outside these fields, the Church has no right to infringe upon the right of free thought (bk. 1, ch. 21, [206]). Consequently, all sciences and arts which do not deal with truths necessary for salvation]). cannot be subject to the doctrinal judgment of the Church. Nonetheless, the Church Fathers and even some councils sometimes opined about questions of science, education, or philosophy. Are these utterances to be understood as authoritative? No, argues Muratori. Since these texts went beyond the limits (*ultra fines religionis*) of religion, even expressions of Church Fathers and councils on such topics must be regarded like those of any other private writer (*privati auctores*; bk. 1, ch. 21, [207]). Although arts and sciences have no intrinsic theological content, they could, however, indirectly contradict (*indirecte*) a religious truth—for example, when they demonstrate that the Bible reports scientific or historical facts incorrectly. This does, however, not damage the credibility and authority of Holy Scripture. Instead of approaching Scripture with an Arminian hermeneutic of suspicion, he suggests that the theologian has to approach the Bible first and foremost as the Word of God, and thus with reverence and love.[50] In cases in which a literal reading of the biblical text leads into a conflict with established scientific findings, the exegete has to follow science and interpret the text allegorically or figuratively, even if this move contradicts the consensus of the Fathers.[51] An example of a conflict in

---

50. Muratori, *De Ingeniorum*, bk. 1, ch. 21, 209. On some Catholic theories of early modern understanding of inspiration, such as Lessius's restricted "real inspiration," which seems to have similarities with Muratori's, see James T. Burtchaell, *Catholic Theories of Biblical Inspiration Since 1810* (Cambridge: Cambridge University Press, 1969), 44–88.

51. Muratori, *De Ingeniorum*, bk. 1, ch. 21, 218: "Rursus eas rationes, eamque evidentiam secum ducere interdum physicae, historia profana, atque aliae Artes possunt, ut prae illis non aeque evidentia, immo dubia sint Scripturae sacrae verba." Bk. 1, ch. 21, 220 about leaving the consensus of the Fathers if questions of morals and faith are *not* concerned: "In reliquis ipsos Patres quidem venerari, aut religiose, & *kata poda* sequi non cogimur: alioqui tot haberemus Haereticos aut saltem temerarios, quot habemus Scripturarum Interpretes."

which the theologian should take the side of science against the Church Fathers is in Muratori's eyes the biblical description of the sun moving around the earth (bk. 1, ch. 22, [221]). Defending the Copernican system, he argues that heliocentrism does not contradict the doctrine of the Church and should therefore be permitted in Catholic school curriculums. After all, since 1616 all books that taught the motion of the earth and the immutability of the sun were proscribed by the Holy Inquisition. Consequently, Copernicanism was only allowed as a *hypothesis*, but could not be defended as a *thesis* by Catholic theologians or scientists. Only in 1757 Benedict XIV decided to drop this rule for future editions of the *Index of Forbidden Books* but did not remove the prohibited books by Copernicus, Kepler, and Galileo.[52]

Muratori's treatment follows his previously established principles of a hierarchy of truths and of ecclesiastical teaching authority. It is therefore clear to him that the Church has no authority to demand religious obedience for her interpretation of astronomical or geographical descriptions in Scripture. Besides, he argues, the biblical authors used colloquial language (*ad opinionem vulgi* and *ad rudis populi sensum*) to explain theological truths to mostly uneducated readers and listeners. Therefore, Joshua's stopping of the course of the sun (Josh 10: 12–15) was entirely about describing God's sovereign power over the universe and not about an astronomical miracle (bk. 1, ch. 22, [222–24]). Every description of celestial bodies must therefore be regarded as accommodation or concession by the author of Scripture to the limited minds of the first listeners. Since accommodative imagery is always obscure

---

52. Maurice Finocchiaro, *Retrying Galileo, 1633–1992* (Berkeley: University of California Press, 2007), 138–39. The report of the consultant for the Congregation of the Index, Lazzarri, states that Copernican astronomy was now well established and accepted everywhere: "There is no need to speak of other books since it is clear and known to everyone of average education that nowadays the prevalent opinion among the most competent astronomers and physicists is that the earth moves around the sun. Here in Rome itself we can find that this is true.... Father Boscovich, who has tried to reconcile the modern discoveries with the earth's rest, has told me several times that he regards his reconciliation and the earth's rest most improbable from the point of view of pure natural reason, and that to believe this it is necessary to bind the intellect in deference to Faith" (Finocchiaro, *Retrying Galileo*, 143). See also the clear endorsement of Galileo in Paolo Frisi, *De Motu Diurno Terrae* (Pisa: 1756).

and often trivial, it can never belong to the deposit of faith or moral doctrine.[53] Accordingly, the theologian is justified in adopting a new scientific worldview and interpreting the biblical texts with its help, just as Galileo and Copernicus had done (bk. 1, ch. 22, [223]).

The most difficult task of an exegete is to find the true meaning of a text. Muratori defends the view that scriptural passages that contain doctrines of faith and morals have only *one literal meaning*, which was handed down by Church Fathers and councils. Literal, however, means more than the plain meaning of a word. It also includes a potentially *figurative* meaning. If for example, a text uses an idiom, a plain literal understanding makes no sense, and the theologian must therefore understand it as a *figure of speech*. Other texts, though, can contain *several literal meanings*. According to Muratori, the theologian is entitled to prefer in such cases the figurative to the purely literal (*proprium*) meaning if there is an acceptable reason. "This does *not* mean to convert the literal, historical sense into allegories, but to recognize this historical, literal sense of Scripture, which agrees well with the matter, the presentation, and the habit of the prophets" (bk. 1, ch. 22, [232]). For example, Lk 19: 44[54] cannot be understood as a literal prediction about the destruction of Jerusalem. After all, some stones in Jerusalem remained on top of each other, even if temple and city were largely destroyed in 70 AD. Therefore, this passage is to be understood in its literal meaning as a figure of speech. According to Muratori, one may assume such a figurative meaning if one does not contort the text (*contorta; violenta*) and does not approach Scripture with the suspicion of error (*omnis suspicio falsitatis ac erroris avertatur*; bk. 1, c. 22, [234]).

Muratori's careful examination demonstrated that the Copernican worldview did not oppose doctrine, not only because the biblical text could be understood figuratively and accommodatively, but also because it did not contradict faith and morals (bk. 1, ch. 22, [234]). Claiming authority in science was after all an egregious overreach of

---

53. Other examples of accommodative speech are, for example, anthropomorphic descriptions of God and his body. Muratori, *De Ingeniorum*, bk. 1, ch. 22, [222–23].

54. "They will smash you to the ground and your children within you, and they will not leave one stone upon another within you because you did not recognize the time of your visitation." Translation according to NABRE.

Church authority, which carried the serious risk of exposing her to public ridicule. The diligent mapping of the borders of the ecclesiastical magisterium therefore serves the reputation and dignity of the Church better than overzealous overreach (bk. 1, ch. 22, [234]).[55] Muratori deepens these reflections in the next chapter by focusing even closer on the freedom of the biblical exegete to interpret texts, but also on the duty of Church leaders to never surrender to the irrational demands of zealots, who wish to condemn scientific theories based on their distorted views of Scripture (bk. 1, ch. 23 and ch. 24).[56]

Book II   The second book continues reflections on wise or excessive restrictions of freedom. Muratori begins by inquiring whether there must be unrestricted freedom to propagate the truth. He agrees, however, only if the proclamation of truth does not violate justice, love, or prudence and thus imposes his standard of moderation. He offers as an example the treatment of heretics. If these propagate their subjective truth claim in a Catholic territory, they act against justice because they cannot be objectively certain of their religion and are not legitimately authorized to preach it (bk. 2, ch. 1). Therefore, a ruler may reasonably restrict their freedom of speech. He acknowledges similar restrictions for cases in which the proclamation of truth violates charity; for example, by publicly shaming an ecclesiastical leader. This principle of charitable discourse also permits ecclesiastical and state authorities to act as censors (bk. 2, ch.2), but only if they themselves follow a charter of personal integrity (bk. 2, ch. 3). Only in rare circumstances is it according to Muratori justified to mention the moral failures of an opponent in public. This distances the librarian of Modena from the standard tactic of Catholic polemicists, who described with delight every moral

---

55. Galileo had already urged this in a letter to Grand Duchess Christina in 1615. See Schüssler, *Moral im Zweifel*, vol. 1, 237–39. Moreover, Galileo had argued that Scripture should be interpreted literally "unless the literal interpretation contradicts propositions that are *capable* of being conclusively demonstrated" (Finocchiaro, *Retrying Galileo, 1633–1992*, 151).

56. Ulrich Weiss (1713–63) repeats this warning about using Holy Scripture to defend one's own physical theories. He charges the Benedictine Ludwig Babenstuber (1660–1726) in Salzburg of his behavior. See Ulrich Weiss, *Liber de Emendatione Intellectus Humani* (Kaufbeuren: 1747), p. 2, c. 17, § 371.

fault in the lives of their opponents.[57] Truth, however, also demands that theologians should not conceal the failures of the Church Fathers (bk. 2, ch. 4). Nevertheless, they should be mentioned with modesty and charity.

These considerations lead Muratori to his fifth chapter (bk. 2, ch. 5), in which he discusses whether bishops and popes have the authority and the moral obligation to censor books. He is convinced that only writings that endanger the public or religious common good, ridicule the faith or contain heretical or immoral teachings, should be proscribed. Furthermore, he openly acknowledges that ecclesiastical censors often fail in justice and charity and treat authors inhumanely. Predictably, he offers in the next chapter (bk. 2, ch. 6) a set of rules that should guide a prudent censor. An ecclesiastical judge, for example, must be able to judge propositions according to the theological notes[58] and thus according to their doctrinal authority. The ability for such discernment differentiates credulous zeal[59] from a faith informed by reason. Interestingly, some of Muratori's suggestions will later be implemented in the reform of papal censorship under Benedict XIV.[60]

From chapter 7 onwards, the thorny issue of freedom for dissenters from the Catholic faith is treated. As a child of his time, Muratori cannot fathom religious freedom as a value. He consequently has little appreciation for the toleration of other Christian churches in a Catholic

57. Johannes Cochlaeus remains a good example for this approach; see for example his *Commentaria de actis et scriptis Martini Lutheri Saxonis chronographice ex ordine ab anno Domini 1517 usque ad annum 1546 inclusive fideliter conscripta* (Mainz: 1549) and closer to Muratori's time the voluminous writings of Nicolaus Weislinger, *Friss Vogel, oder Stirb* ... (Strasbourg: 1722) and his *Ausserlesene Merckwürdigkeiten, von alten und neuen theologischen Marckschreyeren*, 4 vols. (Strasbourg: 1738).

58. Johann Finsterhölzl, "Theological Notes," in *Sacramentum mundi*, ed. Karl Rahner, vol. 6 (New York: Herder and Herder, 1970) 228–29; Sixtus Cartechini, *De valore notarum theologicarum et de criteriis ad eas dignoscendas* (Rome: Gregorian University, 1951).

59. This chapter also contains his remarks about the "censoring" of the Church Fathers in Spanish editions, which William Cave (1637–1713) criticized in his *Scriptorum Ecclesiasticorum Historia Literaria* (London: 1688), prolegomena.

60. Hubert Wolf and Bernward Schmidt, *Benedikt XIV und die Reform des Buchzensurverfahrens zur Geschichte und Rezeption von "Sollicita ac provida"* (Paderborn: Schöningh, 2011).

territory. Relying on traditional arguments he defends the right of Church and state to force heretics (who are baptized Christians) to accept the true religion (Catholicism), but also the need to publicize the truth of the true religion. He argues vehemently against Leclerc's demand for toleration but also his hostile interpretation of Augustine and places the latter's comments on "compelle intrare" ("force them to enter") in their proper historical context (bk. 2, ch. 7). Muratori concedes that some but not all persecutions of heretics were/are unjust (bk. 2, ch. 8; ch. 10). Consequently, he argues, it would be false to describe Augustine as "cruel" since he gave "good reasons" for the intolerant treatment of the Donatists. Furthermore, Muratori compares the Catholic persecution of heretics with the persecution of infidels by Muslims (bk. 2, ch. 9). Defending the measures against the Donatists, the librarian of Modena argues that the early Christians had resisted persecution by the pagans when their accusations were irrational or based on lies (bk. 2, ch. 11). In chapter 12, Muratori refutes Leclerc's claim that the persecution of dissenters by a Christian prince can be used by the Ottoman government to legitimize their actions against local Christians or compared to these.[61] Besides, state governments must, he reasons, care for the religion of their subjects and make sure that the truth of the Catholic faith can be proclaimed without hindrance (bk. 2, ch. 12). Although Catholic princes must not act as strictly against pagans, Jews, and Muslims as they do against heretics, their actions must be shaped by clemency. Nevertheless, if a heretic violates both canonical laws and civic laws, he deserves just punishment (bk. 2, ch. 13, [377]). The differentiation between obstinate heretics and their second- or third-generation followers, who since their childhood

---

61. Cf. Paula S. Fichtner, *Terror and Toleration: The Habsburg Empire Confronts Islam, 1526–1850* (London: Reaktion Books, 2008); Helene Pignot, *Christians Under the Ottoman Turks: French and English Travelers in Greece and Anatolia, 1615–1694* (Piscataway, NJ: Gorgias Press, 2009); Tijana Krstic, *Contested Conversions to Islam: Narratives of Religious Change in the Early Modern Ottoman Empire* (Stanford, CA: Stanford University Press, 2011); Tobias P. Graf, *The Sultan's Renegades: Christian-European Converts to Islam and the Making of the Ottoman Elite, 1575–1610* (Oxford: Oxford University Press, 2017). See also Bruce Masters, "Christen unter osmanischer Herrschaft (1453–1800)," in *Geschichte des Globalen Christentums*, vol. 1, ed. Norman Hjelm et al. (Stuttgart: Kohlhammer, 2017), 177–210.

have been immersed in "false teaching" and do not espouse obstinacy *against* the Catholic Church, is a key element of Muratori's irenicism. He therefore concludes that the latter should no longer be labelled heretics (bk. 2, ch. 13, [384]) and treated with "docility."[62] Especially the tribunals of the Inquisition, whether in Rome or Spain or elsewhere, must show mercy and charity (bk. 2, ch. 13, [385–86]) so that they do not worsen the Church's reputation.

The fourteenth chapter leaves the context of dissent and returns to the question of freedom of thought within the Church. Muratori expresses his profound apprehensions about those who through uninformed zeal (*zelus ineruditus*) claim excessive liberty in questions of faith and Church discipline (bk. 2, ch. 14). By declaring propositions dogmas which are not, they create the "monster of superstition" (bk. 2, ch. 14, [394]) and prepare the way to schism or heresy. While zeal for God is laudable, it becomes dangerous if uneducated people are set ablaze by it and do things that contradict reason, prudence, and Christian charity (bk. 2, ch. 14, [391]). Thus, ecclesiastic leaders must tame such fanatics and educate them, but also prepare the clergy to do so (bk. 2, ch. 14, [393]). In this respect, mere knowledge of scholastic theology, by which he understands speculative theology, is insufficient. Priests and bishops must also study positive theology, by which he means the history of dogma as well as its scriptural grounding and have a good knowledge of the doctrines that separate Catholics from other Christians (bk. 2, ch. 14, [394]). If Church leaders do not discipline the *zealots*, they will run from their shepherds because they see them as dangerous "wolves" and embrace "pseudoprophets" as their teachers (bk. 2, ch. 14, [395]).

Book III The last book investigates specific theological problems in the works of Augustine, which Leclerc finds unpalatable. It is hardly surprising that the first chapter treats original sin. Leclerc not only rejects this doctrine but also seems to embrace a form of Pelagianism, which

---

62. For a discussion of this theological issue, see Eric Demeuse, "The Ecclesial Status of Heretics and Their Baptized Children in Early Modern Ecclesiology," in *Innovation in Early Modern Catholicism*, ed. Ulrich L. Lehner (New York: Routledge, 2021), 111–25.

leads Muratori to suspect that he is a covert supporter of Socinianism (bk. 3, ch. 1, [400–401]). Leclerc's dismissal of infant baptism is treated in the following chapter (bk. 3, ch. 2).

Curiously, Leclerc also charges Augustine with denouncing sexual lust (*concupiscence*) as sinful. This is, as Muratori shows, a misreading of Augustine.[63] After all, for Catholics concupiscence itself is not sinful, while for the major Protestant churches it is.[64] For Catholics, concupiscence was an effect of the Fall and signified that the once good human nature was damaged, but not fully corrupted. The sin of the first parents (Adam and Eve), Muratori explains, has subjected all of humanity to disordered lust, which a person must control through reason and the help of grace. This disordered lust by itself, however, was not sinful, but merely a condition of human life. Had the Fall not happened, sexual lust would have remained ordered and thus reasonable, he argues (bk. 3, ch. 3). Moreover, while Leclerc attributes to free will the ability to achieve salvation, Muratori rejects this as a Pelagian and thus heretical position. Instead, he defends a middle way, which he sees in the Council of Trent, according to which human freedom contributes to salvation but cannot achieve it without grace (bk. 3, ch. 4).[65] Leclerc portrays Augustine as an early Calvinist who teaches

---

63. For an overview including helpful bibliographical details, see Matthew Levering, *Engaging the Doctrine of Creation: Cosmos, Creatures, and the Wise and Good Creator* (Grand Rapids: Baker Academic Press, 2017), 227–72. For a detailed history of original sin in Catholic theology see the handbook of dogmatic history: Leo Scheffczyk, *Urstand, Fall und Erbsünde: Von der Schrift bis Augustinus*, Handbuch der Dogmengeschichte vol. 2/3a-1 (Freiburg: Herder, 1982); Manfred Hauke, *Urstand, Fall und Erbsünde: In der nachaugustinischen Ära bis zum Beginn der Scholastik: Die griechische Theologie*, Handbuch der Dogmengeschichte vol. 2/3a-2 (Freiburg: Herder: 2007); Michael Stickelbroeck, *Urstand, Fall und Erbsünde: In der nachaugustinischen Ära bis zum Beginn der Scholastik: Die lateinische Theologie*, Handbuch der Dogmengeschichte vol. 2/3a-3 (Freiburg: Herder: 2007); Heinrich M. Köster, *Urstand, Fall und Erbsünde in der Scholastik*, Handbuch der Dogmengeschichte vol. 2/3b-1 (Freiburg: Herder, 1979); Heinrich M. Köster, *Urstand, Fall und Erbsünde von der Reformation bis zur Gegenwart*, Handbuch der Dogmengeschichte vol. 2/3b-2 (Freiburg: Herder, 1982).

64. Jairzinho L. Pereira, *Augustine of Hippo and Martin Luther on Original Sin and Justification of the Sinner* (Göttingen: Vandenhoeck and Ruprecht, 2013).

65. On the differing concepts of grace from the Reformation to the twentieth century, see Jose Martin-Palma, *Gnadenlehre: Von Der Reformation bis zur Gegenwart*, Handbuch der Dogmengeschichte vol. 3/5b (Freiburg: Herder, 1980).

that grace forces human freedom instead of preparing and augmenting it (bk. 3, ch. 5 and 6). It is therefore not surprising that Muratori defends the Church Father against this appropriation and against the charge that he misunderstood the different forms of human freedom (*voluntarium; liberum*) (bk. 3, ch. 7). Instead, he offers a detailed exposition of Augustine's teaching that God's grace fully empowers human freedom (bk. 3, ch. 8).[66]

In chapter 9, Muratori defends the teaching about Christ's descent into Hell, which Leclerc rejects (bk. 3, ch. 9), while in chapter 10 Augustine's view of papal authority is explained (bk. 3, ch. 10). Since Augustine's own authority hinges on his faithfulness, Leclerc attempts to undermine the accounts of his and Ambrose's miracles, while Muratori defends their authenticity, but not without acknowledging that no Catholic is obliged to believe these accounts (bk. 3, ch. 11).

Following Protestant polemics, Leclerc ridicules the Catholic veneration of angels and saints as well as prayers for the dead and the evangelical counsel of celibacy.[67] Muratori defends these practices not just historically but also demonstrates that much of Leclerc's criticism is based on a misunderstanding of Catholic doctrine (bk. 3, ch. 12). More creative are, however, the following chapters, in which Muratori is not so much engaged in an apology for doctrine but rather with a critique of Leclerc's methodology. This becomes obvious, when he charges him with misrepresenting texts of the Church Fathers as "lies" (bk. 3, ch. 13), of accusing Augustine of being untruthful because he does not give sufficient evidence for his claims (bk. 3, ch. 14), or of attributing to the saintly bishop excessive self-love (bk. 3, ch. 15). Even more preposterous is in Muratori's eyes the accusation that Augustine's allegorical exegesis should be dismissed because it is not based on knowledge of the Hebrew text and because he taught doctrines *contrary* to the Catholic faith. To buttress his arguments in Augustine's defense, though, Muratori does not cite Catholic apologetics but rather Protestant authorities, such as

---

66. A concise introduction to the Catholic doctrine of grace is given by the late Edward T. Oakes, *A Theology of Grace in Six Controversies* (Grand Rapids, MI: Eerdmans, 2016).

67. Cf. Stefan Heid, *Celibacy in the Early Church: The Beginnings of a Discipline of Obligatory Continence for Clerics in East and West* (San Francisco, CA: Ignatius Press, 2000).

John Drusius (1550–1616) and Hugo Grotius (1583–1645) (bk. 3, ch. 16), and demonstrates in the final chapter that the Church Father is not an inventor of new doctrines but an authentic teacher of the faith (bk. 3, ch. 17).

About This Edition

This edition contains the first thirteen chapters of book one of Muratori's *De Ingeniorum Moderatione*. Since the text refers frequently to questions of proper interpretation of Scripture, the editor decided to add also the twenty-second chapter on Biblical exegesis and the Copernican worldview. The textual basis was the 1779 edition of the Latin text as it appeared in Augsburg, Germany. Muratori's often long-winded Latin was at times broken up into shorter sentences to allow for better readability. Since Muratori does not give titles for his chapters, orientation in the text can become difficult. Therefore, the author decided to add chapter titles. The subheadings within each chapter were also added by the editor; Muratori had placed them all together as a summary at the beginning of each chapter. The editor decided to use these lines as subheadings to give the reader an easier orientation throughout the text. The numbers in [brackets] signify the page numbers in the Augsburg edition. *Sancti patres* was consequently translated as Church Fathers. Since Muratori only sometimes uses *St.* or *Sanctus/Beatus* for other saints, the editor decided to only mention the name (e.g., Augustine instead of St. Augustine), and so forth. The Church was throughout attributed a feminine gender.

The translation aimed at being as close to the original as possible. Wherever suitable, Latin terms are given in [*brackets*] behind their translation to enable the specialist to weigh more accurately the accuracy of the translation. The bibliographic citations of Muratori were corrected where needed. The editor's comments in the footnotes are in [brackets].

Bibliography

I. Editions of *De Ingeniorum Moderatione*

De ingeniorum moderatione in religionis negotio, ubi quae iura, quae fraena futura sint homini christiano in inquirenda & tradenda veritate, ostenditur: & sanctus Augustinus vindicatur à multiplici censura Joannis Phereponi.
Paris: Ch. Robustel, 1714. 548pp.

Subsequent Editions:[1]

Cologne: s.p. 1716.
Frankfurt: Wilhelm Metternich, 1716.
Venice: Sebastian Coleti, 1727; 1738.
Venice: G.B. Pasquali, 1741; 1752; 1763; 1768; 1777; 1793.
The Hague: Joan Swart, 1745.
Paris: Rollin, 1737.
Arrezzo: Michele Billotti, 1770 (*Opere*, vol. X/1).
Augsburg: Matthaeus Rieger, 1779.
Bamberg: 1794/95.
Bassano: Remondini, 1781.
Venice: Cymbularii, 1840.

German Translations:

Lamindi Pritanii oder des gelehrten Herrn Ludovici Antonii Muratori Abhandlung von der Mäßigung der Denkungsart in Absicht auf Religions-Sachen Worinnen so wohl die einem Christen zustehende Rechte als auch derselben Einschränkungen in der Untersuchung und dem Vortrag der Wahrheit gezeiget, und der heilige Augustinus wider den vielfältigen Tadel des Johann Pherepons gerettet wird. 2 vols. Frankfurt: Krauß, 1770.
Ludwig Anton Muratori über den rechten Gebrauch der Vernunft in Sachen der Religion. Koblenz: Bädeker, 1837.

---

1. According to Ludovico Muratori, *De Ingeniorum Moderatione*, ed. Andrea Grandorgaeo (Venice: 1752), XXXVIII; https://www.centrostudimuratoriani.it/muratori/de-ingeniorum-moderatione.

II. Other Sources[2]

Anonymous, *Benediktinermuseum*. *Heft Zwei*. Tegernsee: 1791.
The New American Bible: Washington, DC: United States Conference of Catholic Bishops, 2002. (=NABRE).
The Holy Bible translated from the Latin Vulgate. Douay-Rheims Edition. New York: P. J. Kenedy & Sons, 1914.
Augustine. *Letters*. Vol. 2. Translated by Wilfred Parsons (FC 18). Washington, DC: The Catholic University of America Press, 1953.
———. *Letters of St. Augustine of Hippo*. Vol. 2. Translated by Marcus Dods. Edinburgh: 1875.
———. *The Teacher; The Free Choice of the Will; Grace and Free Will*, trans. Robert P. Russell (FC 69). Washington, DC: The Catholic University of America Press, 1968.
———. *On Christian Belief: The Works of Saint Augustine, a Translation for the 21st Century.* I/8. Translated by Matthew O'Connell. New York: New City Press, 2005.
———. *The Immortality of the Soul.* Translated by Ludwig Schopp et al. (FC 4). Washington, DC: The Catholic University of America Press, 1977.
———. *Opera Omnia*. Patrologia Latinae Elenchus. Online version: www.augustinus.it.
———. *The Trinity.* Translated by Stephen McKenna (FC 45). Washington, DC: The Catholic University of America Press, 1963.
Cave, William. *Scriptorum Ecclesiasticorum Historia Literaria*. London: 1688.
Corpus Iuris Canonici. Vol. 1, 2nd ed. Edited by Aemilius Friedberg. Leipzig: 1879.
Chladenius, Martin. *Disputatio theologica posterior adversus Lamindum Pritanium excutiens ac refellens methodum pontificiorum*. Wittenberg: 1717.
———. *Dissertatio theologica ... adversus Lamindum Pritanium vindicans methodum euangelicorum in inquirenda veritate coelesti quam ....* Wittenberg: 1717.
Cochlaeus, Johannes. *Commentaria de actis et scriptis Martini Lutheri Saxonis chronographice ex ordine ab anno Domini 1517 usque ad annum 1546 inclusive fideliter conscripta*. Mainz: 1549.
Denzinger, Heinrich, and Peter Hünermann. *Compendium of Creeds, Definitions, and Declarations on Matters of Faith and Morals*. 43rd ed. San Francisco: Ignatius Press, 2012. (=DH)
Erasmus of Rotterdam, *The Enchiridion of Erasmus*. Translated by Raymond Himelick. Bloomington: Indiana University Press, 1963.
Feijoo y Montenegro, Benito Jerónimo. "The Problem of Miracles." In *The Catholic Enlightenment. A Global Anthology*, edited by Ulrich L. Lehner and Shaun Blanchard, 77–90. Washington, DC: The Catholic University of America Press, 2021.
———. "In Defence of Women." In *In Defence of Women*, edited by Joanne Barker, 30–81. Cambridge: Modern Humanities Research Association, 2018.

---

2. Names of publishing houses are not given for books printed before 1900.

Frisi, Paolo. *De Motu Diurno Terrae*. Pisa: 1756.
Gaspari, Giovanni B. de. *Vindiciae adversus sycophantas juvanienses*. Cologne [i.e., Venice]: 1741.
Holden, Henry. *Divinae fidei analysis*. Paris: 1652.
Irenaeus, *Five Books against Heresies*. Translated by John Keble. London and Oxford: 1872.
Jansen, Cornelius. *The Predestination of Humans and Angels*. Translated by Guido Stucco. Washington, DC: The Catholic University of America Press, 2022.
Josephus. *The Jewish War*. Vol. 3, books 6–7. Translated by H. St. J. Thackeray. Loeb Classical Library 203. Cambridge, MA: Harvard University Press, 1928.
Leclerc, Jean. *Variorum exercitationes in S. Augustini opera* in *Patrologia Latina*, edited by Migne. Vol. 47, 197–570. Paris: 1877.
Mayr, Beda. *Vertheidigung der Katholischen Religion*. 3 vols. Augsburg: 1787/9.
Marcellio, Henrico. *Ars Interpretandi Scripturas Divinas: Pars Secunda*. Cologne: 1659.
Muratori, Ludovico. *Riflesioni sopra il buon gusto*. Vol. 1, Venice: 1708. Vol. 2, Cologne: 1715.
———. *Della Fallibilità dei pontefici nel dominio temporale* [posthumous], edited by C. Foucard. Modena: 1872.
———. *Della Forza della Fantasia Umana*. Venice: 1745.
———. *Delle forze dell'intendimento umano, o sia il Pirronismo confutato*. Venice: 1745.
———. *De superstitione vitanda, sive censura voti sanguinarii in honorem immaculatae conceptionis deiparae emissi, a Lamindo Pritanio, antea oppugnati, atque a Candido Partenotimo Theologo Siculo, incassum vindicate*. Milan: 1740.
———. *Della regolata divozion de' Cristiani*. Venice: 1747.
———. *Della regolata divozione de' Cristiani*. 2nd ed. Venice: 1748.
Petronius. *Satyricon*. Translated by Michael Heseltine. New York: Heinemann and Macmillan, 1913.
Poiger, Benedict. *De ingeniorum moderatione in rebus philosophicis*. Munich: 1793.
Riccioli, Giovanni B. *Almagestum novum astronomiam veterem novamque complectens observationibus aliorum*. Bologna: 1651.
Salvian. *The Writings of Salvian, the Presbyter*. Translated by Jeremiah F. O'Sullivan (FC 3). Washington, DC: The Catholic University of America Press, 1947.
Simon, Richard. *Réponse au livre intitulé Sentimens de quelques theologiens de Hollande sur l'Histoire critique du Vieux Testament*. Rotterdam: 1686.
Turrettini, François. *Institutes of Elenctic Theology*. Translated by George Musgrave Giger and James T. Dennison. 3 vols. Phillipsburg, NJ: P&R Publications, 1992–96.
Vergil. *Aeneid*. Translated by Theodore C. Williams. Boston: Houghton Mifflin, 1910.
Véron, François. *Regle générale de la foi catholique*. Paris: 1649.
Vincent of Lérins. *The Commonitorium of Vincentius of Lerins*. Cambridge: Cambridge University Press, 1915.

———. *The Commonitory of St. Vincent of Lerins*. Translated by T. Herbert Bindley. London: SPCK, 1914.
Weislinger, Nicolaus. *Friss Vogel, oder Stirb*. Strasbourg: 1722.
———. *Ausserlesene Merckwürdigkeiten, von alten und neuen theologischen Marckschreyeren*. 4 vols. Strasbourg: 1738.
Weiss, Ulrich. *Liber de Emendatione Intellectus Humani*. Kaufbeuren: 1747.

III. Secondary Literature

Al Kalak, Matteo. "La Provvidenza deciderà: Comacchio, Paolo Segneri e i dilemmi di Muratori." *Rivista di storia del cristianesimo* 11 (2014): 115–40.
Antiseri, Dario. *Ragioni della razionalità: Interpretazioni storiografiche*. Vol. 2. Rubbettino: Soveria Mannelli, 2005.
Barnett, Stephen J. "The Temporal Imperative: Criticism and Defence of Eighteenth-Century Roman Theocracy." *History of Political Thought* 22 (2001): 472–93.
Berger, Adolf. *Encyclopedic Dictionary of Roman Law*. Philadelphia, PA: American Philosophical Society, 1953.
Blanchard, Shaun. *The Synod of Pistoia: Jansenism and the Struggle for Catholic Reform*. Oxford: Oxford University Press, 2020.
———. "Liturgical Renewal and the Fight against Superstition." In *The Catholic Enlightenment. A Global Anthology*, edited by Ulrich L. Lehner and Shaun Blanchard, 21–36. Washington, DC: The Catholic University of America Press, 2021.
———. "Proto-Ecumenical Catholic Reform in the Eighteenth Century: Ludovico Muratori as Forerunner of Vatican II." *Pro Ecclesia* 25 (2018): 71–89.
Bragagnolo, Manuela. "Droit et histoire: Muratori et la critique de la papauté à travers ses sources inédites du xvie siècle." In *Droits antiromains xvie–xxie siècles: Juridictionnalisme catholique et romanité ecclésiale*, edited by Bernard Hours and Sylvio De Franceschi, 129–47. Paris: Larhra, 2020.
Braun, Karl-Heinz. "Das Reformprogramm des katholischen Aufklärers Lodovico Muratori." In *Religion und Aufklärung*, edited by Albrecht Beutel and Martha Nooke, 707–17. Göttingen: Mohr Siebeck, 2016.
Burnett, Stephen G. "Western Theologies and Judaism in the Early Modern World." In *Oxford Handbook of Early Modern Theology, 1600–1800*, edited by Ulrich L. Lehner et al., 469–81. Oxford: Oxford University Press, 2016.
Burtchaell, James T. *Catholic Theories of Biblical Inspiration Since 1810*. Cambridge: Cambridge University Pres, 1969.
Caesar, Ann, and Michael Caesar. *Modern Italian Literature*. Cambridge: Polity Press, 2007.
Cartechini, Sixtus. *De valore notarum theologicarum et de criteriis ad eas dignoscendas*. Rome: Gregorian University, 1951.
Charles, Sebastien. "On the Uses of Skepticism against a Certain Philosophical Arrogance: Huet as a Critic of Cartesian Logic and Metaphysics." *Science et Esprit* 65 (2013): 299–309.

Colombo, Emanuele. "Western Theologies and Islam in the Early Modern World." In *Oxford Handbook of Early Modern Theology, 1600–1800*, edited by Ulrich L. Lehner, Richard Muller, and A. G. Roeber, 482–98. Oxford: Oxford University Press, 2016.

Demeuse, Eric. *Unity and Catholicity in Christ: The Ecclesiology of Francisco Suarez*. Oxford: Oxford University Press, 2022.

Eire, Carlos. *War against the Idols: The Reformation of Worship from Erasmus to Calvin*. Cambridge: Cambridge University Press, 1986/1989.

Elliott, Mark W. "Jean Leclerc." In *Handbuch der Bibelhermeneutiken: Von Origenes bis zur Gegenwart*, edited by Oda Wischmeyer et al., 463–74. Berlin: DeGruyter 2016.

Feldhay, Rivka, and F. Jamil Ragep, eds. *Before Copernicus: The Cultures and Contexts of Scientific Learning in the Fifteenth Century*. Montreal, QC: McGill University Press, 2017.

Fichtner, Paula S. *Terror and Toleration: The Habsburg Empire Confronts Islam, 1526–1850*. London: Reaktion Books, 2008.

Finocchiaro, Maurice. *Retrying Galileo, 1633–1992*. Berkeley: University of California Press, 2007.

Finsterhölzl, Johann. "Theological Notes." In *Sacramentum mundi*, edited by Karl Rahner, vol. 6, 228–29. New York: Herder and Herder, 1970.

Franceschi, Sylvio Hermann de. "Catholic Theology and Doctrinal Novelty in the Quarrel over Grace." In *Innovation in Early Modern Catholicism*, edited by Ulrich L. Lehner, 28–47. New York: Routledge, 2021.

Gambarota, Paola. *Irresistible Signs: The Genius of Language and Italian National Identity*. Toronto, ON: University of Toronto Press: 2010.

Garrigou-Lagrange, Reginald. *On Divine Revelation*. Vol. 2. Translated by M. Minerd. Steubenville, OH: Emmaus Academic Press, 2022.

Geerlings, Wilhelm. "Jesaja 7,9b bei Augustinus: Die Geschichte eines fruchtbaren Missverständnisses." In *Fußnoten zu Augustinus: Gesammelte Schriften Wilhelm Geerlings*, 137–48. Turnhout: Brepols, 2010.

Goudriaan, Aza, et al., eds. *Revisiting the Synod of Dordt, 1618–1619*. Leiden: Brill, 2011.

Graf, Tobias P. *The Sultan's Renegades: Christian-European Converts to Islam and the Making of the Ottoman Elite, 1575–1610*. Oxford: Oxford University Press, 2017.

Graney, Christopher M. *Setting Aside All Authority: Giovanni Battista Riccioli and the Science against Copernicus in the Age of Galileo*. Notre Dame, IN: University of Notre Dame Press, 2015.

Hauke, Manfred. *Urstand, Fall und Erbsünde: In der nachaugustinischen Ära bis zum Beginn der Scholastik: Die griechische Theologie*. Handbuch der Dogmengeschichte vol. 2/3a-2. Freiburg: Herder: 2007.

Heid, Stefan. *Celibacy in the Early Church: The Beginnings of a Discipline of Obligatory Continence for Clerics in East and West*. San Francisco, CA: Ignatius Press, 2000.

Heinz, Gerhard. *Divinam christianae religionis originem probare: Untersuchung zur Entstehung des fundamentaltheologischen Offenbarungstraktates der katholischen Schultheologie*. Mainz: Grünewald, 1984.

Israel, Jonathan. *Radical Enlightenment: Philosophy and the Making of Modernity 1650–1750*. Oxford: Oxford University Press, 2001.

Jacob, Margaret. *The Secular Enlightenment*. Princeton, NJ: Princeton University Press, 2019.

Knox, Ronald. *Enthusiasm. A Chapter in the History of Religion*. Notre Dame, IN: University of Notre Dame Press, [1947] 1994.

Kolping, Adolf. *Fundamentaltheologie*. Vol. 1. Münster: Regensberg, 1968.

Köster, Heinrich M. *Urstand, Fall und Erbsünde in der Scholastik*. Handbuch der Dogmengeschichte vol. 2/3b-1. Freiburg: Herder, 1979.

Köster, Heinrich M. *Urstand, Fall und Erbsünde von der Reformation bis zur Gegenwart*. Handbuch der Dogmengeschichte vol. 2/3b-2. Freiburg: Herder, 1982.

Krstic, Tijana. *Contested Conversions to Islam: Narratives of Religious Change in the Early Modern Ottoman Empire*. Stanford, CA: Stanford University Press, 2011.

Laato, Anni Maria. "Isaiah in Latin." In *The Oxford Handbook of Isaiah*, edited by Lena-Sofia Tiemeyer, 489–503. New York: Oxford University Press, 2020.

Law, Timothy Michael. *When God Spoke Greek. The Septuagint and the Making of the Christian Bible*. New York: Oxford University Press, 2013.

Leeuwen, Th. Marius van, et al., eds. *Arminius, Arminianism and Europe: Jacobus Arminius (1550/60–1609)*. Boston: Brill, 2009.

Lehner, Ulrich L. *Enlightened Monks: The German Benedictines, 1740–1803*. Oxford: Oxford University Press, 2011.

———. *The Catholic Enlightenment: The Forgotten History of a Global Movement*. New York: Oxford University Press, 2016.

———. "De Moderatione in Sacra Theologia: Über die Grenzen theologischer Rede bei Ludovico Muratori (1672–1750)." In *Der dreifaltige Gott: Christlicher Glaube im säkularen Zeitalter*, edited by George Augustin et al., 349–64. Freiburg: Herder, 2017.

———. "Päpstlicher als der Papst: Georg Kaiser's (1801–1872) Papalismus." In *Glaube und Kirche in Zeiten des Umbruchs: Festschrift für Josef Kreiml*, edited by Sigmund Bonk et al., 577–95. Regensburg: Pustet Verlag, 2019.

———. "The Semantics of Religious Borders in Early Modern Confessions." *Reformation & Renaissance Review* 26 (2024): 54–79.

Lennon, Thomas M. "Pierre-Daniel Huet: Skeptic Critic of Cartesianism and Defender of Religion." In *Oxford Handbook of Descartes and Cartesianism*, edited by Steven Nadler et al., 780–91. Oxford: Oxford University Press, 2019.

———. *The Plain Truth: Descartes, Huet and Skepticism*. Leiden: Brill, 2008.

Levering, Matthew. *Engaging the Doctrine of Creation: Cosmos, Creatures, and the Wise and Good Creator*. Grand Rapids, MI: Baker Academic Press, 2017.

Livingstone, David N. *Adam's Ancestors: Race, Religion, and the Politics of Human Origins*. Baltimore: Johns Hopkins University Press, 2008.

Ludwig, Walther. "Humanistische Erforschung und Anerkennung nichtchristlicher Kultur und Religion—Schritte auf dem Weg zur Toleranz." In *Wechselseitige Wahrnehmung der Religionen im Spätmittelalter und der Neuzeit*, edited by Ludger Grennzmann et al., vol. 2, 7–58. Boston: De Gruyter, 2012.

Mansini, Guy. *Fundamental Theology*. Washington, DC: The Catholic University of America Press, 2018.

Marschler, Thomas. "Providence, Predestination, and Grace in Early Modern Catholic Theology." In *Oxford Handbook of Early Modern Theology, 1600–1800*, edited by Ulrich L. Lehner, Richard Muller, and A. G. Roeber, 89–103. Oxford: Oxford University Press, 2016.

Martin-Palma, Jose. *Gnadenlehre: Von der Reformation bis zur Gegenwart*. Handbuch der Dogmengeschichte vol. 3/5b. Freiburg: Herder, 1980.

Masson, Gustave. *The French Oratorians. Vol. 1: Richard Simon*. London: 1866.

Masters, Bruce. "Christen unter osmanischer Herrschaft (1453–1800)." In *Geschichte des Globalen Christentums*, edited by Norman Hjelm et al., vol. 1, 177–210. Stuttgart: Kohlhammer, 2017.

Mattison, William C. *Introducing Moral Theology: True Happiness and the Virtues*. Grand Rapids, MI: Brazos, 2008.

Methuen, Charlotte. "Time Human or Time Divine? Theological Aspects in the Opposition to Gregorian Calendar Reform." *Reformation & Renaissance Review* 3 (2001): 36–50.

Mulsow, Martin, and Israel Jonathan, eds. *Radikalaufklärung*. Berlin: Suhrkamp, 2014.

Pereira, Jairzinho L. *Augustine of Hippo and Martin Luther on Original Sin and Justification of the Sinner*. Göttingen: Vandenhoeck and Ruprecht, 2013.

Oakes, Edward T. *A Theology of Grace in Six Controversies*. Grand Rapids, MI: Eerdmans, 2016.

Pignot, Helene. *Christians under the Ottoman Turks: French and English Travelers in Greece and Anatolia, 1615–1694*. Piscataway, NJ: Gorgias Press, 2009.

Rapetti, Elena. "A Man Who Sticks Only to His Own Sentiments: Pierre-Daniel Huet's *Traite philosophique de la foiblesse de l'esprit humain*." In *The Skeptical Enlightenment, Doubt and Certainty in the Age of Reason*, edited by Jeffrey Burson et al., 45–68. Liverpool, UK: Voltaire Foundation and Liverpool University Press, 2019.

Rosa, Mario, and Matteo Al Kalak, eds. *Lodovico Antonio Muratori: Religione e politica nel Settecento*. Florence: Olschki, 2018.

Roth, John D., et al., eds. *A Companion to Anabaptism and Spiritualism, 1521–1700*. Leiden, Boston: Brill, 2007.

Shagan, Ethan H. *The Birth of Modern Belief: Faith and Judgement from the Middle Ages to the Enlightenment*. Princeton, NJ: Princeton University Press, 2018.

Sierhuis, Freya. *The Literature of the Arminian Controversy: Religion, Politics and the Stage in the Dutch Republic*. Oxford: Oxford University Press, 2015.

Scheffczyk, Leo. *Urstand, Fall und Erbsünde. Von der Schrift bis Augustinus*. Handbuch der Dogmengeschichte vol. 2/3a-1. Freiburg: Herder, 1982.

Schüssler, Rudolf. *Moral im Zweifel*. Vol. 1. Paderborn: Mentis, 2003.

Sorkin, David. *Religious Enlightenment: Protestants, Jews, and Catholics from London to Vienna*. Princeton, NJ: Princeton University Press, 2008.

Stickelbroeck, Michael. *Urstand, Fall und Erbsünde: In der nachaugustinischen

Ära bis zum Beginn der Scholastik: Die lateinische Theologie. Handbuch der Dogmengeschichte vol. 2/3a-3. Freiburg: Herder: 2007.

Swanson, Robert N. "*Dubius in fide fidelis est?* Doubt and Assurance in Late Medieval Catholicism." *Studies in Church History* 52 (2016): 186–202.

Swinburne, Richard. *The Existence of God*. Oxford: Oxford University Press, 1979.

Tutino, Stefania. "Jesuit Accommodation, Dissimulation, Mental Reservation." In *The Oxford Handbook of the Jesuits*, edited by Ines Županov, 216–40. New York: Oxford University Press, 2019.

Viola, Corrado. "Le 'Osservazioni critiche' di Giusto Fontanini al 'De ingeniorum moderatione' di Lodovico Muratori." *Studi sul Settecento e l'Ottocento* 15 (2020): 103–21.

Vismara, Paola. "Ludovico Antonio Muratori (1672–1740): Enlightenment in a Tridentine Mode." In *Enlightenment and Catholicism in Europe: A Transnational History*, edited by Ulrich L. Lehner and Jeffrey Burson, 249–68. Notre Dame, IN: University of Notre Dame Press, 2014.

Vranic, Vasilije. *The Constancy and Development in the Christology of Theodoret of Cyrrhus: Vigiliae Christianae*. Suppl. 129. Leiden: Brill, 2015.

Wallnig, Thomas. *Critical Monks: The German Benedictines, 1680–1740*. Leiden: Brill, 2018.

Wirszubski, Chaim. *Libertas as a Political Idea at Rome during the Late Republic and Early Principate*. Cambridge: Cambridge University Press, 1968.

Wolf, Hubert, and Bernward Schmidt, eds. *Benedikt XIV und die Reform des Buchzensurverfahrens zur Geschichte und Rezeption von "Sollicita ac provida."* Paderborn: Schöningh, 2011.

Preface

A Letter to the Illustrious Jean Paul Bignon, Abbot of St. Quentin[1]

[VII] Some years have passed since I completed the present book: *De ingeniorum moderatione*. That it comes to light so late was not caused by the excellent advice of Horace,[2] but by the fact that the manuscript had wandered around for a long time, was finally lost, and by a series of other events (with which I do not want to bore the reader, since they have nothing of interest for him), was found. However, I must not leave this unmentioned, but rather confess aloud that the final publication is owed entirely to the noble sentiments of Your Grace, who has finally snatched it from obscurity and brought it to light. In these days the sciences are happy to have a patron like Louis the Great of France, to whose liberalism they owe so much and under whose auspices they have reached a height that future generations will remember because of the generous care and wisdom of this excellent regent. However, they are no less fortunate that this same prince, who knows how to carefully nurture the spirits, has appointed Your Grace [VIII] as President of the Royal Academy of Arts and Sciences, an office in which You have spared no effort and labor to bring the various branches of science to fruition, here and everywhere. Thus, it has come about that I, too, although far away, have not remained unknown to Your Grace, and among the benefits that I have to thank Him for is not the least that this my writing, however imperfect it may be, has finally been saved from obscurity and is being handed over to the public. I could therefore

1. [Jean Paul Bignon (1662–1743), librarian of Louis XIV.]
2. [Horace, *De arte poetica*, I. 388 famously advised to wait with publishing one's work for nine years to allow the author's ideas to mature: "nonumque prematur in annum."]

dedicate it to no one with greater gratitude than to Your Grace, so that I may leave to posterity, if not a monument of my erudition, at least a monument of my gratitude. Meanwhile, before I invite Your Grace and the reader to pay attention to the subject I am dealing with, I consider it appropriate to preface it with something from which the occasion and the purpose of the book will become apparent.

The works of most excellent authors, which were extremely rare or no longer available, or which could only be obtained at high prices, have already been reprinted in the Netherlands some years ago. The man who had not only succeeded in getting the booksellers in Amsterdam to undertake this enterprise, but who had also put his hands to work so that these books, even if not flawless, would nevertheless be reissued in beautiful editions, has, I must confess, my applause. For why should I withhold my approval from an undertaking that is profitable for science and scholars, merely because it was undertaken by the Dutch? Would I not approve and praise such an undertaking, had it originated in my homeland? However, the enterprise has not stopped there: for one has added to some of the most excellent works, commentaries and critical notes that are not infrequently full of bile and poison. On the surface they seem to have the sole purpose of explaining obscure passages or correcting erroneous views. Yet, since these notes were often filled with immodesty and attacks on the most sacred mysteries of religion, it must be said that the small service done to the classical authors by printing new editions has been outweighed by the gross injustice done to them. It was, in fact, a disservice to Catholic scholars.

Before all the others, I must mention here the notes to the works of St. Augustine, which the editor in question, under the fictitious name of John Phereponus,[3] had published in 1704 [IX] in Antwerp or Amsterdam. How greatly and justly was Augustine's name, genius,

---

3. [*Phereponus*, which means in the original Greek something like troublemaker, was the pseudonym of Jean Leclerc (Joannes Clericus) (1657–1736), a theologian and philologist from Geneva. His interpretation of Scripture, the Christian doctrines and the Fathers was heavily influenced by John Locke and Spinoza and tended to be rationalist. Leaving Calvinism behind, he joined the Remonstrants, at whose seminary he taught in Amsterdam. See Mark W. Elliott, "Jean Leclerc," in *Handbuch der Bibelhermeneutiken: Von Origenes bis zur Gegenwart* ed. Oda Wischmeyer et al. (Berlin: DeGruyter, 2016), 463–74, however focusing on his exegesis and thus not mentioning his *Appendix Augustiniana*.]

and devotion praised! His authority was recognized for centuries by the approval of so many Catholic and non-Catholic scholars. Always, scholars have bowed to Augustine's teachings, and even today they almost universally bow to them, not just Catholics but also Protestants, and peruse his works to support their views with the reputation of such a great teacher. However, in cases where it seemed opportune and advisable to deviate from one of his opinions, it has always been done in a respectful way that did not damage his reputation or his influence on other matters. Those, however, who have put aside all shame and have tried to throw Augustine down from the summit of his reputation, have so far been considered at least audacious people. But nothing could stop Phereponus from challenging Augustine and from attacking him with insults and mockery. He has not rejected individual verses, not individual views of Augustine, but he has declared war on Augustine's reputation. He left nothing untried to portray him to the unguarded reader not only as a sophistical, dangerous, and weak mind, but also as a man who, strictly speaking, in his character was not averse to bad arts, and who conspired to ruin religion.

Therefore, well-meaning and learned men have raised their complaints about Phereponus, who is so hostile to this holy bishop. By despising Augustine, he also despises all the judgments that have been pronounced by so many in his favor. He may succeed in persuading himself or others that he attacked Augustine merely in the interest of truth, which must be more important to man than anything else: but he will hardly succeed in persuading anyone that in this fight he did not exceed the measure of prudent criticism. Moreover, many have not found anything original in his critique. For to make a name for oneself, there is hardly an easier means than to dress oneself up as a critic, especially of writers who, to put it this way, are sanctified by the prestige that antiquity bestows upon them. There are not a few critics who, as soon as they believe they have discovered errors in great men, silently congratulate themselves, as if they now excelled in intellect and judgment over them or flatter themselves that they now surpass those writers who are preferred by so many others.

[X] On the other hand, the language of envy and jealousy finds a willing ear, as Tacitus says in the beginning of his history books, and many readers find pleasure in sarcastic writings in which great men are mocked and ridiculed. Sometimes the criticism of another author's work is useful for us in order to form our own judgment, but it always flatters our ambition, because even the smallest shrub immediately imagines that it has grown when it sees that surrounding tall trees have been bent. Yet, what if such criticism is directed against a celebrated man? This seems to be the most secure way in which a critic can achieve fame, namely adding their critical notes to the works of a celebrated man. Whether scholars want to or not, as soon as they purchase these works they are also buying the critic's words and get to know the man who wants to build his glory on the defamation of great men.

As for me, I disapproved of the work of Phereponus as soon as I got my hands on it and read it, and I was very saddened from the start about his audacious work. I am truly not a man who has any hatred for criticism; on the contrary, I hold it in extremely high esteem as an indispensable characteristic of a scholar, and I will never cease to appreciate the knowledge and proper use of it by others and to wish for it myself. I am talking about the art that helps us to distinguish true from false in science. I am not speaking, however, of the art that goes hand in hand with slander and satire and has a wicked reputation among the uneducated. I also accept the basic assumption that religious differences should not be a reason why we immediately dislike somebody's criticism. But there are people to whom everything is repugnant without distinction and who reject everything that is written by a fellow of a different religious persuasion. For such people it is reason enough to reject a book without further ado as soon as they know that the author is not a Catholic. As far as I am concerned, I will always dislike the ungodly teachings of the heretics; but I will never dislike the truth found even in the mouth of the heretics. Must one consider the works of heterodox scholars false and ungodly without first consulting them? Moreover, one must not condemn Phereponus only because he criticized St. Augustine so harshly. After all, St. Augustine's fame cannot be raised by our praise, [XI] nor his reputation destroyed by wicked words. Even if we prefer St. Augustine to most other Church Fathers, it is clear that the truth itself must be more important to us than his reputation. The individual Church Fathers are not so much teachers, but witnesses of truth, and even if we call them teachers of truth, we will never attach to them the predicate of infallibility. Why then should we be angry about a critic who has truth on his side, and improves our knowledge of St. Augustine? There can be only one justification why I dislike the work of Phereponus—namely, because according to my judgment he has sometimes contested truth itself and has heaped insults and slander upon it. Since public insults that are inflicted on a single truth affect all those who love the truth, and since one must react to dangerous diseases, I have come to the decision to write a pamphlet to save the reputation of St. Augustine and to defend the truth.

Yet, I believed I should not stop here and so I have gradually entered a much larger battlefield, the reasons for which I will not specify further. Everyone knows and experience confirms that criticism is an excellent and indispensable science that can nevertheless be misused and indeed often is perverted. As the healing arts, rhetoric, dialectic, and other arts and sciences that the immortal God has given to humanity, sometimes do harm not through their own fault but through the fault of the one who abuses them, so it is also the fault of the person if criticism, which has the preferential task of defending the truth, sometimes harms it. And indeed, how can we be surprised that so many and so persistent heresies and errors arise and continue to spread every day, when those who deal with science throw off all reins of moderation in the investigation of truth and do not recognize any limits on their ambitious reason [*ambitioso ingenio limitem*]? This should worry us more than the fate of St. Augustine. Nobody will say that I am insulting those people who through a deplorable schism have broken away from their mother, the Catholic Church, if I declare that there is no false and ungodly doctrine that the ancients taught or that was conceived in our days that does not find bold defenders among them. Of course, they will reply that their confession itself cannot be blamed for this. [XII] But if one can think what one likes in matters of faith, if one can go about the investigation of truth without the least salutary restriction—if this, as one assumes, was permitted at least to the founders of their sects, and if now everyone believes that one is permitted to do so just as well as Luther and Calvin were permitted to do it before: What then can prevent us from attributing all this unboundedness (*licentiae*) and all these evils to Protestantism itself?

Yet, non-Catholics do not deserve this fatal fame alone. Even in our own field we can list such accidents. For as soon as somebody believes that he stands above others in spirit, he lets himself be carried away by the lust for fame. He considers it beneath his dignity to agree with the views prevailing among scholars. He resists and rejects and places his hope for fame in the novelty of his teaching. Even if such people do not go as far as to fall away from the Catholic faith and the Catholic Church, their presumptuousness causes all kinds of disturbances that the wise man will prevent and that the righteous man must prevent. From this it is self-evident what the friends of true wisdom must observe: they must not so much seek knowledge *per se*, but rather the method and limit of knowledge [*scientiae modus ac terminus*]. If they do not, they will always strive for true knowledge but rarely come into its possession. Since, however, I am dealing primarily with religious knowledge, because therein lies fulfilment of the Christian life and because all sciences should ultimately arrive at this end, we must stop here, orient ourselves and, above all, make clear to ourselves how far one may advance in the investigation of truth and what *moderation* our mind must observe. Therefore, I could not help but finally decide to compile those rules that Phereponus, to my regret, despised against better knowledge. Scholars should always follow these rules if they desire to not only tame their own presumptuousness, but also avoid danger to their good name and soul and arrive by the safest path at the truth. That there are such rules and that, if they exist, one should carefully follow them, is something nobody will deny. After all, what great fruits can we expect from our studies, and from the careful inquiry of truth, if we have not clearly explored [XIII] how far we are able to proceed in our enterprise, and where our ambitious mind must find a limit? Deny these rules or disregard them only once, and you will see that criticism is no less pernicious than a knife that heals wounds in the hands of a prudent physician but becomes an instrument of murder in the hands of the criminal. It was such considerations that prompted me to undertake this, as I think, very useful work on the *moderation of our reason in religious matters*. May I only be able to complete it in a way that is worthy to meet the needs of some readers!

But even this scope could and must seem too narrow for my task.

Not a few would criticize me as if I wanted to invent new shackles, putting new chains on the mind, since it is already burdened with so many others. Should one therefore not loosen the old before one invents new ones? Certain Catholics will whisper to me in secrecy: Why do you want to recommend and so emphatically urge us to *think with moderation*? Does not the Catholic Church have numerous measures in place, and are they not enforced by manifold and severe punishments, perhaps more than we would like? When we sin, it is certainly not against the freedom of thought and press, but rather because we do not dare to speak out of fear and do not dare to expand the realm of wisdom and truth. Would it not be better to give a speech on the *freedom of the mind*? Why do you speak of reins where spurs are needed? This is the language that individual Catholics use. But a legion of Protestants will confront me with far more vehement complaints and reproaches. For it is customary among them to pity or ridicule Catholics because of their state of science or their doctrine, which they consider unfortunate and contemptible. Is it not a common prejudice among them to consider us no longer free men but wretched slaves? Moreover, do they not claim that our highest Church leaders exercise tyrannical power over the mind and conscience of every Catholic, and that our spiritual inertia is no less intolerable than their tyranny? The Rector of the Academy of Geneva, Johann Alphonsus Turretin,[4] dealt with this point extensively in a polemical speech only a few years ago. After he had brought forward many things to prove that not even a [XIV] shadow of freedom is to be found among us, he continued: "And why do you think that so many respected nations of Europe, which live in mild climates and have by no means been treated stepmotherly by nature, contribute almost nothing of importance to the flowering of science, than through that dreadful Inquisition tribunal or through those laws that can compete with the regulations of the Inquisition, whereby every strength, every intellectual pursuit [*industria*] is broken? Why is it, on

---

4. [François Turrettini (1623–87) was one of the most influential Calvinist theologians of the seventeenth century. His three-volume *Institutio Theologiae Elencticae* (1679–85) is considered a masterpiece of Reformed dogmatics. See Turrettini, *Institutes of Elenctic Theology*, trans. George Musgrave Giger and James T. Dennison, 3 vols. (Phillipsburg, NJ: P&R Publications, 1992–96)]

the contrary, that nowhere are there so many monuments of intellectual education as in some Nordic countries, where mind and body have the use of freedom? For who will promote knowledge, who will take pains to investigate the truth, who put a found truth in the spotlight, when one knows that all striving will end in contempt instead of praise if one deviates even a hair's width from the trodden path—if he receives disgrace instead of recommendation, punishment, and chastisement instead of reward? Who will still give advice if, as Darius very rightly says in Curtius's third book, it is dangerous to offer it?"

Thus speaks Turretin and others in his fold. If we were to pass over these accusations in the present work with silence, those who have an unfavorable opinion of us would feel vindicated, and we would deprive truth of a great advantage. Both *truth* as well as human *reason* [ingeniis] have their rights, and it is the duty of Catholic scholars more than of anyone else, to know and uphold them. For the right to inquire into truth and to make it known publicly is innate in the human person and has been recognized and exercised by all our ancestors. It is a right of such immense extent that we cannot disregard it without committing an injustice. Even if many misfortunes have arisen from immoderate freedom of thought, particularly for the Church, one must state on the other hand the advantages that arise daily from a prudent and truly Christian freedom of thought. The good results of the latter deserve to be praised and recommended to the nations, while one must strive to fight and banish immoderate freedom of thought. If the flourishing of science, the glory of Christian philosophy and of the Church are dear to our hearts, then, I think, it will be immediately understood how much it is our duty to work toward this end, partly so that not only ourselves, but also all other people, may be driven to investigate every truth that exists with virtue, and partly so that we may know for certain how far, how and when it is either permitted or advisable [XV] or obligatory to investigate the truth and bring it to light. Although it is easier to see the usefulness of such a task than to carry it out, I will nevertheless endeavor, as far as my intellectual powers permit, to point out the rights and limitations of freedom of thought. I want to use my faculties to demonstrate that *reason* inherent in human beings may be harmoniously united with *Christian moderation*.

After all, if the first is too restricted, excellent minds that are to promote science and truth will become lethargic and lazy. If, however, the second is despised, the glorious realm of truth and of the Church of the living God, which is the *pillar* and *origin* of truth, will be destroyed by unrestrained freedom of thought.

As for St. Augustine, who I first thought of in these reflections, I will defend him in several places, but especially in the third book, against Phereponus, but in such a way that I do not presume to answer every single point of criticism. Some of them are, however, so insignificant that it would be a waste of time to refute them. Nevertheless, there are also a few things in which I, without sharing the spiteful tendency of Phereponus, tacitly agree with the critic's judgment out of love for the truth. For how many people are there who, if they had not been guided by divine inspiration in their written records, would not at times have been guilty of an oversight? Augustine had an admirable sagacity, but he was a man. With an incomparable erudition he combined a high degree of piety, but he was a man. We should not be surprised, therefore, if in his slumbering or waking state something slipped out of his mouth that one does not approve of, but which one may gladly excuse. However, these remarks are not of such a nature that they diminish the fame of this incomparable man in the least, and they are in no way contradicting Catholic truth. As for the other, more important questions, however, for which Phereponus drags Augustine before his high court and punishes him, I pray to God that he may give me sufficient strength to defend Augustine, the Church, and the truth against him. Neither hatred against Phereponus nor flattery [*assentatio*] for Augustine may lead me away from the duty of a conscientious and sincere writer! If, however, [XVI] it should appear that I have sometimes treated Phereponus more harshly than I would have wished, it is not out of hatred for the person, but out of zeal for the cause of truth, which, as I will demonstrate with many examples, has not infrequently been mishandled by him. For although I do not approve of his contemptuous and bitter attacks on St. Augustine, although I detest the views in which he deviates from Catholic doctrine, I nevertheless do not deny his erudition and praise his understanding, which I have also seen in other respects, wherever such recognition is demanded.

This is all I wanted to say in the preface of the book, which is now yours, Most Reverend Abbot. It now remains for the author to add the plea: May Your Grace forever keep him in the favor and affection with which you have honored him so far. With the wish that Heaven may bless Your Grace, I remain in respectful reverence.

Modena, October 29, 1712

Chapter 1

On Knowledge and Truth

Which Truths Are Necessary to Know?

[1] In this book I will deal with reality and truth. Truth, in so far as it belongs to morality as a virtue and is of decisive importance for the maintaining of justice in society, lies outside the scope of my investigation. Such truth is more correctly called truthfulness, which means that virtue which consists in the conformity of thought to expression; or what is the same thing, which arises when one speaks as one thinks, and when one, even if unconsciously deceiving oneself, does not intend to deceive another. [2] About this virtue others shall write. I will strive to practice it, however, and deal with truth itself as the task of philosophy, theology, scholarship, and other arts and sciences. Since, however, their realm is extensive, I will proceed in such a way that, with the elimination of everything superfluous, I will deal only with what is useful and necessary. My task is therefore divided into two parts: first, I will determine the powers and limitations of those who search for truth, and then of those who teach it.

About the Outstanding Nature of Truth and Goodness

To investigate the reality of a thing means according to scholars nothing other than to investigate whether a thing exists at all, and then how it exists. To find the truth of a thing means again nothing other than to discover whether and how a thing is there. The first is uniquely appropriate to human nature since it is endowed with reason; the latter gives great pleasure. The blissful life and happiness itself, for which man is destined by nature and for which he strives for involuntarily, and which he can attain only through the Christian faith, consists in nothing other than in the knowledge of truth and in the love of the good. For the good and the true exist in God almost like his center [*veluti in suo centro*] or, to express it better, God is truth and goodness itself. For this is how he speaks of himself: "I am the way, the truth and the life" (Jn 14: 6). Since God's eternal goodness decided to create this world and to make humanity a witness of this admirable construction, he also poured out the true and the good upon all creatures, so that everything that *is*, is true, and that everything that is true is—at least in so far as it is true—good. Moreover, God has implanted in humans the impulse to strive for the true and the good, and so it happens that humans are driven toward the former by their intelligence, toward the latter by their will. For this reason, Cicero says that the human spirit has an innate, unfailing desire to see the true;[1] and above all, he states that the investigation and search for truth is peculiar to the human mind.[2] If we succeed in doing this according to the principles of the Christian faith, then we are already beginning to enjoy the highest, perfect, and eternal bliss that we hope to attain in Heaven.

Each Truth Can Be Pursued and Acquired

[3] That one must therefore investigate the truth is demanded by nature and is taught by reason. In my opinion, however, there is in general no truth in the whole range of divine and human things that we are not permitted to investigate and whose discovery would be incompatible with morality. This assertion may seem paradoxical at first sight if one considers how many and great evils commonly flow from the knowledge of individual truths. Yet, the nature of truth itself speaks for the correctness of this assertion. For in general every truth, when we recognize it, makes us see or know something, and enlightens our

---

1. Cicero, *Tusculunae Disputationes*, 1.
2. Cicero, *De Officiis*, bk. 1.

mind [*mente*], sometimes more, sometimes less, but always to a certain extent; this is obviously always extremely useful to humanity. And who would deny that ignorance is a pernicious evil? But this evil, in which everyone participates, is lifted through insight and knowledge, namely through the knowledge of truth. It is therefore clear that truth and its possession are the goods for which one must strive the most. And indeed, when these are bestowed upon us, they form the spirit in wisdom and lead us to that blissful state, to that clarity of mind [*mentis*] (as much as this is still possible after the Fall of our first parents) that we would also have been able to enjoy if the One[3] had not sinned. This is even clearer from the bliss of those to whom God has given eternal life. For all insights, which mortals strive for in vain, are available [*apertum*] to those immortal spirits in God, and thus their blessed state becomes increasingly happier and more perfect. For in that blissful realm of knowledge and truth there is no deplorable ignorance, as is the case with us.

By the way, I believe that there will always be those who doubt what I have said and will bring forth the following arguments against us: everything that is, is also good, and the love of the good is not only natural to God but is also innate in man. This will primarily be our happiness in eternal life. Yet, there are also many things that are pleasant and useful, which humans in this world may not love as goods, and which the moral law commands us to flee and abhor. On the other hand, there can also be truths (and there are indeed such truths) that healthy and educated minds [*rectis probeque instructis mentibus*] must not investigate, because if they are discovered, can only be pernicious to the soul that strives for the sublime. [4] For who cares so little about respectability that he would consider it permissible to investigate the multitude of those true facts and disgraces that have been perpetrated by the lust of individuals, which is so exceedingly inventive [*ingeniosissima in vitiis … luxuria*]? A person would undoubtedly be ill advised if, given the opportunity, one wanted to investigate everything that the emperor Tiberius committed during his seclusion on Capri. Who would not shy away from imagining that chair of secret voluptuousness

---

3. [That is, Adam in Paradise; see Gen 3.]

(to use the words of Suetonius), along with those monstrous kinds of fornication devised by male prostitutes, which this impure emperor engaged in [*monstrosos concubitus a spinstriis excogitatos*]? This would not enlighten the mind, but pollute it, and every unspoiled person would rather not know these shameful things than want to know them. Further, in magic, the mother of heresies and sorceries, there are many lies and innumerable deceptions, but perhaps also some truths; merely to get to know them or to investigate them only from afar is licitly forbidden. The same can be said of other similar things. It seems, therefore, that the proposition is quite wrong that there is no truth whose investigation is not permitted to us and whose discovery would give us illicit pleasure.

Here we must distinguish the rights of the true and the good both in their relation to human nature and in their relation to attaining permitted happiness. The true can only be related to our intellect [*intellectu*]—the good, on the other hand, to speak with the *Peripatetics*, to the will—the true wants to be recognized, the good wants to be loved. Although we recognize the good, we know it only from the side of its truth, which means that we appreciate the truth of a thing in so far as it is truly laudatory, useful, or pleasant. On the other hand, we also love the true; only we love it as something good and in so far as it is good. Therefore, it is part of human nature to recognize what is true and to want or love what is good. There is nothing true that we are not allowed to recognize and nothing good that we are not allowed to want in and of itself. But after human nature fell into that most deplorable state of which everyone is aware, there are two powers that often interfere with and pervert the splendid power of our intelligence and our will. These are the false and the evil; the former has a disturbing and concealing effect on the intellect, [5] the latter on the will. The false produces error in the intellect, if we accept and hold the true for false, the false for true. Evil produces sin in the will, namely when we flee the good as evil, but desire and love something evil as good. Yet since we must assume that the cognition of the true can never be paired with an error of the mind, there is no doubt that it must also be free from the sin of the will. Furthermore, when we come to know the truth of a bad and immoral thing, we do not immediately choose and love the evil itself.

We could merely desire the truth and the knowledge of this thing, and at the same time detest the bad, the ugly, the corruptible, and hate it in others. Therefore, the true in and of itself cannot harm, but it harms because of human wrongdoing, which here abuses something good; and in this sense we also admit that there may be certain circumstances under which it is impermissible for humans to investigate certain truths; namely, if they are investigated with bad intentions, or if the probable danger exists that knowing the truth would draw the investigator either to evil actions or seduce him [*trahat aut etiam solicitet*] due to his weakness. Thus, there are goods which, under certain circumstances, man is not allowed to strive for and which are rightly rejected by reason. Yet, this is not because the true and the good in themselves could ever be something evil, but because human sensuality is disordered and could misuse them or give them a perverted use counter to the order of things prescribed by God and the rules that reason dictates to us.

Objections against This Opinion Are Refuted with the Help of St. Augustine

Therefore, the sins of lust must not be invoked to show from their disgusting sight that the truth can sometimes be dirty [*sordide*]. It is certainly dangerous and possibly criminal to investigate such affairs. But even then the truth remains—considered in and of itself—honorable and useful, and is never evil. It may be present in bad things and be recognized, so that we flee from them, or in praiseworthy things, so that we are encouraged to imitate them. For here, too, as in the recognition of every other illicit and bad thing, two things must be distinguished: the true and the evil. The latter, because it is corrupting the will, must always be abhorred and shunned; the first, because it enlightens [*erudiendo*] the intellect [*intellectum*] and gives insight [*scientiam parit*], is never in and of itself illicit [*improbandum*]. Although I do not wish to encourage anybody to proceed indiscriminately [6] and immoderately with the investigation of truth,, I am nevertheless of the opinion that the evil that sometimes appears in the wake of the known truth is not due to the nature of truth itself, but to the corrupt state of human nature, which carelessly converts medicine into poison. The above can also be proved by examples. For if reason, as we have objected, forbade us to investigate the secrets of lust, they would be doing us a great disservice and would be sinning greatly against the honorable laws of discipline and morality, who have recorded so many incidents of lust in Latin writings and, to use their own words, have put a spotlight on all the nooks and crannies of evil. Also, Catholic confessors would take bad care of themselves when they listen daily to the confessions of their penitents. Finally, those who are charged with the eradication of heresies and the abolition of crimes would be in grave danger, for they must necessarily learn the truth about the many crimes before they condemn them. There are always people who disapprove of the procedures and zeal of certain theologians who bring to light such a multitude of carnal impieties, since the perverse find in their books no less instruction for the bad than the good find instruction for the good. But it is enough for our purpose to know that the investigation of the true is bound to other rules than its communication. Certainly, no reasonable man will blame the confessors and certain authorities, who are employed by the Church to abolish sorcery and other shameful offenses, because they learn certain truths that are better for one not to know. They learn about wounds and diseases in the manner of physicians, in order to heal them in others, not in order to be afflicted with them, and in becoming useful to others they do not fear harming themselves.

What I have said so far in favor of the truth, which in itself is always licit and only through human fault sometimes becomes harmful, can also be proved from the books of authoritative writers. Instead of all the others, I will mention Augustine. In the first book and first chapter of his treatise *De libero arbitrio*, he asks whether the learning [*disciplina sive discere*] of students or the instruction [*doctrina*] of teachers could be harmful. "Who would dare say," Evodius answers, "that learning is something evil? To me it seems to be something good."[4] And [7] Augustine answers him: "It certainly is, since, in fact, knowledge is imparted or awakened in us by learning, and it is only in this way that something is learned." Moreover, Augustine argues that

---

4. Augustine, *De libero arbitrio*, bk. I, ch. 1.2, in *The Teacher; The Free Choice of the Will; Grace and Free Will*, trans. Robert P. Russell (Washington, DC: The Catholic University of America Press, 1968), FC 69: 73.

instruction is never evil, but on the contrary only good, wherefore the objection "Where then does one learn evil?" becomes superfluous. "But if evil is something learned, we learn how to avoid it, how to do it."[5] But since Evodius nevertheless seems to doubt and believe that there is a learning that teaches us to do the right thing and one that teaches us evil, Augustine replies: "Do you at least think that understanding is something that can only be good?"—"So good," replies Evodius, "in fact, that I fail to see how anything else in man can be better, and I could not possibly say that any kind of understanding [*intelligentia*] is evil."[6] Augustine then continues: "If, then, every kind of understanding is good and no one learns who does not understand, then whoever is learning is doing good. For everyone who learns, understands, and everyone who understands is doing good."[7] Yet Augustine, in praising understanding, evidently understands by it the true learning [*veri disciplinam*]; for strictly speaking, one cannot say that one has learned and understood what is false. Thus, one must not waver [*non ambiguendum*], after having recognized this structure in nature [*perspecta institutione naturae*], to state [*generaliter loquendo*] that humans may investigate every truth and rejoice in it when they have found it. Nevertheless, this is only true when this wisdom is impressed on the heart: "It is good to know that everything is good, but it is not good to practice everything that one knows," and therefore one should never strive to know those truths, which do not enlighten the mind but also incite the will to evil.

There Are Two Realms of Truth, Namely Knowledge and Persuasion

We want to go further now. The extremely large area of the good and the true has many divisions. We will pass over many of them but establish the following: There are (1) truths that are known, and (2) truths that are believed. The first we attain by a careful use of our external senses, reflection, and assent of reason, or when reason discovers these

---

5. Augustine, *De libero arbitrio*, FC 69: 73–74.
6. Augustine, *De libero arbitrio*, FC 69: 74.
7. Augustine, *De libero arbitrio*, FC 69: 74.

truths with the aid of the means offered by logic or the sciences. We come into possession of the truths that are believed through acceptable and credible reasons, through alien authority, or through reliable information, which we receive from history, credible witnesses, [8] and contemporaries or other forms of human communication. One calls the knowledge of this second truth persuasion although it has such power and weight that it brings our mind to assent and conviction just as much as the first, which is properly called a science. We do not want to deal with the objections raised by Arcesilaus, Carneades, and Pyrrhus, along with the choir of skeptics who, while they wanted to be the most careful of all philosophers, or at least put on this appearance, were guilty of the greatest silliness and embraced the most delirious mistakes. Since they imprudently denied all knowledge, they did not even admit with Socrates, as they should have done, the certainty that they knew nothing. This philosophical doctrine has already been disgraced by time and right reason [*recta ratio*], and in our days many in the arts and sciences ridicule it, too. To quote from Lactantius in book three, chapter six of his *Divine Institutes*: "We humans cannot know everything, only God can. Yet, we cannot be ignorant in all things because that is a characteristic of cattle [*pecudis*]. There is, however, something in the middle that belongs to humanity [*hominis*], namely a temperate knowledge [*scientia*] that is conjoined with ignorance." As painful as it is we must agree with this statement. After all, human knowledge is in relation to its ignorance very limited and will always remain so. Just as the moral good, which we must strive for, is easy to recognize but difficult to carry out, so the true is easily desired and wanted by all, but difficult to find and know. Nevertheless, many truths can be recognized and known—a fact only an imbecile would deny. The area of those truths that we do not know but believe on the basis of opinion and not knowledge is also very extensive. In the middle, between persuasion and knowledge, stands divine faith, which is the firm conviction of the truth of religion and participates in both. It has many characteristics in common with persuasion but surpasses even knowledge in reliability, since it came down from Heaven and is thus based on divine authority. It appeals pleasantly to the human mind, takes complete possession of it, and seizes it with such determination that no act of violence, no terror of death, could destroy or weaken it. Just as there are grades in the love of goods, [9] so there is an order of truths: the lowest place is occupied by those that relate to the corporeal world, the middle place by those that relate to the rational soul, and the highest place by those that relate to the eternal bliss of the soul and the body awaiting its resurrection. But since nothing can be beautiful and perfect without order, we are instructed and admonished daily, both by the precepts of the Creator and by nature and reason, with the help of an inner instinct, to observe this order in the investigation of truth. For according to the precepts of the Gospel, the kingdom of God should be sought first and foremost, and to this end belongs the investigation and knowledge of those truths that make it possible for us to enter the kingdom of God. After this, we must pay special attention to the education of our mind, the splendor of scholarship, and worldly wisdom. We must cultivate them so that we, who are elevated above the animals by means of our reason, do not sink down to their level through shameful ignorance. In addition, we must cultivate the knowledge that provides for the well-being of the body, for its adornment and for its licit enjoyment. But how small is the number of people who observe this glorious order! Most people only strive for the acquisition of the lowest class of this knowledge. They do not care about educating and enlightening their soul [*illustrando beneque informando per sapientiam animo*], about true wisdom. They seem to put all their happiness in the recognition and enjoyment of the physically pleasant and the comforts of earthly existence. Others devote themselves to individual sciences and arts but bury themselves in them to such an extent that they seemingly forget the main tasks of human life, even if they do not despise them. If they can show that they are capable philologists, that they are learned jurists, physicists, and mathematicians, that they are ingenious fiction writers, and if they can display their acumen in disputations and are satisfied with themselves, these scholars often put aside all other studies through which a human becomes virtuous in this life and obtains beatitude in the next. Both, then, sin—not because they concern themselves with the truths of the lowest and second-lowest order (for to investigate the truth, as we have shown, is in itself nothing evil), but because they do not devote as great or greater diligence to the study and contemplation of the higher truths. Thus, they pervert the divinely instituted order, either by [10] their laxity or by their ambition. In the eleventh chapter of *De utilitate credendi*, Augustine says that "Understanding [*intelligere*] is always without fault. For the understanding of deep and honorable, nay even divine, matters is a most blessed thing. The understanding of superfluous things, however, is not harmful, but perhaps the learning was harmful in that it took up the time of necessary matters."[8]

There Is an Order among Truths

Within the great realm of truths, one therefore has to distinguish between those that give pleasure and those that are necessary [*delectabiles a necessariis*]. For it is not laudatory to ignore the first, but it is never considered a sin. Yet, not knowing necessary truths is not only a sin, but also often dangerous [*maximas miserias*]. For this reason, one will never have to fear admonition from a reasonable person if one has not learned to sing, to paint, or to cook [*ciborumque Apiciana industria*], although all these faculties can give manifold pleasures. On the other hand, one will be called extremely unwise if one does not know and does not want to know what is harmful to the body, what is necessary for the preservation of health, and what is to be avoided in this respect. For who does not know how much nature recommends that we take care of our bodies? Yet to disregard one's body without a particularly important reason, to rid oneself of it for any reason other than duty, virtue, or religion, is something only a coward or a delusional person would do. It is forbidden by the laws that God and nature have prescribed for us. Likewise, it will not be considered a sin if we do not occupy ourselves with the study of mathematical sciences, liberal arts, secular history, or natural science, even though they are suitable for forming the mind in a truly pleasant way and expanding our knowledge. On the other hand, we deserve admonition [*nemo nos excusatos*] if we do not know and do not want to know what the laws prescribe,

---

8. Augustine, *De utilitate credendi*, ch. 11.25 in *The Immortality of the Soul; The Magnitude of the Soul; On Music; The Advantage of Believing; On Faith in Things Unseen*, trans. Ludwig Schopp et al. (Washington, DC: The Catholic University of America Press, 1947), FC 4: 424.

partially for the moral and virtuous life, partially for the preservation of human society. After all, since nature created us not as irrational brutes, but as rational beings, it did not instruct us to live in solitude but in relationship with our relatives, friends, fellow citizens, and all mortals in our houses, cities, and diverse juridical and commercial ties. Thus, we are obliged to know and understand all things through which the welfare [*honestatem vitae*] and wisdom of humanity is augmented, and which bring about the proper fulfillment of our duties.

Especially the Truths of Religion Must Be Pursued

[11] Nothing must therefore be dearer to a human heart than the thorough knowledge of true religion. Only one religion can bring us to eternal bliss, namely by believing what we should believe about God, and worshiping and loving God in the way he wants to be worshiped and loved. It is therefore our duty to examine, before anything else, the true religion and then the truth of its individual doctrines; among which, however, some are necessary and others useful and pleasurable. Compared with this truth, all the splendor and all the advantage that the occupation of secular human sciences can offer is vain and to be regarded as nothing. For this reason, one would not go wrong to call so many philosophers and wise men of antiquity, whose immortal names have come down to us, unwise and unhappy, because they disregarded or neglected the true religion and are therefore in God's eyes contemptible beings. If then, the business of religion is such an important matter that, in contrast to it, everything else is to be disregarded and pushed aside, there can be no doubt that we must make it our utmost concern to convince ourselves of its truth. Therefore, we must see to it that we do not spend our whole lives in the investigation of truth and in scientific studies, and yet remain ignorant of those things that are the most necessary to know. It is these truths, which I have in mind and confess. For innumerable people are, due to negligence, not aware of the true religion because they do not search enough. Others, because they go too far in their investigations and let themselves be carried away by ambition, suffer shipwreck by it. How far, then, can the human mind go in these investigations and where must it stop? That is the task we

shall now discuss. If I succeed in saying something by which a safe and straight path is shown, on which one is led not only to the belief of the necessary truths of religion, but also to those truths whose scientific investigation creates usefulness and pleasure, then the author will not regret having written this work, and perhaps the reader will not regret having read it.

Chapter 2

On Prudent and Imprudent Doubt

Is It Necessary to Begin the Search for the True Religion with Doubt?

[12] By my assertion that there is absolutely no truth whose investigation would not be permitted in and of itself, I have acknowledged a wide field for the activities of the human mind [*amplissimum campum humanis ingeniis*]. Yet, at the same time I stated that it is not only honorable but obligatory to investigate truth, in so far as it is religious, and to make it one's own. If it is therefore a duty to get to know the true religion, it also follows that it is permissible, indeed that one is obliged, to take that path that leads us most surely to it. Some might suggest now that the most suitable start for such an investigation is doubt. After all, how can one seek and find the true religion if one does not first begin to doubt whether the religion one professes is the true one, and whether one is caught up in error? If one does not doubt and ask which of the various religions that humans profess is false, and which is the true religion? This method of investigating truth, in which reason abstracts from all preconceived opinions [*omnibus anteceptis opinionibus*] and accepts nothing but what it has proved with clearly argued reasons [*perspicuis argumentis probatae*], was first established by Socrates and praised by other highly esteemed academics and scholars. Yet it was reintroduced and mightily improved during the last century by Descartes. In the recently published philosophical works it is found on almost every page, as it helps to find the truth, or at least to avoid error.

According to this view, it would therefore be licit to doubt one's religion and to subject it to an examination. To others, however, it seems different; for if anyone is allowed to doubt his religion, how many disadvantages must arise from this for the true religion itself, and how many errors will this allow to enter through the gates of faith [*erroribus janua aperiatur*]! He who begins to doubt and has the principle of accepting as true only what he sees and understands [*nonnisi evidentibus & perspicuis rebus assensum*], and he who always fears that he may be deceived, will either, like the disciples of the skeptics, eternally doubt everything or will reject together with the errors also many truths, as it usually happens unfortunately to ambitious minds. Moreover, he who has begun to waver in the true religion and is undecided about his faith [13] is already unbelieving and renounces a certain good to seek an uncertain one. Therefore, since everybody is convinced that his religion is true and all others false, no one will consider it licit to doubt his faith and to fight against errors that he can never defeat, as long he considers it irreligious to doubt religion itself.

The Necessity of Doubt for the Avoidance of Error and the Danger of Losing the Truth by Doubt

Thus, right at the beginning of our investigation, we encounter such great obstacles that, if we fail in clearing them out of the way, any hope of proceeding is cut off. However, this will be all the easier for us if we first establish a few things that are necessary for the solution of this important question. *First*,[1] it is a generally acknowledged fact that all human beings have a natural desire to protect themselves from error, or if they have carelessly fallen into it, to remove it. For to err and to accept falsehood as true is contrary to the very nature of man, and it can bring him into the greatest calamities, even regarding his eternal fate. *Second*,[2] from this right follows another, which states that everybody is permitted to make use of those means, which reason as well as nature and afterwards the honest arts [*honestae artes*] as they are taught by wise

---

1. [The italics to indicate the steps of the argument are the editor's.]

2. [Consequently, Muratori regards the human need to protect from error or to remove it also as a right, even if he did not label it as such in the previous sentences.]

and learned men, offer to avoid or remove errors. One can even say that the sciences and arts are really nothing but such means [*subsidia*]. The arts and sciences, however, require special other means, through which they guide [*regnant*] themselves and their practitioners [*se suosque cultores*]. If these are not observed, they often lead not to truth but to error, and become unsafe means for recognizing truth and removing error. These special means are called criteria of truth, and their knowledge can be called criticism [*critica*] if this term is understood in a wider sense than usual. Such criteria exist in every science and art, and with their help we investigate everywhere and frequently discover through them what is certain, what is probable, what is doubtful, what is fictitious and what is false. If we use these criteria as our guiding principles and most carefully examine and distinguish all circumstances [*singula*], we often learn which errors have been produced and are still being produced by a logical flaw [*perversa ratiocinatio*]—by the power of prejudice [*praejudicatae opinionis*], by the rule of our affects [*affectuum*], by an undue reverence for antiquity [*nimium erga antiquitatem obsequium*], by too great [14] a love for innovation [*recentiorum temporum amor*], by immoderate trust in our senses, our teachers, our ancestors, history and other testimonies of mankind, which all can be erroneous. In a word, these aids enable us not to believe anything imprudently, not to accept what is doubtful for true and certain, not to accept what is certain and true for doubtful and false. Since both reason as well as truly enlightened men advise us to use these tools in the fight against error and in the investigation of truth, there is no doubt that their correct application is, on the one hand, quite permissible and necessary; but on the other hand, sometimes necessary for all those who desire to find the truth and want to avoid error.

Third, all these remedies to avoid and eradicate error would be useless if we were not allowed to doubt those things and views [*sententiis*] whose truth we investigate. There would even be no end to error and no prospect of coming into the possession of truth if we were not allowed to doubt and examine so many opinions or concepts of things that have impressed themselves onto our imagination and soul either through our thoughts [*cogitationem*] or corporal senses. After all, many of these turn out to be false and unreliable as soon as we doubtfully examine them by the proper criteria. Consequently, it belongs to the principles and laws of nature, which always tries to avoid error, to first doubt objects and perceptions that have not yet been scrutinized, and then investigate them with the help of the praiseworthy tools of criticism, so that we are not deceiving ourselves or persisting in old errors.

Fourth, in addition to these natural rights of man [*insita homini jura*] there are also certain other natural laws [*insitae etiam sunt quaedam leges*] that nobody can transgress knowingly without either slight or grave guilt, and ignorantly without incurring great or at least some harm. For just as sound reason [*rectae rationis*] demands that everyone avoids deception and falsehood, it also contradicts reason when a person [*homo*] renounces truth, impairs it, or resists it. Therefore, a person who is only anxious to avoid error will fear to believe what is true, and not feel obliged to seek the truth himself because he fears everywhere deception, but this way falls also into error [*impingit in errorem*]. We wonder which of the two is more miserable—the one who [15] falls into error through lack of caution or the one who forgoes the truth out of excessive caution. It is, however, certain that the first falls in pardonable ignorance; the latter, however, in insufferable arrogance [*intolerandam superbiam*].

Fifth, reason dictates that truth should not be resisted, that it should not be destroyed, but that we must accept and preserve its unsurpassable light. Moreover, we are obliged to use all tools that prevent us from harming or resisting the truth and must renounce all impediments that can impair our progress into the realm of truth. This rule does in no way contradict the abovementioned rights to doubt. On the contrary, it is in harmony with them if one uses them according to the guidance of reason and thus keeps them within their proper boundaries. For both those who go too far in doubt and those who believe too easily are equally sinning [*peccant*] and in a miserable situation because both are carried away by the excessive desire to either escape error or to resist the truth. Even the aids and criteria of truth by which a person is secured against error can, if those who use them are not simultaneously prudent and humble, be used to reject the truth as well as to scare away error. Therefore, it is necessary to moderate [*perpetuo temperet*] the rights to doubt, which can sometimes degenerate into imprudent provocativeness [*in effraenem audaciam interdum assurgentia*], and to take care [*timor*] that one does not incautiously expunge [*exscindamus*] with the errors also the truth. The obstacles that stand in the way of the recognition of truth, however, and the means of attaining this recognition, must be elucidated now insofar as our task demands it.

The Praise of Prudent Doubt and the Rejection of Imprudent Doubt

In the meantime, it follows from these laws that reason approves of prudent doubt and disapproves of imprudent doubt. For since reason gave us the power to doubt, to save us from error and to bring us to the truth, one cannot conclude that it is permissible to doubt anything without further distinction [*sine discrimine cuicumque, & de quibuscumque rebus*]. After all, all natural rights [*naturae jura*] have certain limits that cannot be transgressed without offending the creator [*conditorem*] of nature. In the same way, the innate rights of human affects [*innata affectuum jura*] also have their boundaries and measure. Nature obliges us to do nothing so much as to love and practice virtue, but the same nature also forbids us to transgress the boundaries and order of the various virtues. Our affects, as well as all our virtues, can only be guided and directed by wisdom. [16] All passions and virtues must be guided and moderated by prudence, as well as everything else, especially if one makes use of one's right to doubt, so that one does not abuse it, but uses it correctly.

Although there is no more difficult task than to determine when, to whom, and in which cases reasonable doubt is permitted (for wisdom, as the philosophers say, reveals itself in particular cases, and these are innumerable), I will not leave unmentioned that there are some general rules that can be applied to almost all individual cases. The first of these rules is this: *Do not doubt imprudently the highest and self-evident [per se nota] principles that are testified as true either through experience or the testimony and consensus of all men and ages.* The second is this: *Inexperienced and thoroughly uneducated people should not enter into any dispute about the truth of things and opinions that learned men have taught and have demonstrated.* All those, not excluding the most astute men, who have claimed that they have no certainty even in regard to the first principles, have hardly ever been called wise but mostly unwise. After all, which rational man will, if he wants to act somewhat prudently, doubt whether he lives, whether he thinks, whether he eats, whether he speaks, whether he writes, since he is most certainly conscious of all this? Who will reasonably doubt whether dry firewood, when thrown into the flames, can burn? Whether a heavy body, when nothing holds it up, will fall from the air to the earth? And then would it be prudent for someone to disbelieve, without any reason, everything that he is taught in the sciences and liberal arts, and what is reported in history through credible witnesses, because it sounds strange to him?

Therefore, it is extremely important to state here again that there are two kinds of doubt, of which one is absolutely in agreement with reason and the other not at all. The difference between the two lies in aim [*in fine*] and the cause [*causa*] of doubt. Some people doubt the most obvious things, not because the truth of these things is doubtful or suspicious to them, but in order to put the truth in a brighter light [*in meliori ... lumine*] with the help of doubt and investigation, and to remove the doubt more from others than themselves. No one, in fact, will disapprove of this way of doubting; rather, it deserves to be praised: for it does not actually mean to doubt, but only to take on [*induere*] the role of a doubter. [17] Therefore nobody has ever disapproved of the excellent writers who, following this principle, doubted *whether there was a God, or whether the Christian religion was true, whether the basic principles, which have been approved and confirmed by men throughout history, are true and well founded.* The unlearned are, however, entitled to be taught by the more experienced so that they, too, may thereby become more adept at believing these sublime and hidden truths. It is, however, in conflict with reason when people doubt with no other purpose in mind than to show off their perspicacity. These men consider themselves experienced and wise, although they only believe their own views to be valid and despise the convictions of others. These demonstrate greater ability in tearing down than in building up. They approve of nothing or approve only of that which flatters their desires and is evident only to their perspicacity.

Chapter 3

On Doubt in Religion

Doubt in Religion

[17] It would lead us too far away from our topic if I intended to determine all limits of doubt. It is, therefore, sufficient here to show only briefly the general foundations on which licit [*aequa*] doubt is based, before returning to our main point. For this purpose, it is important to carefully examine which path we must choose to reach the true religion. It is well known that humans can easily make mistakes in such an important matter and persist in them, since as experience sufficiently teaches, innumerable people have erred and still err in embracing a religion to which they are usually led not by reason but convinced by education or by the example of their parents or fellow youth. Therefore, one cannot doubt that it is not only honorable but even necessary to somewhat doubt [*aliquam dubitationem movere*] the truth of one's religion. After all, how else would it ever be possible that [18] Muslims, Pagans, Jews, or followers of another such sect [*hujusmodi sectarum genera*], which we regrettably subsume under the false religions rejected by God, denounce their false convictions and deeply ingrained errors or are converted [*revocare aut per alios revocari*] by others, if the right to reasonably doubt [*prudentis dubitationis*] was considered sinful [*piaculum*]?

For this very reason we recommend reasonable doubt [*prudentem dubitationem*], and advise not to digress from the most just laws [*aequissimis legibus*] to which, as one says, the right to doubt is bound.

Nevertheless, there are—so God help me—probably only a few people who know how to make use of this freedom, or who want to make use of it. After somebody has professed a religion since his youth, he will begin to despise all others, consider them false, regard their teachers as unreasonable, claim that only his religion is in harmony with reason and truth, and consequently will think it imprudent to cultivate doubt about his opinion. I must therefore hasten to the investigation of which followers among the great diversity of religions [*tanta religionum diversitate*] must reasonably doubt their religion and who must not. Everything will depend on this part of our argument [*Heic rei maximae cardo vertitur*] and once we have proved it, we have the best hope that it will fortify those who stand in the truth and to awaken those who slumber in error. The word "religion," insofar as I use it here for the superstitions of the heathens [*gentium sectarumque*], is used only καταχρηστικῶς, or abusively since not several, but only *one* can be the true religion. Incidentally, this designation is also used by Holy Scripture, which although it establishes with gleaming truth [*fulgentissima veritate*] the one God, often describes false idols also as gods [*sub deorum appellatione*].

Not Everybody Is Allowed to Doubt One's Religion

We therefore state that the person who realizes [*perspicit*] easily that his religion is based on certain principles and foundations [*certissimis principiis & fundamentis*] may refrain from doubting. There are two foundational principles, namely *reason* and *authority*. By reason we understand the power [*vim*] and light of the mind to distinguish true from false, good from evil. It is also the power [*vim*] through which a rational soul [*rationalis anima*] deduces something certain with the help of particular true premises and convinces herself or others of this truth. By authority we mean the power that—contained in the statement of another [19] and communicated to us either orally or in writing—convinces us [*persuadendum*]. The firmer these foundational principles are, the stronger the truth that rests upon them and the more brightly it shines and convinces a person. Thus, being convinced [*persuadendum*] of the true religion relies on the harmony of both [*conspirant*], even if they differ in importance.

Reason and Authority in Religious Questions as Well as Their Importance

However, we cannot deny that reason contains seeds [*semina*] of the true and the good that were implanted by nature herself, as one can see from children who feel natural shame when they become aware of the evil they have committed and pain about having been deceived. Most clearly, however, we can perceive these seeds when we carefully observe the inner processes [*penetralia rationis*] of our reason, and when we consult the excellent books and the company of those people who awaken [*excitare*] in our consciousness the latent ideas of the true and the good—or if one prefers this way of speaking—infuse us with alien and new ideas [*peregrinas et novas*]. Once these ideas or seeds of the true and the good are awakened in a person, then reason (although it always suffers from weaknesses) can advance not only in the knowledge of nature and the properties of the visible, but also of the invisible world. There are as many examples of such progress [*progressus*] as there are ideas among the ancient philosophers. They understood with the light of their reason alone many things that we were shown later [*patefacit*] through a higher [*melior*] light.

How to Determine Which Religion Is True

It is generally known what great importance [*pondus*] authority has both in ordinary life and in the individual sciences [*disciplinis*], especially in history. If we were to believe nothing other than what reason found by itself [*invenit*], not only would a great part of human science and learning be lost, but also immense disadvantages for mankind would ensue. We must therefore rely on the statements [*narrationibus*] of others and trust [*fidem*] them, unless we are willing to consider all that has been handed down to us from previous centuries in word and deed [*libri et fama*],[1] as dreams [*inter somnia computare*]. Only a

---

1. [Muratori seems to carefully avoid the Latin word *traditio* here.]

dreamer and fool would do that! Besides, there is a double authority: one is divine, the other human; the former never deceives, the latter deceives often, very often. Among the first and most certain precepts of reason [*rationis evidentissima praecepta*] is therefore according to universal consensus this one: *All that is certain, true, and [20] unshakable, is revealed and taught by the highest truth, which is God.* For, as Salvian says: "God's word is his own witness, because whatever uncorrupted Truth says must be undefiled testimony to truth."[2] Yet since people err and are fallible, since they can mislead and be misled, one may not utterly trust [*non continuo fidendum*] their authority without further inquiry. Reason or prudence, aided by experience, criticism, and the other arts, can show and determine with good success [*feliciter*] when one must trust the words of others and when not. It is therefore the business of reason to investigate whether people, who orally or in writing proclaim something as divine revelation and teaching, are deceiving us or themselves. In this case our reasonable doubt and suspicion [*prudens dubitatio atque suspicio*] is not about God, who is eternal truth, but about humans, who deceive partly out of ignorance, partly out of dishonesty. Therefore, the Apostle John urges with great wisdom in 1 John 4:1 not to believe everyone who pretends to proclaim divine teachings: "Do not believe every spirit," he says, "but test the spirits to see whether they are from God, for many false prophets have come into the world." Furthermore, humans can deceive themselves and others in understanding, communicating, and explaining an authority that they believe to be divine. One must therefore also consult reason whether they are erring in this regard. During this inquiry, one must follow this order: *First*, one must ask whether the religion one professes contradicts proper reasoning [*rectae rationi*]. If it does, then one must not only doubt its truth, but immediately reject it [*in ipsam protinus dicenda sententia*]. Yet, if it does not contradict reason in any way, then one must examine *second*, whether it originates in God or humans. This means that one must ask whether this religion has been introduced [*inducta*] by a divine or a human authority. If it originates in human authority, then one must doubt its truth; if it originates in God,

---

2. Salvian, *De gubernatione dei*, bk. 3.1, in Salvian, *The Writings of Salvian, the Presbyter*, trans. Jeremiah F. O'Sullivan (Washington, DC: The Catholic University of America Press, 1947), FC 3: 69.

then any doubt about its truth must be excluded, for the divine authority has power over reason [*supra rationem*] and is free from any suspicion of deception. But even then, it remains to be examined, and *third* must be doubted, whether that which we rightly believe to be revealed [*an quae Deum tradidisse*] by God is also correctly understood and interpreted by us. Once we have done this by means of reason or by more reliable means—if God has offered them—it is prudent [21] to rest [*prudentis erit conquiescere*],³ so that we do not put ourselves in greater danger by imprudent doubt [*inconsulta dubitatione*].

Pagans, Jews, and Muslims Must Reasonably Doubt Their Religion

Presupposing all this, we state that the older and newer pagans [*ethnicos*] not only could and can prudently doubt the truth of their religion but had to and must do so [*debuisse et debere*]. For if they can consider with a sincere mind [*sincere animo*] on what principles the opinion [*opinio*]⁴ rests, which has been implanted in them since childhood [*a teneris unguiculis*], they will clearly [*evidenter*] recognize their shaky grounds [*nutare statim*]. Neither the first principles of reason nor divine authority, which alone is firm and reliable, can help alleviate their doubt. On the contrary, they will find that their religion has offended proper reasoning [*recta ratio*] in several ways and that its basis is merely a deceitful human authority that only an imprudent person [*inconsulte*] would trust, since reason vehemently warns against such action. And what could contradict reason more overtly than the belief in several gods who are at odds with each other? Can one conceive something more irrational than transferring the worship owed to the One God to humans, stars, elements, and various other works created by nature or by human hands, and to believe that the human will is subject to inescapable fate? Is it not illogical to deny—as some did and some still do—that the rational soul [*rationali animae*] does not survive the death of the body, and even attribute ignorance, lust, licentiousness, and other human defects [*indigna facinora*] to God? All this should be

3. [That is, in such a case it is prudent to "rest" (abstain) from doubt, and to assent to this faith.]
4. [Muratori uses here *opinio* to indicate the falsity of this religious conviction.]

so obvious to a thinking person [*in oculos meditantium*] that we do not need to speak any more of these offenses, which the religion[5] of the pagans not only permits, but even praises and rewards. In addition, their doctrine has not been established by a divine authority and thus by the highest truth, God Himself, but through games of eloquent lies conceived by poets; or the uncertain, inconsistent, and deceitful tradition [*traditio*] of humans, especially old women, or uneducated minds [*immo & anicularum, rudisque popelli*]. Trusting such accounts without prior examination is not prudent, but foolish. The pagans may and must rightly doubt the truth of their religion, but if they do so and compare theirs with the truths of the Christian religion, they must, if they do not want to renounce laws of reason and prudence, conclude that ours is the only true and perfect religion, and that others are dedicated to idol worship and contain the most reckless [*crassisimis*] and intolerable errors. Even before the birth of Christ, some philosophers came to this insight merely [22] through the light of reason. Yet never has this become so obvious as when the power and truth of the Christian doctrine began to shine far and wide and permeate the entire earth. Its faithful [*cultores*] were not even defeated by torture or fire and convinced through their fortitude, where reason alone could not convince [*ratio sola persuadere poterat*]. For at that time the heathens, and especially the people who cherished the life of the mind and the sciences [*ingenio et literarum cultura*], were not converted by the force of torture, nor by the fear and terror of the sword [*armorum terrore*], but by the power of the truth, and consequently attached themselves [*Christo adjunxere*] to Christ.

The Rational Basis for Their Doubts

As far as the religion of the Jews is concerned, there is nothing in it that is contrary to reason. That their religion was given by God Himself is proven by so many valid arguments, including the assent of Muslims and Christians, that it would be foolish to doubt them. These arguments are thoroughly treated in a number of excellent books to which I refer the reader instead of paraphrasing them here superficially. The

---

5. [Muratori uses here explicitly the singular of *religio*.]

Jews, however, cannot be satisfied with the abovementioned claim since reason and prudence admonish them to inquire further [*progrediendum*]. Therefore, they must doubt whether they correctly understand and interpret the teachings of Holy Scripture, since foolish reasoning [*imbecilla ratio*] could have led them into error. Such doubt must arise even more among the Jews when they realize that so many noble nations that are admired for their genius [*ingenio*], judgment, and scientific education, and are incomparably more learned than the Jewish people, care about the truth of religion at least as much as they do and venerate the sacred scriptures of the Jews as no less sacred themselves. Moreover, these are unanimously convinced that all contemporary Jews are struck with shameful blindness [*turpissime caecutire*] in the interpretation of their holy books. After all, is there something more clearly and more frequently mentioned in Scripture than that the Messiah will come, and do they not even admit this? Does prudence therefore not demand that they seriously examine whether he has not already come, whom so many people proclaim as such, based on the firmest reasons and greatest miracles? Reflecting on their current fate should furthermore increase their doubt. They are the most hated and despised people in the world, are robbed of their prophets, without priests, without a temple, and not just for a few years but for almost seventeen centuries.[6] Can somebody think of a more justified cause [*justam causam*] [23] for their great misfortune than their rejection of the Messiah due to their misinterpretation of their laws, and that they have ceased to be the people of the living God? Certainly, if any Jew with an unbiased and truth-seeking mind [*sincere docilique animo*] doubts whether he understands the Law correctly, and carefully examines the origin, evidence, and the reasons of the Christian religion, still does not realize that so many prophecies have been clearly fulfilled in Christ and his religion, and thus continues to persist in his earlier conviction [*sententia*][7] then any prudent man will consider him the blindest and most obstinate of human beings.

    6. [Here, Muratori shows himself falling into anti-Jewish sentiments.]
    7. [For the religious conviction of pagans, Muratori used the noun *opinio*, here however *sententia* (sentence or doctrine), probably to indicate the compatibility of Judaism and reason.]

Many things could be said about the followers of Mohammed, but we will be brief. Muslims will only with difficulty be moved to doubt whether there is anything in their beliefs that would conflict with sound reason, and we do not want to bother the reader with this problem. Yet since they pretend that their faith has been established by divine authority and rely often on this proof, they act against the first principles of reason and prudence if they do not want to believe without further inquiry anybody who claims to be the Messiah and to have received his teachings or writings directly from Heaven. Even they will not deny that one must be on one's guard against impostors. At least there will be nobody among them, if such a person knows the precepts of prudence, who would immediately accept a new religion proclaimed by a man, even if this lawgiver taught nothing contrary to reason or displayed great piety or insisted constantly that he was sent from Heaven as a herald of truth—unless this man proved his credibility and the truth of his doctrines and teachings by true miracles, by holiness of conduct, by ancient prophecies, by the excellence of the doctrine itself [*optima doctrina*], and by other signs of a divine mission. There is, however, another more important reason to doubt the mission of Mohammed. According to his explicit confession, the writings of the Old Testament, as well as those of the New Testament, are of divine origin. Moreover, he confessed that Moses and Christ have proclaimed the true religion, and that the Law and their teachings have been the real teachers of truth until the end of the sixth century (when Mohammed was born). How imprudent would it be to believe a man immediately and without examination, who abolishes a religion that according to his own words was in former times the best and even a divinely revealed one, and who afterwards condemned this religion, unless one could prove convincingly that he is acting on God's behalf and prove by undeniable signs that he is a true [24] prophet and divine messenger! Given these circumstances, the doctrine of the Qur'an will not have a long reign, if one can believe anybody who preaches a new, heavenly approved religion.

If the credibility of Mohammed is subject to doubt, and reason dictates that his alleged divine authority must be subjected to examination, then a Muslim (at least in my opinion) will very soon give up his opinion [*opinione*] and be persuaded, if he wants to be persuaded.

It will then soon turn out that the impostor Mohammed did not possess a single reliable sign that could confirm his divine mission and did not perform a single miracle to authenticate his new doctrine. After all, the statements of some individuals that Mohammed worked miracles are refuted by directly contradicting claims of the Qur'an, the false prophet himself, and some wiser [*sapientiorum*] Muslims. Moreover, from reading the Holy Scriptures of Jews and Christians, it will become apparent that nothing could be falser than Mohammed's assertion that his teaching was quite often predicted in them, and that the Qur'an teaches nothing but what Moses and Christ have proclaimed. One will also realize that it is impossible (which, however, this deceiver pretended) that the Holy Scriptures, which have been proclaimed by Jews and Christians, spread all over the world, and translated into several languages, were mutilated and falsified by the unanimous and secret agreement of all these people [*secretissima tot populorum conspiratione*] to eradicate passages in which Mohammed's mission and teachings had been predicted. How credible can this be if he himself did not know these passages and does not even mention them, although he would cite them if they had been in his favor and had known them! Moreover, the Qur'an's doctrine of faith and morals is inferior to that of Christianity with respect to sanctity and moral perfection. The latter is based on the spirit, the former on the flesh; the latter teaches peace, the former teaches war; the latter intends the true bliss of the spirit, the former sensual and carnal pleasures. Therefore, one cannot think of a reason why God, as Mohammed claims, would have wanted to change the perfect religion of Christ into a less perfect, even highly imperfect religion, which suffers from several vices that are contrary to the revealed [*tradendis*] moral [25] and dogmatic teachings of Holy Scripture. Moreover, this religion has been introduced and spread by the force of the sword [*vi armorum*] and not by the persuasive power of its truth, and according to its own doctrine must be spread by force [*vim*]; it also forbids all disputation about religion, so that it is impossible to ever discover deceit or eliminate error. It is evidently clear that Mohammed invented all this due to his sexual desires [*libidine*] and his ambition, and that the book, which Muslims regard as thoroughly divine—although it contains a lot of tasteless fables and lies—is so full of superstition that it is impossible that God could be its author, and that it does not deserve the faith it is given, as soon as one consults common sense, or compares the light of the Gospel with the darkness [*tenebris*] of the Qur'an.⁸

> 8. [Muratori operates with arguments against Islam, typically used at the time, relying probably on apologetic treatises and not on firsthand knowledge of Islamic theology. For an overview see Emanuele Colombo, "Western Theologies and Islam in the Early Modern World," in *Oxford Handbook of Early Modern Theology*, ed. Ulrich L. Lehner, Richard Muller, and A. G. Roeber (Oxford: Oxford University Press, 2016), 482–98.]

Chapter 4

On Doubt in the Christian Faith

Whether a Christian Can and Should Doubt His Faith?

[25] Finally, let us move on to Christians and examine whether they, too, may reasonably doubt the truth of their religion, or whether they should. I know in advance that there are minds of such delicate complexion, which feel a shudder just at the fact that I raise a doubt whether one may doubt such an established fact. Yet I ask you not to be terrified by empty shadows and words. We all reject unreasonable doubt, we all approve of reasonable doubt. After all, just as it is foolhardy and ungodly not to guard oneself against the first, so it is nonsensical to reject and condemn the latter altogether. Whatever one may think of the question, it is obviously connected with [26] many uncomfortable misgivings: For if we allow the Christian to subject the truth of his religion to doubt, how can faith in this religion still exist? Then God would have given him in vain the glorious gift to believe without doubt that the Christian religion is the only true one. And indeed, persons who begin to doubt whether what they believe is true or false, seem to have already lost their faith. Therefore, it is said of the heretics: "Whoever doubts the faith is already an unbeliever."[1] Moreover, it is a very daring enterprise to doubt such an important object. For

---

1. [This is a dictum from canon law. See for example, Robert N. Swanson, "*Dubius in fide fidelis est?* Doubt and Assurance in Late Medieval Catholicism," *Studies in Church History* 52 (2016): 186–202.]

although the Christian religion commends itself more than any other religion to reason by its excellence, its holiness, and its truth, due to the weakness of human reason it can easily happen that somebody who has begun to doubt its truth will not stop doubting. Moreover, it can happen that such a man is furthermore deceived by his own judgment and led astray by sensuality, and consequently takes up the banner of another religion, which is nothing other than sacrificing a certain good for a certain evil out of ill-consulted curiosity [*inconsulta curiositate*].

It Seems Licit That a Christian Can Doubt, but It Is Connected with Grave Dangers

If, on the other hand, we maintain that the Christian must not doubt the truth of his religion, how unjust would this be to the pagan, the Jew, and the Muslim! For they will demand of us what we have rightly demanded of them. If we reject doubt under the pretense that we are unshakably convinced of the faith, that truth is on our side and error on theirs, then they will respond to us with the same words whenever we demand that they doubt theirs. Or they will respond to us: You Christians might be convinced of your faith and its truth, but you cannot have certainty that this religion is what you think it is, unless you have compared it with the other religions, and have obtained afterwards the conviction that it is perfectly in harmony with reason and based on divine authority! And why are you so afraid of doubt, they would say, if the truth of your religion is so certain and obvious? Only those who are stuck in error [*stultitiae*] are terrified and consider it too burdensome to liberate themselves from the serfdom of error and be guided to the realm of truth.

A Christian Can Doubt, but How Should He Do This and Not Endanger the Gift of Faith?

In order to answer this question, we have to consider not only the right to investigate the truth but also the danger of losing the truth, and therefore we must remember what has been discussed in the previous [27] chapter. First, uneducated and ignorant people should not doubt the truth of things that have always been taught by the wisest men. Second, everyone, if he has a good *intention* [*honesto fine*], can doubt even the most obvious things, not as if their truth seems suspicious, but to see their reasons and causes and their truth more clearly. This, however, is permitted not only to learned and ingenious people but also to inexperienced and ignorant ones; on the condition, however, that the latter confine their doubts within the bounds that have been harmoniously stated by prudent men [*intra limites concordi prudentum consilio statutos*], and that they turn with their doubts to faithful and wise teachers and let themselves be instructed by them. Consequently, it is allowed to somewhat doubt or to inquire how firmly the law of religion is founded on reason and authority. Nevertheless, their goal in this enterprise should be the illumination of their intellect. Therefore, it is necessary that during this exercise they do not abandon their certainty about the truth of the law, and that they make proper use of instruments designed to bring about a correct judgment. Thus will the glorious gift of faith, which Christians receive from God in the sacrament of baptism, be preserved intact even in the midst of doubt, and will the truth of the Christian religion shine even more splendidly and be more firmly grounded in human hearts.

But do not let the pagans, Jews, and Muslims say to this that what we demanded of Christians is easy compared to the difficult things we demand of them. We want to stand in the same line with them: they should not doubt their religion for any other purpose and under any other conditions than Christians should doubt their religion. From this diligent form of doubt, we gain—so we are firmly convinced—a happy, albeit contrary, result on both sides if the examination is made impartially, and if reason, amid the two parties, freely pronounces its verdict. For then the Christian, whoever he may be, will be more firmly grounded in his religion, and he will be more skillful and courageous in defending it against its enemies, which is exactly what St. Peter urges all Christians to do when he writes in his first epistle, chapter 3: "Always be ready to give an explanation to anyone who asks you for a reason for your hope" (1 Petr 3: 15). Those, however, who did not believe in Christ until now, will be converted to the Gospel or they will reveal that only stubbornness [*pervicacia*], earthly considerations, or other unpraiseworthy motives kept them [28] from embracing in name and mind the Christian religion.

The Truth of the Christian Religion Is Based on Reason and Authority

And this is indeed the peculiar merit and privilege of this religion: that it is, I will not say more credible than all others, but that it is the only one that is credible and in harmony with nature and reason. Therefore, one may, as much as one may like, examine its foundations and principles. One will not find a single dogma that would not enjoy the approval and homage of reason. However, there are individual mysteries about the nature of God and his decisions that are beyond the comprehension of human reason [*captum humani intellectus excedunt*], and therefore cannot be fully understood and clearly interpreted [*perfecte intelligi, dilucideque exponi non possunt*]. But everyone will see that these are not found to be against reason, but above it; and it is not at all surprising that a finite being is not quite able to grasp the infinite essence of God and make it comprehensible. Nevertheless, these are not against reason but beyond it. It is not at all surprising that a finite being is unable to comprehend the infinite nature of God and to understand it. We know, however, with certitude that we believe these things because they were revealed by God according to his own testimony, and we are convinced that God really revealed them, especially because they do not at all contradict proper reasoning [*ratione recta*] but are confirmed by it.

As for divine authority, there is so much evidence in favor of the Christian religion that only an imprudent person could deny that it is revealed by God. For its founder, Christ, was prophesied beforehand by several prophets, which are recorded in books that the Jews, hostile to Christianity, have venerated for so many centuries. Moreover, the truth of this religion is confirmed by the absolutely divine way of life and the mores of Christ as well as the undeniable and innumerable miracles that both he and his disciples, on whom he bestowed his power, have performed. Furthermore, one must add the purity and holiness of the teachings, the excellence of the moral precepts by which the Christian religion, like no other, urges humans to practice all kinds of virtues, leading them from the earthly to the heavenly, and not only teaches them to believe worthy things about God, but even to worthily worship God as best and greatest being. One should also consider that this religion was not proclaimed for the sake of gain, advantage, or fame, since it was not spread by force over almost the whole world, but was first preached by uneducated men and afterwards defended by an infinite number of weighty reasons [29] and proclaimed through scholars and martyrs, who endured incredible torments and persecution. They taught things that were not easy to grasp for human reason nor pleasant for the will and desire—namely, the law of the cross and the mortification of desires, with which they finally defeated the stubbornness of many Jews and convinced many other nations. If these and many other proofs and reasons for belief [*motiva credibilitatis*], as they are called, which are presented at great length by those who speak of the truth of the Christian religion, do not furnish obvious proof and do not lead a person to the reasonable assumption that this religion is from God, what else can be demanded? Certainly, no other religion has so many consistent proofs of its divine origin, and if one must profess any religion (which is certainly not subject to doubt), the person who does not see that the Christian religion, whose *testimonies have become extremely credible* (Ps 93:5), is far preferable to all others, will not see anything else either.

Why Christians Could Reasonably Forgo Doubt and Just Embrace Their Religion in Tranquility

But since for so many centuries thorough scientific studies (especially the study of theology and religion) have flourished and still flourish, since everything that sound reason and theology have ever taught, both about the confirmation and interpretation of the holy books of the Old and New Testaments and about morals and the perfect dominion of intelligence and human will, has been published by Christians who excel no less in piety than in virtue and scholarship, and since all this is still treated and examined especially in schools and churches, one can state: the common Christian people are freed from the duty that reason prescribes to each person, namely to investigate thoroughly the principles and foundations of religion. For it would obviously be an imprudent and harsh demand to expect all people to study theology, the various languages and other disciplines that are necessary to explain the sacred documents, and to engage in a thorough examination of religion. An innumerable number of pastors and teachers of the Church, however, have done just that, and still do, with great diligence. Since Christians have so many careful leaders (to pass over other things in silence that speak for us [Catholics, U.L.], but not for others), [30] it would be imprudent to accuse them of believing unwisely.

In the Catholic Church, Scholarly Research of Religion Is Mainly Done by the Clergy

For this reason alone, however, we cannot absolve all Christians from this duty. For we believe that the ministers of the Church and all those who are called to teach the Christian people have the duty to carefully examine the foundations and principles of the Christian faith and to acquaint themselves with them, so that they may recognize not only the truth of their religion but also the falsity of other religions. We consider this to be a greater duty when the Christian people live in the vicinity of pagans and other religious parties, where opportunity brings it about, or where love often commands them to fight not only against superstition but also for their true religion. After all, if the Christian people, as we have shown, can rightly rely on so many insightful, credible, and pious men of ancient times, who have proclaimed the doctrine revealed by God and approved by reason, then who else will safeguard the sacred heritage if the people are fed with doubt, or if doubt arises in any other way, or if the truth of the Christian religion is contested by opponents? This is undoubtedly the duty of the clergy, who are familiar with the care of the flock. But how will they avert danger from the flock if they are—due to their ignorance—not even able to protect themselves from the invading wolves? Since the people of God are given shepherds and teachers for no other reason than that they may instruct them in sound doctrine, fortify them in the truth, and preserve them from error, it necessarily follows that they must also acquire the ability to fulfill their office and mission. The precept that the apostle Paul gives (Ti 1:9) on this point is very clear: "The bishop must be able to exhort by sound doctrine, and to rebuke those who contradict." And in the second letter to Timothy (2 Tm 4:2): "Proclaim the word; be persistent whether it is convenient or inconvenient; convince, reprimand, encourage through all patience and teaching." The Church Fathers and the Councils teach the same. Now, if we extend these requirements to the entire clergy of the Christian Church without distinction of rank, we shall not be reproached for being overly severe. For it is the duty of every single one of them to feed and shepherd the flock. I do not deny that this can also be done by deputies and paid assistant clergy, but this is only morally permissible if the shepherds are incapable of doing so and choose suitable persons for this position. The pastors have to devote the greatest care to their flock, use the sciences, [31] wisdom and piety, and never be merely content with the name and honor of the shepherd all the while frustrating with their ignorance and lethargy the highest of all shepherds, Jesus Christ.

Chapter 5

On Faith and Its Reasons

Is Authority or Reason the Beginning of the Acceptance of the True Religion?

[31] From what has been said so far, it follows that reason and authority must be consulted and that both must work together [*confluere*] so that one either retains the [previously, U.L.] accepted true religion, or embraces it. But since most people do not pay attention to this rule or disregard it, they are guided only by a deceptive human authority. Unsurprisingly, then, it happens that many countries persist in old errors and never convert to the true religion [*cultum*] of God. It is especially the Christian religion that prides itself on being founded on authority and reason, and which, supported by incontrovertible evidence, claims that the other religions lack one or both of these foundations. The apostles and their successors, the Church Fathers and the other Christian teachers, have spread this belief over almost the entire earth by no other means than by showing that it is revealed by God and in harmony with reason. They proved this with arguments that satisfy [*acquiescat*] human prudence [*prudentia*], unless one prefers to listen to the Flesh rather than to the Spirit.[1] Therefore, at first sight it seems that Phereponus does not unjustly blame Augustine, who in his book *De utilitate credendi* endeavors to prove that the Christian religion must first be accepted without reason in order to grasp its truth

---

1. [Listening to the Spirit means trusting reason and the guidance of the Holy Spirit; obeying the Flesh, however, means giving in to the rule of concupiscence.]

with the help of reason afterwards. Augustine says: "For unless those things are believed, which later, if he has succeeded and been worthy, each one attains to and perceives, and without a certain weighty power of authority, true religion cannot at all [32] be rightly entered upon."[2] Phereponus[3], in his notes to the book in question, combats the view of Augustine with the following words: "How could Augustine prove that one must believe certain things beforehand without reason (for that is how he must be understood), which would only be grasped afterwards? Could not a merchant of lies and fables [*mendaciorum et fabulorum propola*] demand the same, and afterwards, when somebody wants to refute his tales answer that he was unworthy to understand them? Could not the Jews and the pagans use the same argument when they are challenged by Christians on the grounds of reason?"[4] Furthermore, he goes on to show that those who want to convert to Christianity can rightly demand that the truth of this belief be proved based on rational grounds before they accept it as true. Proceeding in any other way would be preposterous. Moreover, if one embraced Augustine's opinion, one could lure [*pertrahi*] people into every conceivable superstition.

Phereponus Has Attributed an Absurd Opinion to St. Augustine

Yet Phereponus imputed an absurd view to Augustine, and what happens to him is what happens to many others who, by examining an author as their opponent, discover errors and blunders that the opponent

---

2. Augustine, *De utilitate credendi*, ch. 9.21, or "The Advantage of Believing," in Augustine, *The Immortality of the Soul*, ed. Ludwig Schopp et al., *Fathers of the Church* (Washington, DC: The Catholic University of America Press, 1977), FC 4:416–1794.

3. [Pseudonym for Jean Leclerc or Le Clerc (1657–1736), a Calvinist Biblical scholar and historian from Geneva, who later joined the Arminians. Muratori and others accused him of Socinianism (anti-Trinitarianism). See Martin I. Klauber, "Between Protestant Orthodoxy and Rationalism: Fundamental Articles in the Early Career of Jean LeClerc," *Journal of the History of Ideas* 54 (1993): 611–36; M. C. Pitassi, *Entre croire et savoir: Le probleme de la methode critique chez Jean Le Clerc* (Leiden: Brill, 1987).]

4. Jean Leclerc, *Variorum exercitationes in S. Augustini opera* in *Patrologia Latina*, ed. Migne, vol. 47 (Paris: 1877), 197–570, at 509.

is often not guilty of, but which the critic has dreamed up and which have arisen from his zeal. We, who examine Augustine's view with greater impartiality, will show that no demand is fairer and more appropriate than the one Augustine made of the Manichaeans. We will also show at the same time how great the weight of reason [*pondus rationis*] is and how it must proceed in matters of religion. As we have already said, true religion must be derived from authority or divine revelation. Since God cannot want to speak to each individual human being in order to make his true religion miraculously known, it follows that humans have to turn to reason and human authority in order to convince themselves of the truth of divine revelation. Human authority, however, no matter how great its reputation [*quamquam multum polleat*], must be brought before the judgment seat of reason and subjected to its scrutiny [*rationis tribunal & examen*]. From the approval or disapproval of reason we learn about its strength or weakness. Thus, reason can bring about the knowledge of divine revelation in a twofold way: (1) by way of demonstration or intrinsic proofs [*argumenta intrinseca*], or (2) by way of trust and reasonable faith [*credulitatem & persuasionem prudentem*]; that is, by extrinsic proofs [*extrinseca argumenta*].

The Boastful Manicheans Are Refuted

The Manichaeans invited people to their religion with pompous words and promised each new follower that they would demonstrate and explain perfectly the truth of all their mysteries and dogmas [33] before they demanded any faith. In fact, if their success corresponded to their promise, these people could see through reason and intrinsic reasons alone the truth of that religion, which they then accepted by means of faith, so that reason itself was really the principle of faith. Catholics, on the other hand, claimed that one must first believe to be able to understand [*intelligi*] later some difficult dogmas and mysteries by means of reason and intrinsic reasons [*per rationem et per intrinseca argumenta*]. This way of leading people to true wisdom was haughtily scoffed at by the Manichaeans, the stupidest [*stultissimi*] of all heretics. They believed that there was no other way of proceeding than by believing nothing until reason had made the intrinsic truth of all dogmas and mysteries comprehensible through convincing demonstration [*evidentem demonstrationem*].

Augustine exposes in his works how unjust [*injusta*] the Manichaeans' approach is, and how just, on the other hand, that of Catholics. First, he remarks that the heretics themselves did not accomplish what they promised; for, he says in the first book, first chapter of *De utilitate credendi*, that they were "more fluent and eloquent in refuting others than they were strong and sure in proving their own beliefs."[5] And in the sixth chapter he asserts that their disciples were "forced to cherish and believe under the false pretense of reason, untold thousands of fables."[6] In his *Contra epistolam Manichaei* chapter 5 and chapter 14, he reports that those teachers themselves were quite incapable of giving an account of their own teachings and of substantiating them. In his other writings against these heretics, he deals with this specifically. Second, the Manichaeans admonished their followers that they believed in Christ and followed in this regard the example of the Catholic Church. They promised to prove and demonstrate the truth of all that Christ had said and all that was written in the Scriptures according to Manichaean principles. Third, since some divine mysteries and dogmas are beyond the comprehension of human reason, not contrary to but above reason, Catholics taught that faith must pave the way to reason, so that having obtained divine assistance through the obedience of faith, one could penetrate its depths and secrets with the help of reason. Fourth, Catholics showed that if humans could comprehend the mysteries of God and Holy Scripture with mere reason, it was nevertheless the business of a few men to grasp the intrinsic reasons that led humans to a reliable knowledge of all divine things. [34] But should we deny religion to those people who do not have such fortunate ingenuity [*felici ingenio*], such a lively capacity for comprehension, and withhold it from them? Should we not lead them to the acceptance of truth by faith? If we assert this, then the uneducated and intellectually limited people [*tunc rudes et crassa minerva afflati*], convinced that one cannot believe other than on rational grounds and demonstrations, will never come to the true religion, since they will never attain a sufficient comprehension

---

5. Augustine, *De utilitate*, ch. 1.1; FC 4:393.
6. Augustine, *De utilitate*, ch. 6; FC 4:409.

of certain dark and difficult [*obscura et ardua*] doctrines of religion. Finally, Christ himself, to pass over Augustine's other arguments, did not attract humans in any other way; he demanded of them nothing so insistently, nothing so emphatically than faith in his person, since they were not yet fit to grasp the divine mysteries [*percipienda secreta*]. The Catholic Church has held firmly and holds until today nothing other than this, wherefore departure from this practice is certainly fraught with danger and is certainly a fruitless endeavor. "This," says Augustine in the tenth chapter of *De utilitate credendi* "is the foresight of true religion; this has been divinely commanded; this has been handed down to our blessed forefathers; this has been kept even to our own day. To desire to pervert and disturb it is nothing else than to seek a sacrilegious way to the true religion. As to those who do this, even if their desires are granted, they cannot arrive whither they intend. For whatever kind of excellent ability they may have, unless God is present they creep along the ground. And He is then present when those who tend toward God have at heart the interests of human society. No surer way to heaven can be found than this step."[7]

Extrinsic Reasons of Faith [*motiva credibilitatis*] Precede Faith: For the Acceptance of Dogmas, One Cannot Demand Demonstrative Proofs

What has been said so far is not enough to remove all doubt from the reader. I have not yet presented the arguments of Phereponus, have not yet dispelled his error. When the reader hears that the ancient Christian Church and Augustine demanded that those who joined the true religion should first believe without reason to pave the way for arriving at an understanding of the mysteries of faith, he must not believe that they were demanded to believe without any reason at all. It was demanded that they should accept the Christian faith as true, but they were also given proofs for why they should believe, proofs on whose grounds they could accept it as reasonable. These reasons, however, were what in the schools are nowadays called reasons for belief [*signa,*

---

7. Augustine, *De utilitate*, ch. 10.24; FC 4:422.

On Faith and Its Reasons 91

or *motiva credibilitatis*].[8] As such, these are extrinsic, but according to general consensus, excellent and powerful proofs [*sed proposito fortissime probando omnium consensu idoneae*]. Some of these proofs we have already touched upon above. The mysteries and dogmas of the Christian religion were presented and explained to the unbelievers at the same time as the books of the Old and New Testaments. [35] The intrinsic reasons, however, were passed over because they are very difficult to grasp and can only be understood after extensive study and with special divine assistance for which one may hope only after the divine infusion of faith through the grace of baptism. "For I not only judge it," says Augustine in chapter 14, "most healthful to believe before using reason (since one is unfitted to comprehend reason), and, with faith itself, to prepare the ground to receive the seeds of truth, but I believe that such is the way, generally, by which safety can alone return to sick souls."[9] Christian priests, who preached the faith among unbelievers, did not intend to create baccalaureates of theology—to use a barbaric expression—but to make Christians [*Christianos facere*]. Through such cogent reasons of credibility [*praeviis igitur argumentibus efficacibus*], the unbelievers were moved to believe in the Christian religion. Once the foundation had been laid and the truth of divine revelation had been recognized, what was presented to them as part of this heavenly religion was believed as true and held; even if they did not understand these truths, they were not offered intrinsic causes and reasons for them, nor did they sufficiently comprehend them. Nevertheless, they believed these things, because they had had been revealed by God, who cannot deceive, through his true religion [*a Deo mentiendi impotente in ea vera religione traditum*]. In this way the extrinsic reasons prepared

---

8. [For the classic Thomistic explanation of the *motiva credibilitatis*, written in the first half of the twentieth century, see Reginald Garrigou-Lagrange, *On Divine Revelation*, trans. M. Minerd, vol. 2 (Steubenville, OH: Emmaus Academic Press, 2022). Therein, on intrinsic motives, 1–11; on extrinsic motives, 17–46; on miracles as motives, 47–142. For an approach that takes positively into account both the Second Vatican Council as well as twentieth-century religious philosophy, see Adolf Kolping, *Fundamentaltheologie*, vol. 1 (Münster: Regensberg, 1968), 282–342, or Guy Mansini, *Fundamental Theology* (Washington, DC: The Catholic University of America Press, 2018), 184–212.]

9. Augustine, *De utilitate*, ch. 14.31; FC 4:432.

the mind for the faith, while the mercy of God conferred upon a person so prepared the grace of baptism and of salvific faith. When a person's soul was finally permeated [*imbutus*] by divine grace, he became, as much as such is possible for a finite being, quite capable [*aptissimus*] of understanding the dark and hidden mysteries and dogmas.

The Custom of the Catholic Church Is Praised, Which Does Not Demand Anyone to Believe without Reason

The Manichaeans accused Catholics of nothing else than demanding faith without offering intrinsic reasons and without having proven every dogma and mystery before somebody entered the Church. As we have seen from Augustine's words, the Manichaeans were wrong to demand this, even impious and unreasonable. It was much more prudent, safe, and expedient to lead people to the faith by means of the *motiva credibilitatis*, the extrinsic reasons. Phereponus, who did not pay attention to this, immediately concluded (because he heard that in the Manichaean system reason precedes faith) that Augustine taught the opposite and that consequently the Catholic Church imposed the yoke of faith on the future faithful without offering them any reasons beforehand. But what on earth does Augustine condemn in the Manichaeans other than that before faith "they will give them a reason for things that are very obscure," [36] as he says himself in the ninth chapter?[10] Then, secondly, that they claimed that one should not believe "unless they can give a reason that cannot be doubted,"[11] and that "they contend that nothing should be believed without their showing to fools a complete disclosure of reason as it concerns God."[12] Augustine thus endeavors to prove nothing other than that one can and must believe rationally, even before one has understood certain dark and difficult divine mysteries. And is it not prudent and sufficient to enter the true religion after being led to her by extrinsic arguments, when the religion of Christ [*Christi Religio*] has so many convincing ones to offer? For as soon one

---

10. Augustine, *De utilitate*, ch. 9, FC 4:417.
11. Augustine, *De utilitate*, ch. 14.32, FC 4:434.
12. Augustine, *De utilitate*, ch. 14.32, FC 4:434.

realizes that a religion is true, one also realizes that it only contains true doctrines, even if one has not seen a demonstration of the truth of each individual doctrine. The reasons that moved Augustine and others to accept the law of Christ [*Christi legem*] are listed in the fourteenth chapter of *De utilitate credendi*. He says he believed in Christ's presence on earth, because he did "believe no one except the affirmed opinion and the widespread report of peoples and nations."[13] This was confirmed by "a report which had the strength of numbers, agreement, and antiquity."[14] Then, in the sixteenth chapter, he says that we must find reasons for belief partly in the astonishing miraculous signs of the Christian religion, which only impudence can deny, and partly in the fact that there is such a large number of believers, who in Augustine's time spread over almost the entire world: "And for a man that cannot see the truth, authority is at hand to make him fit for this, and to allow him to purge himself. And no one doubts, as I said before, that authority prevails, partly through miracles, partly through the crowds that accept it."[15] In the following chapter he enumerates the many *motiva credibilitatis*, with which one moved and still moves unbelievers to accept this reasonable faith [*prudenter credere*]. This, he said, "is the work of Divine Providence, achieved through the prophecies of the prophets, through the humanity and teaching of Christ, through the journeys of the apostles, through the sufferings, the crosses, the blood and the death of the martyrs, through the admirable lives of the saints, and in all these, at opportune times, through miracles worthy of such great deeds and virtues."[16] These are the reasons and grounds on which the unbelievers believed, before they were led by a demonstration of the inner reasons to the comprehension of the individual doctrines and mysteries of the divine law. Augustine continues: "When, then, we see so much help on God's part, so much progress and such fruit, shall we hesitate to bury ourselves in the bosom of that Church? [37] For starting from the apostolic chair down through the successions of bishops, even unto the open confession of all mankind, it has possessed the

---

13. Augustine, *De utilitate*, ch. 14.31, FC 4:432.
14. Augustine, *De utilitate*, ch. 14.31, FC 4:432.
15. Augustine, *De utilitate*, ch. 16.34, FC 4:437.
16. Augustine, *De utilitate*, ch. 17.35, FC 4:440.

crown of authority. And the heretics who lurked around her in vain were condemned, in part by the judgment of the people themselves, in part by the weighty decisions of the councils, and also in part, by majestic miracles."[17] Other such extrinsic evidence that kept Augustine in the bosom of the Catholic Church, he has developed in more detail in his *Contra epistulam Manichaei*, chapter 4.

The Difference between Knowledge and Faith

Now, Phereponus may appear and say what he writes on page 596 in his *Animadversiones*: "Could not a merchant of lies and fables [*mendaciorum et fabulorum propola*] demand the same? Could not the Jews and the pagans use the same argument that one must first believe and not understand, when they are debated by Christians on the grounds of reason?"[18] Which merchant of lies and fables, which pagan or Jew has, however, ever been able to list so many profound *motives of credibility*, or could prove that his religion was not only of divine origin but had also been preserved by God in its original laws and rites, other than the religion of Christ?[19] Neither Augustine nor the Catholic Church has to fear to be admonished for their statement that one must first believe rather than understand everything intimately [*quam intime evidenter omnia intelligerentur*], since the other religions cannot offer such a great quantity of efficacious and congruent arguments, that they could even demand faith before comprehension. Therefore, Phereponus goes much too far when he attacks Augustine in his other notes as if he teaches that one must believe Christ, the Christian Church, and her priests without any reason [*nulla ratione*]. "Whoever believes without any reason that a religion is the true one, or that God wants to be worshipped by humans, has either lost his mind or is so dull-witted that there is almost no difference between him and a fool. He who believes you without reason will, if he desires it, also withdraw his faith from

---

17. Augustine, *De utilitate*, ch. 17.35, FC 4:440.
18. Leclerc, *Variorum*, 510.
19. [Thus, Muratori acknowledges that in principle other religions also could use this argument, but he denies that their motives of credibility match those of the Christian Church.]

you without reason. He will without hesitation convert to the Arians, if they come to power, or, what is worse, he will join the Muslims,[20] which the Africans actually did after the times of Augustine."[21] This is not the place to investigate why, apart from Asia and Greece, also Africa converted to the Muslim superstition [*Muhammedanum superstitionem*], but I have to reject as false the prejudice that the Africans had come to believe in Christ without reasons [*sine ratione olim credidisse*], learned this religion without reasons [*sine ratione didicisse*], and confessed it for several centuries without reasons [*sine ratione servasse*]. Nor do I want to examine how many exceptions exist to the rule, "He who believes you without reason [38] will also easily withdraw his faith from you," nor how one explains them. For the descendants of Jews and Muslims usually believe their parents and ancestors without reason when they are taught their religion, and yet they are not easily dissuaded from their faith and conviction. If this happens with Jews and Muslims, with how much greater right does it happen and should it happen with Christians! For even a person who, without proof, believes in Christ and is incorporated [*conjungitur*] into the true religion through the baptismal bath honestly and without hypocrisy, will receive without doubt heavenly virtue as assistance, which can keep such a person steadfast in his faith even without reason.

I do, however, not waste more time with this argument and will admit Phereponus's opinion that the nineteenth chapter of the Book of *Ecclesiastes* states as such: "Whoever trusts too quickly has a shallow mind."[22] Yet, what does this have to do with the teaching of the Catholic Church, which has propagated the holiest religion from the time of Christ until today by referring to so many reasons and causes that explain why one should trust Christ and his priests? Phereponus must consider all people who are famous for their genius [*ingenii*] and who have attached themselves to Christ [*ad Christum hucusque adjunxerunt*] as delusional and silly [*bardos plane stupidosque*], if he believes that they have accepted the Christian religion without reason. After all, he thinks they were not perfectly convinced by reasons

---

20. [Muratori uses the term *Mohammedani* to signify Muslims.]
21. Leclerc, *Variorum*, 512.
22. Sir 19:4.

before they began to believe! Phereponus, however, also states that Augustine demands one must not believe because of reasons, but because of the demand of the clergy. If pagan priests claimed this right for themselves and held what Augustine teaches about the profit of believing against Christians, what could we answer them? The Christian would shout back that it was intolerable [*intoleranda*] to demand such a thing! "Therefore," adds our critic, "what is regarded a correct conclusion in Africa will be considered a false conclusion at the source of the Euphrates."[23] If the priests of the Gospel had demanded that one must believe them without any reasons, one could admit Phereponus's statement [*percontatio*]. But as we have seen, the story was quite different [*aliter sese res habuit*]. The Christian priests, apart from their own sincere character [*animum non fictum*], offered such weighty reasons with which they proved the obvious credibility of their religion, that one had to accept them even if one had not understood every single dogma and mystery. The Manichaeans, however, were so obstinate that they neither believed the Catholic clergy, despite their honest efforts, nor their most convincing arguments from extrinsic reasons. [39] They claimed that they did neither want nor could embrace the faith [*vellent ... negarent*] before understanding [*cognoscerunt*] all the mysteries of the divine law and its documents through certain intrinsic proofs. Thus, any comparison of Christian with pagan priests is unwarranted.

Augustine raises in the twelfth chapter of his treatise *De utilitate credendi* the questions: "For, I ask, if what is not known need not be believed, how are children to be subject to their parents? And how are they to love with mutual affection those whom they do not believe to be their own parents?"[24] Phereponus, however, argues that these things are not similar at all. "For," he says, "the parents and also other people can know, and truly know, which are their own children, and which belong to others. Nor do they have any interest, at least usually, in accepting alien children as their own. The priests, however, who demand to be believed in matters of religion are, if they have no reasons, no more convincing than other people. Moreover, they usually do not enlarge

---

23. Leclerc, *Variorum*, 511.
24. Augustine, *De utilitate*, ch. 12.26, FC 4:425–26.

their flock without a great advantage for themselves."[25] Yet this example reveals what Phereponus has not understood. Since he is a master in the art of criticism, he should accept my advice to read the books of others more carefully [*diligentius*] to determine their intention [*mentem*] before he pronounces a judgment about them. After all, Augustine had mentioned three things in the eleventh chapter: Understanding, believing, and opining [*intelligere, credere, opinari*]. Understanding, he says, is as much as knowing, or possessing something on the basis of reliable knowledge. Then he adds this: "But everyone who understands also believes, and everyone who has an opinion believes, too; but not everyone who believes understands, and no one who merely has an opinion understands."[26] Yet in order to show that the Manicheans were mistaken when they asserted that one must believe nothing but what one knows, he cites the example of children, who evidently can never know by reason and demonstration that these people, whom they love and honor, are their parents. After all, they are moved by extrinsic reasons, by authority, to believe just that. "Yet we believe, and we believe without any doubt, what we admit we cannot know."[27]

Now what does Phereponus object to such a foregone conclusion? "Parents," he says, "and others too, can and do know who their children are." I do not even want to mention that even parents cannot always *know* this with scientific and logical accuracy [*per scientiam certamque mentis cognitionem*], which is the meaning Augustine intends here for *knowing*: After all, do children know their parents through intrinsic reasons and [40] scientific insight? Certainly not. For, to use the words of Augustine: "For this cannot in any way be known through reason, but is believed of the father on the authority of the mother; but, as to the mother herself, it is not she, for the most part, that is believed, but midwives, nurses, and servants. For cannot she from whom a son can be stolen and another substituted, having been deceived herself, deceive others?"[28] Phereponus, however, argues that Augustine wants to

---

25. Leclerc, *Variorum*, 511. [Leclerc argues here that the clergy has financial and other interests in increasing the number of followers.]

26. Augustine, *De utilitate*, ch. 11.25, FC 4:425.

27. Augustine, *De utilitate*, ch. 12.26, FC 4:427.

28. Augustine, *De utilitate*, ch. 12.26, FC 4:427.

prove by this example that one must believe the Christian priests without reasons, but these are two totally different things. Who would dare to claim that children believe that this or that person was their father without having any reason for such a belief? Augustine only cites this example to show that nothing remains intact in human society if we decide not to believe anything that we have not directly observed [*perceptum*]; that is, anything about which there is no certain knowledge. Augustine and the Manicheans argued about the question: whether one can and must reasonably believe certain things on the mere testimony of authority [*argumenta credibilitatis*] or whether it is necessary to acquire knowledge of these things first [*earum rerum scientiam prius habere*] to believe reasonably [*prudenter*]. No one will deny that the children, if they have similar reasons, prudently believe and must believe that these or those are their parents. Nor will anyone dare to deny that unbelievers could reasonably come to believe a Christian priest, who offers the reasons for the faith [*motiva credibiliatis*] even if he has not proved to them the truth of certain doctrines through intrinsic reasons. These examples are, however, also dissimilar in a way quite different from what Phereponus considers. After all, children, as is obvious, can easily be deceived regarding whom they take for their parents, but the unbeliever who believes a clergyman who gives so many reasons for faith is able to consult his reason so that he is not deceived even if the clergyman was thinking of his own material gain. How ethical [*modeste*] and true this attack of priests is, will Phereponus see. For the arguments for the credibility of the Christian religion have such strength [*vis*] that one can reasonably and without difficulties believe [*prudenter et sine difficultate credere*]. For a person who has encountered this evidence, it is very difficult to withhold assent. Phereponus, because he did not know at all what Augustine understood by *knowing*, concluded all too hastily that in former times the clergy had demanded belief without any reasons. [41] Yet, he could have informed himself about it through the passages we just cited. After all, he saw in the fourteenth chapter some things correctly, but here he has gone clearly off the rails [*sed qui extra orbitam cucurrerat, se in viam revocare non valuit*] and was unable to return to the right path.

Miracles Are Extrinsic Reasons

Augustine defended the teaching of the Church that demanded that one must believe before the intrinsic reasons were given, pointing to the example of Christ who, as he says, demanded nothing more urgently, nothing more insistently, than to believe in him. "By faith," he says, "he guided fools; you guide them by reason. He praised those who believed in Him; you revile them."[29] Phereponus comments that his excellent moral precepts and his miracles constitute two valid motives by which this divine teacher procured faith in himself, even though the Jews understood nothing of what he said. Yet, has our learned critic [*censor*] proposed anything new? Does not Augustine write in the same place: "For what other purpose had His miracles, so numerous and so stupendous?"[30] But why then did Phereponus not see that the extrinsic reasons for belief [*argumenta credibilitatis*] are sufficient to believe reasonably [*prudenter credendum*] in the Christian religion, and that the ancient Christians, in so far as they themselves believed and preached the Gospel to the unbelievers, knew and accepted these reasons? Even Christ did not point out the intrinsic causes and reasons of some of the most exalted dogmas [*altissimorum dogmatum*], and yet he demanded to be believed. The miracles alone, which no one else had performed, took the place of all other reasons, so that the Jews could and had to [*debeant*] reasonably believe in Christ. Miracles, however, are not, as is generally known, intrinsic but extrinsic reasons to prove the truth of the doctrine. Thus, Phereponus could have learned from this that Catholics would have made themselves ridiculous if they had referred to the example of Christ and demanded that one should believe him not only without intrinsic but also without extrinsic reasons, since the Son of God only demanded faith in his person on the basis of his extraordinary miracles, which were the weightiest extrinsic reasons by which the Jews were brought to believe but not to understand. Let our critic see for himself whether he is right when he concludes with the following words: "Augustine, therefore, could not cite the example

---

29. Augustine, *De utilitate*, ch. 14.32, FC 4:435.
30. Augustine, *De utilitate*, ch. 14.32, FC 4:435.

of Christ as proof that the Catholic Church rightly demands to be believed without reason."[31]

Phereponus's Other Opinion That Catholics Demand Belief without Reason

Phereponus could have easily learned from other writings of Augustine, what his intention [*mens*] and the tradition [*consuetudo*] of the Catholic Church were. Here he had a beautiful opportunity [*bella occasio*] to prove his genius [*exercendi ingenii censorii*] as a critic, but he was too fond of his own fictitious idea [*figmentum suum nimis amasset*]. In the twenty-fourth chapter of *De vera religione* Augustine says: "So it is that the very healing of the soul, which by God's providence and his inexpressible kindness is being applied step by distinct step, is also of the greatest beauty. It is divided, you see, between authority and reason. Authority (and one might add the arguments for credibility)[32] demands faith and paves the way for people to use reason. Reason leads on to understanding and knowledge, although reason is not entirely wanting in authority, when one considers who precisely has to be believed, and certainly the Truth itself, once perspicuously known, has supreme authority."[33] In his 120th letter, chapter 1, he expresses the view of the Catholic Church more precisely: "Therefore, we must refuse so to believe as not to receive or seek a reason for our belief, since we could not believe at all if we did not have rational souls. So, then, in some points that bear on the doctrine of salvation, which we are not yet able to grasp by reason—but we shall be able to sometime—let faith precede reason, and let the heart be cleansed by faith so as to receive and bear the great light of reason; this is indeed reasonable."[34] That these words are absolutely correct was also emphasized and confirmed by Phereponus himself, although he later confessed that he did not

---

31. Leclerc, *Variorum*, 511.

32. [This is an insertion by Muratori.]

33. Augustine, *De vera religione*, ch. 24.45, in *On Christian Belief: The Works of Saint Augustine—A Translation for the 21st Century* I/8, trans. Matthew O'Connell (New York: New City Press, 2005), 58.

34. Augustine, *Letters*, vol. 2, FC 18:302.

understand how this could be reconciled with what Augustine taught elsewhere about authority. Yet this would have been an easy task for him, had he studied the works of Augustine with an amiable instead of a hostile mind [*amantis potius, quam inimico animo*], and if he had chosen to illuminate his thoughts rather than to slander [*insectandi*] him.

Phereponus is all too charming [*lepidus*] when he guesses in his daydreaming why during Augustine's time faith was demanded without reason.[35] The first is this: "Because the Christians were not sufficiently skilled in philosophy and criticism to defend the Scriptures properly against the objections of the Manichaeans and others." The second: "Because they knew well that they taught many things which were in contradiction with sound reason, such as the doctrines of grace and predestination, and other related dogmas, which were presented by Augustine as major elements of the faith [*capita fidei*] which had to be embraced." Finally: "This was the language of a party that had become aware of the strengths [43] and numbers of its members. Augustine often demonstrated this by belittling those who dissented as insignificant due to their small number." Behold, the perspicacity of Phereponus has succeeded in discovering a multitude of accusations against the Catholic Church! However, as for the first cause, we deny that the ancient Christians, especially in Augustine's time, were so ignorant of philosophy and criticism that they were incapable of properly interpreting and defending Holy Scripture. I refer to the writings by which they have defended the truth and holiness of the holy books against the objections of the pagans, the Manichaeans, and other enemies. The fact that such a large number of Manichaeans, many other sectarians, and innumerable pagans have been converted from their superstition to the true Christian religion, is proof (if we do not want to consider all of them oxen and blockheads) [*pecora stipitesque*] that the supervisors and shepherds of old [*praesules et pastores*] diligently studied the sacred writings, and correctly and successfully defended and interpreted them. Secondly, we maintain that the special criticism [*illam criticam*] and philosophy that Phereponus demands was neither necessary in the past nor in the present to lead someone legitimately to the acceptance

---

35. [Muratori's use of *charming* is ironic, just as of *perspicacity* a few lines after.]

of the Christian and Catholic religion. After all, there is abundant evidence to demonstrate the prudent, even obvious, credibility [*prudenter credibilis, immo evidenter credibilis*] of the Christ's religion. Even Christ did not make use of other proofs, and neither did the apostles, their successors, and the other teachers of the Catholic Church in the proclamation of the Gospel. Origen, too, in the first book against Celsus, a man who preceded Phereponus with this accusation, asserts that no other proofs are needed. A great harvest was brought about by the efforts of so many workers [*agricolarum*] in God's vineyard, who—if we want to believe Phereponus—did not understand anything about philosophy and criticism [*criticae*], although history testifies the opposite. Whether the paths laid out by Phereponus and his highly praised criticism [*commendata ars critica*] are suitable to win many believers for Christ may be decided by others. I can, however, affirm that if people refrained from assenting to faith in Christ (whether in the past or present) until all difficulties from Holy Scripture and doctrine have been perfectly resolved, they would either become Christians too late or never at all. For neither untamed, nor curious or weak reason are ever [44] satisfied. No people are in more discord than the ones that worship criticism [*enixam dat operam criticae*], where people doubt everything and accept nothing as trustworthy unless it has been clearly proven. Every one of them [the critics, U.L.] thinks he has understanding in abundance [*sensu abundat*], opines knowing more than others, and therefore knows that he can only trust himself. Therefore, it has always been more prudent [*tutior*] and more laudable to preach and proclaim the Gospel in the way Christ himself and our ancestors did it and still do. Perhaps Phereponus would not have denied this, had he—and he could have achieved this easily—better understood Augustine's view on this point. Yet I want to talk about the right use, abuse, and necessity of criticism as well as about the science of patristics in another chapter.

As for the other reason, namely, that the ancient Christians and Catholics avoided giving reasons because they were "aware that they taught some things that were contrary to sound reason," contradicts the truth in every aspect. We have already mentioned that in the Catholic religion several things are taught that are above human reason, such as those Christ revealed about the nature of God. That individual doctrines contrary to sound reason [*rectam rationem*] would be taught therein without Christians even being aware of this, was—God forbid!—never believed by a Catholic other than erroneously. No one, unless a foolish Catholic, would ever dream of believing something like this [*nullus, nisi stultus, somniavit*]. On what authors does Phereponus base, I ask, this tasteless view that he imposes [*imposuit*] upon the Catholic Church? Perhaps he will cite for us some old and new heretics, with whom he agrees, as authorities for his assertion? Yet, what rule of criticism has taught him to believe our opponents when they assert what we most emphatically deny [*constantissime negamus*]? Moreover, since Augustine was drawn into this dispute, Phereponus should prove that he was well aware that what he presented about grace and predestination contradicted sound reason! I have not the slightest doubt that Augustine, if one had asked him, would not only have denied ever having held such an absurd opinion [*absurdae opinionis*], but he would have shown with invincible reasons that his teaching [*sententiam*] was in harmony with sound reason or at least not in conflict with it.[36] His books speak for him. There, he specifically proves that no other view of grace and the election to grace is in harmony with Scripture and reason than his own and that of the Catholic Church.[37] [45] If he had held the view the Calvinists attribute to him (let us assume this to be quite untrue), we would not deny that he conflicted with sound reason. Yet even if this was admitted, there is no doubt that Augustine would not have been aware of how much his teaching contradicted proper

---

36. [Muratori juxtaposes here *opinio* with *sententia*. While the first and thus invalid view is attributed to Phereponus, the latter true one is presented by him.]

37. [Nevertheless, even among Catholics it was hotly debated who understood Augustine's view correctly. Thus, in the seventeenth and eighteenth centuries, Jansenists clashed with other interpretations. For an overview see Thomas Marschler, "Providence, Predestination, and Grace in Early Modern Catholic Theology," in *Oxford Handbook of Early Modern Theology, 1600–1800*, ed. Ulrich L. Lehner, Richard Muller, and A. G. Roeber (Oxford: Oxford University Press, 2016), 89–103; Sylvio Hermann de Franceschi, "Catholic Theology and Doctrinal Novelty in the Quarrel over Grace," in *Innovation in Early Modern Catholicism*, ed. Ulrich L. Lehner (New York: Routledge, 2021), 28–47; Cornelius Jansen, *The Predestination of Humans and Angels*, trans. Guido Stucco (Washington, DC: The Catholic University of America Press, 2022); José Martin-Palma, *Gnadenlehre von der Reformation bis zur Gegenwart: Handbuch der Dogmengeschichte III/5b* (Freiburg: Herder, 1980).]

reasoning [*non advertisse Augustinum, quantopere hujusmodi sententia adversaretur*]. For even the Calvinists, although they really do teach things contrary to reason on this point, cannot be brought to believe that they teach things contrary to reason and are persisting in their miserable error. Augustine's real view becomes obvious in his book *De utilitate credendi*: "Belief," he says in chapter 11, "is then blameworthy, either when something is believed about God which is unworthy of Him, or when, in the case of man, such belief is too readily held."[38] I must confess that one could not have a more unworthy [*indignius*] view of God than that which Calvin attributes to Augustine—namely, that God creates human beings who in antecedent necessity are driven, like by fate [*non secus ac fato*], to good and evil and subsequently punished by God for their sins, which they are not forced [*non coacti*] to commit. Nevertheless, since they are without their fault not among the elect and thus deprived of the power to resist sin, they can never avoid these sins! Such ideas are unworthy of God and contradict reason. Suppose Augustine really had the view of grace and the election to grace that the newer heretics ascribe to him, and that he was aware of how contrary to reason and unworthy of God his view was: If he had been so witless [*mentis inops*] would he have asserted then that a man who believes something unworthy of God is blameworthy? Yet Augustine has been wrongly explained by Calvin; he did not teach anything unworthy of God, and much less was he conscious of believing something that was in contradiction with reason.

Finally, Augustine writes in the 143rd letter, which was not unknown to Phereponus, since he called it—perfectly rightly—a golden letter, the following: "On the other hand, if, against the most manifest and reliable testimony of reason, anything be set up claiming to have the authority of the Holy Scriptures, he who does this does it through a misapprehension of what he has read, and is setting up against the truth not the real meaning of Scripture, which he has failed to discover, but an opinion of his own; he alleges not what he has found in the Scriptures, but what he has found in himself as their interpreter."[39] The same author

---

38. Augustine, *De utilitate credendi*, ch. 11.25, FC 4:424.
39. Augustine, *Letters of St. Augustine of Hippo*, trans. Marcus Dods (Edinburgh: 1875), 2:222.

also asserted with clarity in the fourth book of *De trinitate*, chapter 6: [46] "No sensible person will decide against reason, no Christian against the Scriptures, no peaceful man against the Church."[40] He speaks in a similar way also in other places. Now we would like to ask Phereponus how he can claim that Augustine was aware of teaching in the matter of grace and predestination things that were in conflict with sound reason, without claiming that either Augustine, a man of such an enviable mind, was delirious, or that this extremely pious man was the most infamous deceiver, since he himself did not know what he should hold to be true and certain, or that he believed in his heart things of which he taught the opposite in order to deceive others! Phereponus must assume this, or admit that Augustine, who teaches that one must not believe anything that is contrary to sound reason, was not consciously holding views that conflict with sound reason or, if Phereponus prefers: that Augustine had violated reason, but was not conscious of his error.

It would not be difficult for us to show that Augustine was not mistaken in the argument about grace and the election to grace, and that he did not propose anything that was in conflict with reason. But this task has already been undertaken by learned Catholics, and through the learned diligence of the same it has also been brought to light how much St. Augustine's teaching differs from that of the Calvinists. Here it is sufficient to note that Augustine wrote the book *De utilitate credendi* while he was still a simple priest. At that time, however, the dispute about grace between him and the Pelagians had not yet taken place, and it is therefore an unfounded claim that Augustine had put forward unreasonable views about grace and predestination. Far from it! Augustine had at that time nothing more important to do than to defend human freedom of will against the Manichaeans, about which, as some mistakenly believe, he was later guilty of errors in his writings against Pelagius. Augustine himself, however, testifies that at that time he was carelessly inclined to the view that was later taught by the Semipelagians, namely that the beginning of faith is to be attributed to the merits of man, not to the grace of God. Since it is clear that, at

---

40. Augustine, *De trinitate*, bk. 4, ch. 6, in *The Trinity*, trans. Stephen McKenna (Washington, DC: The Catholic University of America Press, 1963), FC 45:144.

least at the time when Augustine wrote this book, his views on the doctrine of divine grace [47] were not in conflict with reason, it is also clear that Phereponus could not have argued anything more improper than that Catholics had demanded that faith should precede reason, because they were aware that they taught certain things that were quite contrary to sound reason. The same thing that has been said about the doctrines of grace can be applied to some other doctrines of the Catholic Church that Phereponus believes to be in conflict with sound reason, and which he would also (I fear) have liked to cite here, had he not thought it more appropriate to spare his countrymen, who do not approve of all of his views and his licentiousness, such a reading.

The third reason why Catholics demanded that faith should precede reason is, according to Phereponus, that they had already felt their strength and trusting in their great numbers had despised the small number of dissenters. "Such people," he says, "cannot stand that they are contradicted by a small number of individuals, and demand to be believed as soon as they open their mouths."[41] I do not know whether our clever critic [*ingeniosus*] implicitly accuses here the Synod of Dordt, but I do know that what he says about Catholics is quite correct, namely that they referred to their large number in the dispute with the Manichaeans. Nevertheless, just like in the foregoing, he treats us shamefully [*contumeliose*]. The esteemed Commonwealth of Catholics [*Catholicorum Respublica*][42] certainly claimed that the pagans should believe them; however, not because of their words alone but because, as we have seen, their teaching was perfectly credible, even without proving its intrinsic reasons. This is what Phereponus never learned to consider. Wherever one fights heretics, a suitable proof for the knowledge of the true faith is the great number of faithful members. For there the question arises which of so many parties [*sectas*], each of which claims to be in possession of the true religion of Jesus, is the orthodox, legitimate religion. Catholics, besides other arguments from credibility, which favor only them, are also aided by the fact that they have been Catholic in fact and in name [*in re et nomine*], and this since

---

41. Leclerc, *Variorum*, 510.
42. [Interestingly, Muratori avoids here the use of church (*ecclesia*).]

the times of the apostles. This means that the Catholic religion has been diffused over the whole world and by divine decree [*divino munere*] and is today everywhere present [*latissime pateat*]. No heresy so far has achieved this and will not achieve this before the last day of judgment. If we assumed (which I do not admit) that something like this could, however, happen, it would in no way affect the truth of our religion, which had hitherto been the only Catholic one. Everybody can see that. [48] This characteristic [*tessera*]⁴³ contributes to the others that are found present in the church of Christ and distinguish her from false and heretical churches. Therefore, this characteristic has most wisely been used in the sacred creeds [*symbolis*] by the ecumenical councils, and most efficiently by the writings of the Church Fathers in the fight against heretics. Yet we will deal with this more appropriately in the following chapters.

I would like to conclude this chapter with the remark that Phereponus declared war on Augustine whenever he mentions his *De utilitate credendi*. If one remembers what I have so far laid out, one will recognize how poorly equipped he is for this battle, since he does not understand the state of the question [*statum quaestionis*]. It is therefore obvious that the weapons he prepared for this battle are blunt and his strikes imprudent [*incaute*]. Therefore, I am spared the trouble of refuting his remarks on the seventh chapter of the book *De quantitate animae*, on the second chapter of book one of *De moribus ecclesiae Catholicae*, and on the second chapter of book one of *De libero arbitrio*. There is only one thing I cannot leave unmentioned, which he remarks on at the latter occasion. Here he ridicules Augustine by citing these words from Isaiah 7:9, "*Nisi credideritis, non intelligetis*" (If you do not believe, you will not understand).⁴⁴ From these words

43. [Literally "piece." *Tessera* signifies the part of a bigger whole. In the ancient world sometimes a coin or amulet was broken up and became *tesserae*. These tokens (*symbola*) were then handed to spouses or friends. They symbolized that the carriers of the pieces belong together. Moreover, *tessera* was also an official token of identity among Roman soldiers, and thus figuratively a characteristic. Cf. Adolf Berger, *Encyclopedic Dictionary of Roman Law* (Philadelphia: American Philosophical Society, 1953), 732.]

44. [Augustine quoted the *Septuagint* (LXX), a Jewish Greek translation of the

he intends to prove that one must first believe rather than understand. Yet the words of the prophet, says the new critic [*novus censor*], do not matter here, because according to the correct transcription of Jerome and others, they have a different meaning, namely: "*Nisi credideritis, non permanebitis*" (If you do not believe, you will not remain).⁴⁵ Thus, the meaning of this prophesied passage would be quite different from how Augustine understood it. "Instead of the view of the prophet," says Phereponus, "the good man has cited a fabrication [*figmentum*] of Greek translators. He believed that this was the meaning of the scripture passage before he even knew whether he could trust in everything the translators of the *Septuagint* had written, or whether they had translated this passage correctly."⁴⁶ I do not want to detain the reader any longer with the dispute whether the translation of the *Septuagint* can still be defended, since other learned Fathers have also found this meaning in the words and which even Jerome does not reject. Whatever the correct meaning of this passage may be, so much is clear, as we have seen, that Augustine wanted to prove a truth with it [*probare voluisse*]. A true doctrine, however, remains true and certain, even if useless arguments are used to prove it. Incidentally, it has been accepted as a rule that if a passage from Sacred Scripture allows various interpretations, [49] it is not licit to use it as the foundation of a doctrine [*non ad fundandum*], but only as an illustration [*illustrandum*].

Hebrew Bible dating to the third century BC. For a first overview of its history, see Timothy Michael Law, *When God Spoke Greek: The Septuagint and the Making of the Christian Bible* (New York: Oxford University Press, 2013).]

45. [The Church Father Jerome (ca. 342–420) translated the Bible into Latin. This translation is called the *Vulgata*. On his translation of Isaiah, see Anni Maria Laato, "Isaiah in Latin," in *The Oxford Handbook of Isaiah*, ed. Lena-Sofia Tiemeyer (New York: Oxford University Press, 2020), 489–503. The best analysis of Augustine's use of the verse, which also includes an overview of its aftermath in scholasticism, is Wilhelm Geerlings, "Jesaja 7,9b bei Augustinus: Die Geschichte eines fruchtbaren Missverständnisses," in *Fußnoten zu Augustinus: Gesammelte Schriften Wilhelm Geerlings* (Turnhout: Brepols, 2010), 137–48. On the varying interpretations of this scripture verse in the post-Reformation period, see Ethan H. Shagan, *The Birth of Modern Belief: Faith and Judgement from the Middle Ages to the Enlightenment* (Princeton, NJ: Princeton University Press, 2018), 65–97.]

46. Leclerc, *Variorum*, 220.

Thus, there is no danger that such meaning, even if it is not very useful [*non prosit*], will harm a doctrine whose truth can be shown from other more obvious passages in Sacred Scripture. Augustine, however, did not have to wait for Phereponus teaching him about which version of translation was more certain [*diversa illius versione*], as is evident from the twelfth chapter of the second book *De doctrina Christina*, which, as we know, he only wrote two years after *De libero arbitrio*.[47]

47. [Muratori successfully refutes Leclerc's claim that Augustine did not know other translations of the verse. Cf. Laato, "Isaiah," 493; Geerlings, "Jesaja 7,9b."]

Chapter 6

On the Weakness of Reason and Judgment

The Weakness of the Human Mind and of Human Reason

[49] So far it has been shown to what extent a human being can investigate the truth before choosing a religion, and that it is sufficient and even obligatory for anybody, who acts reasonably, to accept the true religion on the basis of so-called extrinsic reasons (*argumenta credibilitatis*) of faith, even before one is able to understand all of its doctrines and mysteries. Yet even today there are still people who follow the bad example of the Manichaeans, who, blinded by the vanity of their mind [*mentis ambitione*], falsely believe they can understand all things, and excessively exalt the powers of human reason [*rationis humanae*]. To destroy this pernicious view at its root, we must turn against the main bulwark of all errors, which means we must make humans aware, as briefly as possible, of the weakness and foolishness [*infirmitas ... stultitia*] of created minds [*creaturarum mentium*]. From this must be derived our precepts and maxims how to restrain the mind [*moderandi ingenii*]. The sages of this world teach us we should get to know ourselves before [50] everything else. And indeed, we must not expect any progress toward the true knowledge and love of God, unless we have first arrived at the insight of our own weakness [*imbecillitatis nostrae cognitio*], and unless humility, which is granted to us by God, turns us toward Him by correcting [*castigans*] human pride and enabling us to receive or ask for the greater gifts from Heaven.

How Easily Humans Fail—And the Reasons for That: Negligence of Scientific Education and Lethargy in the Search for Truth

When we say that the human mind and reason [*mentem atque rationem*] are feeble and weak [*infirmam esse atque imbecillem*], we mean to say that persons, although endowed with reason, find it difficult to come to the knowledge of truth and to correct judgments by their own efforts, because they are easily carried away into folly and remain in it. This weakness and impotence seem to flow from a double source: The first of these is that humans do not want to seek the truth and do not want to use the expedient means to find it. The second is that even if a person does seek the truth, such a person often will not find it, since the truth is difficult to discover and reason often used incorrectly [*inepto rationis usu*]. We will discuss these causes one by one, so that human reason may learn to see its vulnerabilities [*vulnera*] more clearly, and so that our mind [*ingenia*] may finally get rid of its pride and impudence.

All know, and no one denies, that a human leaves the motherly womb wrapped in crassest ignorance. Soon afterwards, this ignorance seems to disappear if the person uses the outer senses and begins to reason [*sensibus et meditatiane pollere*]. Whether the ideas of things are innate [*ingenitae*] to us or whether they are communicated to us from the outside is a question about which philosophers argue; we leave it at that. Yet this much is certain: The use of the senses is necessary either to develop the innate ideas in us or to communicate new ideas to the mind from the outside. Therefore, Seneca says in his ninety-fifth letter: "The soul carries within itself the seed of everything that is honorable, and this seed is stirred to growth by advice, as a spark that is fanned by a gentle breeze develops its natural fire."[1] We call it thinking [*meditari*] when the soul [*anima*], being in a lively body [*vegeto corpore*], to put it this way, directs [*intendit*] vigilantly its sharpness [*ipsa vigilans aciem suam*] to objects, their essence, their causes, their effects and qualities. The use of the senses, experience [*experientia*], contact with parents and other people as well as other mechanisms [*instrumenta*] of

---

1. Seneca, *Letter 94 l.* 29, in Seneca, *Epistles*, vol. 3, trans. Richard M. Gummere (Cambridge, MA: Harvard University Press, 2014), LCL 77: 30–31.

human life, gradually form the uncultivated mind [*rudem intellectum*] whether one wants it or not, and communicate to it a certain notion of truth. Yet of what share [*quota pars*] of the vastness of truth can this be said? And with how many errors and wrong views is this notion still mixed and infected? Thus, we usually acquire only knowledge of common things [51] discoverable by the senses; indeed, we learn nothing more than the surface [*superficies*] of these things. If, therefore, human beings stop at this and neither want to explore the immeasurable field of other truths nor ponder what they have already learned, such *bipeds* would differ only by body posture from *quadrupeds*. In such a case truth is not intended and the necessary and expedient means to discover truth are neglected. Some do this out of indolence and aversion to work and because they are under the spell of their disorderly inclinations, others because they have surrendered entirely to the pursuit of earthly concerns and goods. Others despair over finding truth, while again others believe they know what they do not know, and so on. It is universally known how many errors subject and dominate people. When it concerns things that go a little beyond the affairs of common life, some people appear just like children. Their mind [*mens*] is caught within the narrow circle of a few finite objects and cannot rise above them without drifting into error. Since these people are still dominated by the innate ignorance from which they might have been able to free themselves if they had wished so, it is not surprising that their reason [*ratio*] is very weak [*imbecillima*]. After all, they allow themselves to be carried away daily by false and foolish opinions, never discard old nonsense [*vetera deliria*], consider themselves incapable of discovering things that are not obvious, cannot solve difficult and intricate problems [*quaestiones dirimendas*], and finally fail to think correctly [*rite meditandum*] because in innumerable cases they cannot distinguish [*distinguendum*] truth from falsity.

Bodily Weakness, Lack of Aids to Find the Truth, and the Abuse of Such Aids

Much sadder, however, is the other case—namely when people, although they seek truth and science and the paths that lead to both, cannot find them. Three causes best explain this phenomenon—namely the body, the nature of scientific tools, and the inner faculties of the soul [*animae*]. As far as the body is concerned, the fact is that the bodily organs sometimes do not correspond well with the activities of the mind [*animorum*][2] and cannot be improved by any effort or diligence. Thus, countless diseases can daily afflict the body and exert thereby a detrimental influence on the mind [*animo*]. The mind [*animus*] must necessarily feel [*sentire*] the pains and discomforts of its prison [*carceris*], and consequently everybody must feel to what great extent the [52] mind [*mentem*] is weakened by an incapacitated, weak, and sick body, and how great the darkness is with which the purest light of reason [*lucidissima rationi*] is surrounded in this dark bodily mass [*massa corporis*]. For this reason alone, many people remain in the state of their original ignorance [*pristina ignorantia*][3] and cannot rise to nobler education [*nobiliores disciplinas*], even if they want to. Moreover, dull and shallow minds [*obtusis crassisque ingeniis*], which also cannot remember anything accurately [*nulla memoriae tenacitate*], should not be allowed to have a say in exposed or concealed truths [*obviis atque reconditis veritatibus*], nor give a judgment about difficult or uncommon affairs.

Now I come to the weakness of human reason [*rationis*], which stems from the lack and inadequacy of any means by which the truth can be recognized, and error avoided. In this case, too, the lot of such mortals is lamentable. Many lack the means and facilities to attain knowledge. For how many countries are there in the world who have access to a liberal arts [*liberales disciplinae*] education and suitable teachers? Only a few! In many of them there are not even the slightest traces of the arts by whose help one arrives at the truth, and which enable the instructed and educated mind [*eruditus atque excultus animus*] to somewhat protect itself from the grossest errors. Look at Africa, Asia, America, and even all the countries close to Hyperborea

---

2. [While Muratori uses the feminine noun *anima* to describe the soul, he switches here to the masculine *animus* to describe the physiological aspect of the soul, best translated as mind.]

3. [The use of the adjective *pristina*, describing an undefiled state of purity, is seemingly ironic.]

under the Seven Stars of the Bear.[4] Then look at the happiest region of all, Europe itself! How many of its people are blessed because of its climate [*natura*], to gather around teachers and pursue education [*doctoribus affluant & disciplinis*]? And how many are there who truly dedicate themselves to this work or even desire it? In truth, they do not care at all for the arts or the teachers, and never learn because the impediments and demands of life keep them from it. But no one doubts that such great barbarism and such a dearth of linguistic learning [*doctrinae linguarumque inopia*] encourages natural ignorance and opens the door to countless mistakes.

Unfortunately, however, the means of knowledge that serve the discovery and learning of truth also not infrequently serve error. Since humans are either, because of their evil disposition, inclined to lie to others or deceive them, or are deceived and led astray due to the weakness of their minds [*mentis*], it follows with necessity that humans are constantly led astray and deceived by contact with other people, even the erudite ones. First our parents, then our nurses, soon our elders, and then our equals teach us fairytales from the earliest age and fill our impressionable mind [*mentem*] with distorted judgments [*perversis judiciis*] [53]. Later on, when they have introduced new swaths of errors, the learned masters corrupt the mind—sometimes by their very own books and lectures with the result that we have a far worse [*deteriorum*] knowledge [*scientiam*] or understanding [*intelligentiam*] of things than through our previous knowledge.

Weakness of Memory and Untamed Imagination, Especially When the Mind Is Moved by the Passions

However, there are even more important causes that prevent people from recognizing the truth. This becomes apparent when we consider the hidden depths of our minds [*animorum*] and reflect on those obstacles to truth that belong intrinsically to the mind [*animo*]. The first source of error can be attributed to imagination and memory. For as

---

4. [Muratori uses this phrase to signify Northern Europe.]

soon as an extremely vivid image [*vivacissima imago*] rushes [*irruit*] into our imagination [*phantasiam*], it is powerfully inscribed [*inscribitur*] into it, and the soul [*anima*] can only with difficulty abstain from contemplating the image that is inflicted upon her even against her will [*nolenti passim ingerit*], which is the most powerful faculty of the soul [*objicit potentissima illa facultas*]. Since these images [*phantasmata*] that are impressed onto the mind are observed with vividness by the soul's inner eyes [*oculos animae internos*], they seize control of the free activity of the soul, interfering with it in such a way that it is not able to contemplate other images, whose examination is necessary for proper judgment. Moreover, the soul can be so occupied or forced by an impression that it sometimes does not, and sometimes is not even able to, properly examine the ideas (*rationes*) of other things, to separate the true from the false by good judgment [*placido consilio*], and to choose good instead of evil. Consequently, the stronger the power of one's imagination and the more frequent or fiercely [*ferocius*] an image enters, the more the soul's ability to investigate and find truth is weakened. And so it happens that that faculty, which is destined by nature to help reason gain its dominion, not infrequently turns this reason into a slave and deprives it of its dominion in a human being.

Imagination and memory hurt the activity of reason, when the images of sensory or intellectual objects, are disturbing the mind or the affects [*animi perturbationibus sive affectibus*]. For objects which are perceived through the senses or which are conceived by the intellect do not usually cause any, or if so just an insignificant affect or perturbation [*nullum aut levem creant in anima affectum sive perturbationem*], unless they enter the soul with a mighty impact [*ingenti cum impetu*]. For then they implant [*infigi*] themselves deeply into the soul, where they occupy the inner contemplative faculty of the soul [*internum animae intuitum*]. We see and hear a great many things every day that, [54] because they always occur, we hardly notice; these things come into our imagination [*phantasiam*] and remain in it, but without causing any grave commotion in the soul. If we, however, think or perceive with our senses things that excite in the mind the affects [*affectiones*] of love, hate, fear, hope, terror, pain, and so forth, they affect our imagination much more intensely [*concitatius*] and leave a lasting impression.

Hence it comes about that, as often as the mind [*mens*] contemplates images of this kind (which it often does of its own accord, and indeed is sometimes forced to do so), not only the image itself but also the associated affect is imposed upon the soul [*animae*]. Therefore, the image of an enemy will always be presented to the soul with renewed traces of hatred. Likewise, the cheapskate always thinks of robbers and simultaneously fears them. A lover always recalls the image of his beloved, fanning the flames of love in his mind [*animo*]. Yet, if it is such an extremely difficult task to control the affects of the mind [*animi*] and to subjugate them to the rule of reason [*normam rectae rationis redigere*], and if nothing is truer than that only a few people will discover and prevent all temptations, all seductions, all secret deceptions in their affects, and if it is certain that the soul is against its will carried away by imagination [*recusantem rapi ad intuendas*] to meditate and contemplate images of things that are accompanied by passionate affects, an important insight arises: Who does not see that both imagination and memory, as well as the excitements of the mind [*animi*], are often not only obstacles for grasping the truth, but also become sources of many errors? Certainly, this evil may appear in ordinary life and business, but most frequently one finds it in the Republic of Letters [*Eruditorum Republica*]. For example, if the image of Plato, of Epicurus, of Aristotle has taken hold of our souls, and if their views and philosophies have become known to us, if their image is accompanied by admiration, love, and reverence, then the mind [*animus*] is so excited and dominated by this image that from now on it only appreciates the views of Plato, of Epicurus, of Aristotle, and despises all others. The opposite occurs when, instead of love and admiration, we are taken by hatred and contempt for another writer or view [*sententiam*]. As long, however, as such vivid images rule over imagination and memory without any restraint [*sine fraeno*] [55] and inner affects are dominated by errors, the soul will remain subject to error. After all, only sound reason can regulate and guide affects and imagination, because she subjects them to a thorough inquiry about their just or unjust origin.

The Perversity of the Will

Yet also the perversity of the will often causes errors. All people have a desire for happiness [*velle esse beatos*]. This natural desire [*appetitu*] gives rise to a multitude of affects of the will. However, the affects of the mind [*animi*] are nothing else than movements of the will toward a good that one would like to acquire or that one already possesses, or toward a good that one has lost or that one has not yet acquired. We love [*amamus*] when we want to be united with a good or to remain in union with it. We desire when we wish for a good. We hope when we have the prospect of acquiring a good soon. We rejoice when we have acquired it and fear losing it. We are filled with anger and hatred against a person who robs us of a good or attempts to do so. We mourn when we have lost a good. The same is true of the other affects. If the will was always striving for the one true good and if its movements were always guided by prudence, the intellect would have no reason to be angry with it and would have nothing to fear. However, since the depraved human will constantly strives for objects that only appear to be good, but are in fact evil, it often diverts the mind [*animum*] from the true good and keeps it away. Consequently, the intellect falls into slavery and thus into a most deplorable state and becomes subject to a thousand errors. As a result, the will strives for bodily pleasures, for riches, and for transient honors, which—as it persuades itself—grant happiness to the earthly part of the human person [*terrenae hominis parti*], with which it is conjoined through an intimate bond of love [*arctissimo vinculo et amore*]. The will is either possessed by the desire [*appetitus*] for glory, from which derives the lust [*libido*] for innovation [*novitatis ardor*] or domination, or other such desires [*cupiditates*], all of which Holy Scripture subsumes under *concupiscence*. This way, however, the intellect is carried away by the dominion of the delirious and dissipated affects of the will and forced to go along with this delusion. By behaving badly and serving the body beyond good measure, the mind [*menti*] cannot investigate the truth and bring those errors to light but is merely intent on seeking the means [*rationibus*] through which the counterfeit goods [*apparentia bona*][5] are

---

5. [Muratori makes clear that these goods are not really good but only appear to be so. Therefore, the editor chose the translation *counterfeit*.]

revealed to the will. After all, it is only concerned with how the will can obtain these false goods. And even if the mind were eager to do this, its efforts would often be in vain, [56] since disordered affects [*male sano affectu*] do not allow the formation of proper judgment. Moreover, the will is going to make the weak intellect [*intellectus*] either openly or covertly support and approve its desire.

Narrowness of Human Judgment, Ignorance, and Obliviousness

Finally, there are two more impediments to proper and certain judgment. The first is that the mind [*mortalium mentes*] of the mortals, although it appears to be quite powerful, is in comparison with the minds of the angels quite limited, not to mention of course God, with whom human minds can in no way be compared [*nullo pacto*]. There are many things that remain inaccessible to our intellect, even to the most gifted, as long it is enclosed in this mortal body, despite the bravest efforts and ingenuity [*meditationis intentio et ingenii solertia*]. Many of these are found in physics, astronomy, and medicine but also in the other arts. The intellect attempts to perceive and recognize what is probable and extremely likely [*probabilia et verisimilia*] in these affairs, but never the intrinsic truth of things. To this category belong also those things that are believed but not known, and thus everything that is dependent on the testimony of history or reputation. Since the finite human mind has not always existed and has not been present in all places—could not and never will, since this is God's business alone—we will, if we want to know what contingently happened [*non necessario contigerunt*] in the past and in places where we have not been, use the sharpness of our thought [*cogitationis aciem*] in vain where our sensual perception has failed and what it could never reach. In order to get to know these things [*percipiendis*], the intellect [*intellectus*] must therefore trust [*fidat*] in the uncertain and erroneous opinion of other people and books. Even if one reaches the truth this way quite often, reason will nevertheless not enjoy the same decisiveness and certainty that would dissolve any suspicion of error. The same defect is noticeable when one must investigate the inner thoughts of other people and wants to know the secrets of the heart [*arcana cordium*]. From the outer appearances one may well infer internal things, but who knows with certainty what is going on in the interior of other minds [*animis alienis interius*]?

There is no better way to exhibit the narrowness of the human mind [*mentis*] than [57] by contemplating an infinite object or one that borders on the infinite. The sharpness of the mind will vacillate quickly and be replaced by darkness and confusion. Now the deficient eyes of the mind finally recognize their impotence and audacity! After all, the mind will have tried in vain to measure and embrace something infinite with its finite power. You may measure the globe in feet and cubits, if the measurement is repeated as often as necessary, for the earth has borders. Yet if you inquire about the infinite, whatever finite measure you may use is useless. Even if we advance in measuring, there will always be a far bigger part—or more appropriately said—an infinitely big part left. In physics and in geometry we find things of which we form an idea [*quidem ideam*] by means of reasoning; which, however, can never be compared to the unlimited width of the objects themselves [*numquam rerum interminatae amplitudini*]. Yet, leaving other things aside, there is one "thing" that is absolutely infinite [*revera omni ex parte infinitum*]—namely, the all-good and all-powerful God [*Deus optimus maximus*] and whatever is in God, specifically his power, his wisdom, his providence, his goodness, his justice and the other qualities [*dotes*] or attributes of the infinite being. Nothing is more certain than this simple truth; nothing is more obvious to the more rational part of humanity [*pars hominum sanior*]. If, however, human reason should desire to fully comprehend the divine nature, the divine attributes, and judge them according to human measurements, it is doubly unsuccessful: either it immediately realizes its limitations, acknowledges its defeat, and stands in awe before the infinite light; or it is carried away on an audacious course to a thousand absurd opinions and follies.

Choosing the False Principles for Judgment

The second impediment for correct judgment, which the mind can overcome only with difficulty, derives from ignorance and forgetfulness, or from the choice of false principles that are necessary for proper judgment. There are certain ideas, certain principles of reason, certain first truths [*primae veritates*] that are so firmly grounded either in nature or in divine and human laws, or in the universal consensus of humanity, that no one can withhold assent or obedience to or deny them, even if he wanted. The ideas and truths of things are judged according to these principles. To judge means nothing but using these principles, universal truths, and ideas, as a reliable measuring stick [*veluti ad regulam certamque ad amussim exigere*] for every single thing [*singularia & particularia*]. If there is proportionality, [58] equality, or similarity between these principles and the individual things compared with them, we call them good [*dicimus istas bene se habere*] and in agreement [*consentire*] with truth or rectitude. If they do not agree [*sin secus*], we declare them false or distorted [*falsas aut perversas*].[6] *Every human is an animal*, that is a principle, a rule. We now bring various humans under this rule and measure them by it—for example, Peter and John—and we recognize at once that since they are human, they are also properly called animals. Yet if the correctness or truth of a first principle or concept is doubted, it must be established by other, even more general and certain principles and ideas. By comparing these with the less certain principles and ideas, one can establish either the truth or falsity of the latter.

There may well be many people who flatter themselves in their arrogance that they have grasped all principles, all first truths and the ideas of things, and that nothing hinders them from proceeding to a judgment with certainty. Yet, those who claim this seem to be completely ignorant of a fundamental fact that is not only taught to us by the sacred and divinely revealed Scriptures, but also by the pagan philosophers and by reason; namely, that there is always far more that is unknown than known.[7] A thinking person [*homini meditanti*], who is eager to learn something new every day and compares himself with

---

6. [The full Latin sentence: "Si proportio, aequalitas, similitudo comperitur inter has regulas, atque inter collatas seu comparatas cum his regulis res particulares: tum dicimus istas bene se habere, & veritati aut rectitudini consentire. Sin secus, falsas aut perversas pronuntiamus."]

7. ["... [p]lura nempe semper esse, quae homini cuicumque nesciantur, quam quae sciantur."]

other persons distinguished in knowledge, will be able to realize this truth lucidly through his own experience. Nevertheless, there is a real danger that a person will be led to wrong judgments out of ignorance of a principle, a first truth or idea. This is certainly the main cause for the mistakes in judgments among the uneducated. Yet I liberally concede that some astute and learned men know everything that is required for correct judgments. They know all the axioms, principles, and rules according to which judgments must be made. Nevertheless, their mind has not eliminated all grounds for error, for it sometimes happens that persons do not remember all necessary principles and rules or choose one principle mistakenly instead of another, or apply a principle to a wrong object. Indeed, for a judgment to be correct, one therefore must carefully consider an object from every side, inside and out. One must direct the sharpness of the intellect [*aciem intellectum*] to [59] causes and effects, an object's inner qualities and its external relations, to all kinds of modifications and forms of existence. Moreover, one must see under which fundamental rule, under which principle of reason (of which thousands may exist and be consulted) this object falls and must be judged. Yet, it happens quite frequently both that one fails to recognize all the particular circumstances, modifications, relations, and causes because either imagination [*phantasia*], memory, or will are too deficient or weak to offer the intellect the principles and axioms that are necessary for this intellectual operation. Even if they offer them, the weak and incautious intellect often mistakenly chooses one principle instead of another and will thus be unable to refrain from error. Unquestionably, everything has in some respect similarities with a number of principles and ideas. In the concrete world,[8] however, the object concurs perfectly [*omnimodam integramque*] only with one thing in similarity, proportion, or equality. If one therefore used instead of the rational principle, which in such a case must be the only measurement [*mensura unice*], another, inappropriate principle, one will be deceived by the [superficial, U.L.] appearance of truth and correctness, and pronounce an incorrect and false judgment. One will, I say, pronounce a wrong judgment, not because the fundamental principle

8. [Literally, Muratori, writes "occasionibus datis," in given events. He seems to distinguish here abstract from concrete reality.]

failed, but because it was used for the wrong object [*sed quod ea in re illud*], or because one only used this one [*unum dumtaxtat principium ante oculos habuisti*], and consequently neglected other axioms [*documentis*] that would have been far more appropriate for right reasoning.

The importance [*dignitas*] of the matter prompts me to give one more example. This is a basic axiom of political law, which is in no conflict with reason: *Whoever kills a human unjustly must be put to death.* With this general principle in mind, a judge will consider the crime of a murderer and find perfect [*integram*] similarity and proportionality between this principle and the case at hand, and thus sentence the murderer to death. Nevertheless, the judge errs if the public good requires the preservation of the murderer's life, or if his death would bring great disadvantages for the common good. In this case, another law or principle is more appropriate [*opportunius*], namely: *A person may not be punished with death for a privately committed crime if the State has a strong interest in the accused remaining alive.* Likewise, among Catholics it is an established axiom considered in perfect harmony with religion, to say: *One owes reverence to places consecrated to God.* [60] Because of this principle, not only bishops but even kings have permitted to such places the right of granting asylum for people who are guilty of certain minor offenses. In certain countries this privilege was later extended to almost all other crimes, and in the opinion this would please God, to all places consecrated to God. Yet a number of scholars maintained that such a great number of asylum-granting institutions [*tantam asylorum amplitudinem*] should not be tolerated, for they have considered this subject from the perspective of a different axiom, namely: *God must be more pleased with the punishment of crime and the preservation of public peace and justice than with the immunities[9] of the churches.* After all,

9. [Such immunity included the right to grant asylum. It led in many places to outright abuse of this privilege, for example in Naples: "Every church, every chapel, the convents, their vegetable and flower gardens, the houses, shops, and bakers' ovens, which had a wall in common with or were adjoining to the church, and the houses of the priests, all furnished an asylum to criminals; so that, among so many places for shelter, upon the commission of a crime, an asylum was sure to be at hand, protected by the bishops or clergy, and by the furious zeal of the mob, who defended these mockeries, as if they had formed a part of religion" (Pietro Colletta, *The History of Naples: From the Accession of Charles of Bourbon to the Death of Ferdinand I*, trans. S. Horner,

churches would be desecrated if they all became the sanctuary of criminals, and this would endanger the safety of innocent people and render ineffective the justice that God had charged worldly princes to execute. Therefore, these scholars claim that the right of asylum must be judged according to the latter principle, not according to the earlier one. This consideration, however, has its place in the judgments of politics, morality, physics, and theology, as well as in the remaining wisdom of human life as well as the other sciences, in which reason alone can be teacher and moderator [*magistra et moderatrix*]. For we not only fall into error if we subsume particular cases under false and doubtful principles that we consider to be true and established and measure the truth of a matter with a false yardstick, but also if we apply to a particular problem, which we have to judge, a principle that is established and true but does not fit the matter.

---

vol. 1 (Edinburgh: Edmonston and Douglas, 1860), 60). A new concordat with the Holy See in 1741 curtailed these privileges. It was especially Enlighteners who favored the abolition of these privileges. For overviews of the history of the ecclesiastical asylum, see Karl Härter "Vom Kirchenasyl zum politischen Asyl: Asylrecht und Asylpolitik im frühneuzeitlichen Alten Reich," in *Das antike Asyl: Kultische Grundlagen, rechtliche Ausgestaltung und politische Funktion*, ed. M. Dreher (Cologne: Böhlau, 2003), 301–36; Karl Shoemaker, *Sanctuary and Crime in the Middle Ages, 400–1500* (New York: Fordham University Press, 2011); Susanne Pohl-Zucker, *Making Manslaughter: Process, Punishment and Restitution in Württemberg and Zurich, 1376–1700* (Leiden: Brill, 2017); Wilhelm Liebhart, "Kirchenasyl am Beispiel von St. Ulrich und Afra in Augsburg," *Zeitschrift für Schwäbische und Bayerische Rechtsgeschichte* 1 (2017): 89–100; Elizabeth Allen, *Uncertain Refuge: Sanctuary in the Literature of Medieval England* (Philadelphia: University of Pennsylvania Press, 2021). For the specific context in Naples, see Pietro Lo Iacono, *Chiesa, Stato e popolo nel Mezzogiorno dei Lumi: la legislazione ecclesiastica dei Borboni di Napoli e di Sicilia tra istanze regaliste e tutela dell'ordo spiritualis 1734–1739* (Cosenza: Pellegrini, 2012).]

Chapter 7

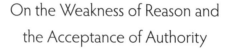

On the Weakness of Reason and the Acceptance of Authority

The Weakness of Human Reason according to Common Experience

[60] It should be obvious from the previous chapters how many things can prevent human reason from making correct judgments. [61] It would be great foolishness not to realize or to deny the many causes why people err, and outrageous pride to consider them beyond the suspicion of error. Experience proves it! No country has ever been without religion, or is without one, although many countries have been without the true religion and still are. After all, there is no opinion delirious enough that it was not conceived and adopted by a people somewhere and turned into their religion. I do not even want to start speaking about the many monsters [*tot monstris*]! But how could such a forest [*silva*] of errors have grown and spread almost over the whole Earth? What causes exist for this deplorable misery [*miserandi excidii*] other than the ones I have pointed out so far?

Nobody should, however, attribute the silly ideas and dark concepts in which so many people are entangled only to human lethargy and ignorance, and not to the weakness of the human spirit! As if these people had never investigated the truth or had never been aware of the innate powers of reason [*ingenitasque rationis vires*], did not feel them [*stulte non senserint*], or perniciously neglected them [*igniominose neglexerint*]. The Indians have had their Brahmans and Gymnosophists, the Persianstheir magicians, the French their Druids, the Egyptians and the Chaldeans had men educated in art and science, and above all, the Phoenicians have gained a reputation for their scientific culture. How much progress [*in disciplinis... processerint*], though, Chinese science has made can be seen from its present state. Not excluding the Scythians, who have given us the admirable Anacharsis,[1] there were very few or even no people anywhere in the vast continent of Asia where in ancient times the sciences would not have been cultivated. From these Barbarians, as Clement of Alexandria shows in the first book of the *Stromateis*,[2] flowed [*fluxit*] the sciences to Europe, for which the world later admired the Greeks and Romans. How much the ancient Greeks and Romans have achieved in the sciences is well known. Antiquity has produced many geniuses [*ingenia*], excellent philosophers, experts in all realms of knowledge, and all of them in such great numbers that posterity, until the end of the fifteenth century of our time has not seen anything comparable. One could say that at that time nature showed what it was capable of and what human genius [*humana ingenia*] could achieve.

Consequently, the people before the times of Christ were not at all stupid or infantile, irrational, or intellectually unconcerned [*incuriosos*] [62], but people who had attained an admirable degree of distinction in all sciences. One could even say that they outclass us [*saltem in re nobis praeferendos*] since they invented [*fecerint*] the arts and sciences and have not just received [*acceperint*] them [from a previous generation, U.L.], and still enlighten [*illustrent*] our age with their genius [*ingenio*]. We would have never progressed this far had their light not preceded us![3] Nevertheless, we are not only aware of the fortunate fate [*felicitas*] of these great minds, but also of their unfortunate fate [*infelicitas*] in the attainment of the noblest of all truths—I mean the truth of religion. Although the ancients, because of their never-ending scholarly

---

1. [Legendary Scythian prince. U.L.]

2. Clement of Alexandria, *Stromateis, Book 1–3*, trans. John Ferguson (Washington, DC: The Catholic University of America Press, 1991), FC 85: 23–156.

3. [The original Latin sentence runs from the beginning of the paragraph to here and was broken up for easier readability. U.L.]

quarrels, also missed many truths in physics, ethics [*moralibus*], astronomy, geography, history, and other such sciences, it is true that they diligently investigated the divine nature, providence, and the power of God, how God should be worshipped, what duties humans have toward him and what obligations humans have to each other [*quidque homo homini debeat*]. But, by God, what absurd and impious opinions did they come up with! Never has the weakness [*imbecillitas*] of human reason been more clearly revealed. For what they opined [*senserunt*][4] was either unworthy of God or of humans, and their religion was idolatry. Those among them who considered themselves the most perspicacious either denied the existence of God or the immortality of the soul and have thereby fallen into ghastly vices [*scelus*] and misery. Others recognized the falsity of their religion with the help of philosophy. Cicero's statement is known: "Would that I was able to find the true as easily as I refute the false!," but it is a fact that [the ancients, U.L.] did not acquire true religion this way. Lactantius therefore states: "Those more wise, lest they fall into error, do the same thing, either because they do not know the true, or because they continue in those which they know to be false so that they may seem to hold to something, or because they worship nothing at all, when this very thing is the greatest error—to imitate the life of beasts under the form of man."[5] The Apostle Paul described the foolishness of the ancient philosophers in his epistle to the Romans (Rom 1:21–23) this way: "For although they knew God they did not accord him glory as God or give him thanks. Instead, they became vain in their reasoning, and their senseless minds were darkened. While claiming to be wise, they became fools and exchanged the glory of the immortal God for the likeness of an image of mortal man or of birds or of four-legged animals or of snakes." He writes in a similar way in the Epistle to the Ephesians (Eph 4:17).

[63] What is the use of this disputation, and why do I continue to prove by examples the calamities that befall the human mind in its investigation of truth? Is there any alternative to befriending academic

---

4. [The verb literally translated means "feeling," but it can also mean "to have an opinion."]

5. Lactantius, *Divine Institutions I–VII*, bk. 2, ch. 3, trans. Sr. Mary Francis McDonald (Washington, DC: The Catholic University of America Press, 1964), FC 49:105.

skepticism [*academicis et scepticis*] and asserting that there is no certainty and no truth under the sun? I am far from doing something as silly and dangerous as that. Yet those who believe they are able to achieve everything through the power of reason, are just as silly and appalling as those who believe they can achieve nothing with it. Nothing in my arguments entices a reader to choose such a path, and nothing in them can be used to justify it.[6] I have not said that the human powers of reason are destroyed, but only that they are weakened, and that therefore truth can only be found with great difficulty, but I have not rejected the hope that we can find her. For if we wanted to fully comprehend—while our soul is bound to a mortal body and constrained by it—the things that transcend the sharpness and capacity of our intellect, or if we believed we could comprehend them, we would be ridiculous in the eyes of truly wise men. Therefore, I do not exclude genius [*ingenium*] and reason from the study of true religion, but only recommend all reasonable people moderation [*moderationem*] in their use. What such moderation should look like, I will explain later.

Humility Is Necessary for Our Reason to Recognize the True Religion: Wisdom and Strength Must be Asked from God

First, a person must recognize the weakness of mind and reason [*mentis rationisque*], which is extremely easy if one considers how many and great obstacles there are that keep one from recognizing the truth and lead one into error. Such a person should consider the examples of so many excellent men, with whom he would never compare himself in genius and erudition [*ingenio et eruditione*], and above whom he would not, unless in silly pride, elevate himself. Yet, these men have failed in discovering the true religion despite their perspicacity or, even if they have discovered it, have not embraced it, and have obviously defended countless errors and ridiculous opinions. This is ample proof for what one can hope to achieve with the powers of reason alone. Moreover,

---

6. [The editor chose to translate this sentence a bit more freely. Literally translated it states: "Our arguments are not leading an attentive reader there and cannot lead him there."]

reason itself will advise such a person not to presume too much, nor to trust oneself too much. For who would believe he possesses the sharpest mind and best judgment? Who would consider himself free of every prejudice? Who would believe he possesses all the scientific means and instruments and always uses them properly? Who would believe that neither the disordered movements of the body nor the will are harmful to reason and judgment? Who would not agree that the will must be free of all evil desires and deceptive effects to judge properly? Who would furthermore claim to not only have found all principles, first truths, and all concepts, on which correct judgment is necessarily based, but also to remember them at every moment perfectly, and to always choose from them the right and suitable one for the decision of a question, and that he has never applied a wrong one for his judgments? Even if there exists someone who really affirms such a grand view of himself before the tribunal of his mind, such a person might be honest with himself but could not be absolved from arrogance and rashness.[7]

Secondly, after a person has recognized and conquered inner pride, reason demands that humility and modesty [*animi depressio*] take its place, for whom the desire and hope for help is the only consolation. Due to our weakness, we cannot expect such help from ourselves, but neither from others who can be deceivers or deceived. Therefore, the only hope that remains is to turn [*convertat*] our mind in humility to God, the parent of all [*omnium parentem*] and the creator of all that is good, and to ask wisdom and understanding [*sapientiam atque intelligentiam*] from him. This is what the Apostle James teaches (1 Jm 1:5) when he writes: "But if any of you lacks wisdom, he should ask God who gives to all generously and ungrudgingly, and he will be given it." If all this has been observed, then human reason can proceed with greater acuity to investigate a religion wherever one can find one. Often, divine

---

7. [Muratori seems to allude here to the possibility of an erring conscience but avoids the term *conscientia*. In the Catholic understanding of an erring conscience a person can be fully convinced of doing the right thing even if it is objectively wrong. Following one's conscience reduces the person's culpability in the offense against the objective norm, but not for the offense of malforming one's conscience. Thus, a person might have such a grand view of one's powers, but the consequences of this view are not fully culpable. Nevertheless, it is fully culpable that the person became arrogant and rash in the first place.]

grace also reveals this religion to those who do not seek it through good books or through the teachers of divine truth. Consequently, it cannot be denied that the way to true religion would be very easy and safe if God revealed it directly [*immediate*] to a human. For how could reason waver under such a teacher, that is, if the highest truth itself taught? Yet it would be an audacious demand, and even more audacious to hope that God would depart from the established laws of nature to lead *you*[8] by means of a prodigy to the truth. Rather, you may hope that the most merciful God [*clementissimum Numen*] tells a few truly pious persons and his prophets what to believe and how to worship him. "The LORD knows the plans of man; they are like a fleeting breath," as David says in Ps 93:11.[9] Since we must assume that he created humans primarily for the purpose of [65] being loved [*amaretur*] and glorified by them, we may also assume that he revealed to them some kind of religion by which men are instructed how to truly love and truly honor their creator. This was appropriate for his wisdom and clemency, but such assistance was also necessary due to our weakness. Nonetheless, it is not reasonable to assume that God would conceal the truth of his religion with such secrecy [*in loco tamen abdito*] that human reason could never reach it. On the contrary, one must assume that he has made the arrangement that we, if we make the right use of his assistance and the natural powers of reason, can reach this truth with certainty [*tuto*]. He invites [*advocat*] humans who are endowed with reason and wants them to come to him through his grace [*per gratiam suam*], but not entirely without the use of reason [*sed not sine ratione*]. Although the powers of the human mind are weak, if they are aided by divine grace, they are strong enough to recognize the revelation of the true religion and to distinguish it from false and invented ones. Thus, one must steer a middle way between the extremes of complete disregard of reason on the one side, and complete presumptuousness [*nimiamque ambitionem ingenia*] on the other. For if one gives in to one of these, one could easily end up [*periculum subest*] with no religion at all or a false one. About the powers of human reason and how to use them best, reason will teach us.

8. [Muratori switches from the third person to the second person.].
9. [Muratori counts the Psalms according to the Vulgate. In NABRE it is Ps 94:11.]

What Is Knowledge, What Is Belief, and What Is Reasonable Faith?

I have stated above that there are two ways of arriving at the truth: either by knowledge [*scientia*] or by belief [*persuasione*] and reasonable faith [*credulitate prudenti*]. The first is based on demonstrations and syllogisms that conclude from certain premises that something is necessarily the case or has been the case, or that something must necessarily be or ought to be. Knowing something this way means knowing it from *intrinsic reasons*.[10] The second is based on the belief [*fidem habemus*] that other people tell us that something was the case, which did not happen by necessity, but contingently. One considers their account to be true not because of a demonstration, but highly probable and plausible *extrinsic reasons*, which establish that these people could not and did not want to deceive us. This I call reasonable faith [*per prudentiam credere*]. There are, however, certain basic principles that can and do lead us to knowledge or reasonable faith in this life. Many of them are taken either from the light of nature [*naturae lumine*] or the consensus of educated and uneducated people and are so widely diffused and approved all over the world that nobody with a sane mind would not know them, would deny them, or refuse to endorse them. [66] "For," says Cicero in the first book of *De natura deorum*, "that must be true on which all men agree."[11]

The First Principles for the Guidance of Reason and Wisdom in Their Search for True Religion

Nobody will fail to comprehend [*cognoscat*] the truth and necessity of the following propositions even if he has not thought much about them, or at least understand them when they are presented [*edoctus non statim intelligat*]: *There must be a first cause of all things and all other causes. Such a first cause must be revered and loved by humans. Humans, however, cannot attain bliss by themselves and without the friendship of God. The assumption that there are several gods is contrary*

---

10. [Editor's italics.]
11. Cicero, *De natura deorum*, bk. I, 44.

to the light of nature. *It is wrong to attribute unworthy and sinful things to God [indigna ac nefanda tribuere Deo] and to worship creatures in his place. It is likewise unworthy to assume that the human will is drawn to good or evil by fate and preceding necessity.* Will not everybody agree that it is moral and good to never inflict violence [*contumeliam*] on somebody, to give everybody what he needs [*suum cuique tribuere*], *not to do to another what we do not want done to ourselves*,[12] and many more truths like this. Prudence likewise has its rules and is guided by principles such as these: *One must believe that a thing really happened or happens, if this is reported by people who correctly judge in this matter, and if there is no probable [verisimili] reason to assume that they themselves have been deceived or have wanted to deceive us.* For example, somebody tells that there is a certain city or a certain mountain, or that a certain battle has been fought, a comet has appeared, or that a certain king or other man has lived and has done this or that. One must also assume that a book is correctly attributed to an author, if his authorship has been accepted from the very beginning, if his authorship has been attested by other contemporary writers and never been denied, and if no other probable reason exists to assume the opposite. If, however, something is reported that transcends [*superet*] the powers of nature or is advantageous to the person who recounts it, one must not believe it without truly compelling reasons [*rationibus ... urgentibus*]. Likewise, one must never believe a person who proclaims to have received new revelations from God and boasts of a heavenly mission, if this person's teachings and morals clash with honest and pious behavior [*honestate ac pietate*]. Should they not clash, one must not believe such a person until the truth of his teachings is proved by obvious signs [*evidentibus signis*]. No rationally thinking person will want to reject these and similar principles!

Reason and Authority Prove That Christianity Is the Only True Religion

If somebody investigates the truth of a religion or is asked to embrace a religion, one must answer two questions, namely: Is this religion in fact

---

12. [These and the following italics are Muratori's.]

revealed by God? [67] What is the content of this revelation that has to be known [*sciendum*] and believed [*credendum*]? Whether the religion in question has been revealed or not can be decided by prudence alone, albeit assisted by God. For all humans, unless they are children or fools, are prudent enough to grasp the general principles and rules through which everybody can realize whether such a revelation must be embraced or rejected. There are, however, so many clear proofs that only the Christian religion has been revealed by God as the fulfillment of the Jewish religion [*ad Judaicae complementum*], while all others have been either invented or corrupted by humans, that nobody can reasonably refuse to believe them. At this point, then, one must therefore examine what God has revealed through the Christian religion. This revelation contains many things that human reason can grasp [*pervia*], but there are also things that seem incomprehensible [*impervia*] not only to the uneducated [*rudibus*] but also to the most perspicacious minds—for example, the doctrine of the Trinity of God, that the Word of God became flesh, that humans will be reunited with their bodies at the Last Judgment, and the like. Consequently, it is important that such an investigation remains modest, and remembers the weakness of human reason. What can be demonstrated as true by means of conclusions [*syllogismos*] can be fully understood, but what cannot, must be believed. This is the right use of human powers [*humanarum virium*], but I do not know whether this approach demonstrates greater obedience to the revealing God or prudential consciousness about the weakness of reason. Be that as it may, whoever proceeds differently displays arrogance, audacity, and an unhealthy ingenuity of mind [*insani ingenii*]. After all, the divine exceeds the human power of comprehension, and thus the human mind [*mortalium menti*] must receive the divine with reverence and not arrogantly subject it to its own judgment. For is there something sillier than humans who do not want to believe anything about the nature or will of God [*nihil aliud credere velle*] unless they have fully comprehended [*intelligere*] them? Can he only want things whose causes, effects, and order [*causae, effectus, ordo*] one understands? An unlearned person would certainly be called a fool, if he doubted or denied the truths that philosophers and astute men consider as absolutely certain, only because he cannot comprehend them. How much more foolish [*major illorum est dementia*] is it than not wanting to consider what God, the source of all truth, has revealed as true and certain [68] only because it transcends human intelligence [*acumem excedant*]?

Such people might object that they do not doubt the truth of what God has revealed, but only whether those who claim these teachings to be divine revelation have not been deceived and whether they do not also deceive others. Even I have argued that we should not carelessly believe other people. However, they argue that although one should submit to divine authority without reason, one should not immediately follow a human authority that demands belief in a divine revelation without reason. This is because human authority can often be deceitful. If we accept their arguments, they would be willing to accept teachings that surpass human reasoning, only if they are certain that they were revealed by God. As I have demonstrated before, the Christian religion can be proved to be revealed by God through the so-called *arguments from credibility* [*motiva credibilitatis*] so convincingly that no prudent person could deny assent. What more do they require to accept these doctrines, which are taught as divine revelation with the utmost certainty in the most credible religion? Even though the Christian Law has a few doctrines that seem impervious to human reason, they are still credible because they are based on reasons. Reason teaches us that everything revealed by God is true. Just because something surpasses human understanding, it does not necessarily mean that it is false. Divine truths are beyond human comprehension, but we should not doubt that anything that clearly contradicts [*aperte contraria*] right reason is false. The dogmas of the true religion, which is Catholicism, are therefore not in contradiction with reason. They contain nothing that contradicts right reason, as many learned men have demonstrated, and every reasonable judge [*judex*], even if he does not profess Christianity, will concede. For it is evident that there is no contradiction in what is taught about the unity and the trinity of God, since unity refers to the nature and the essence, while trinity refers to persons. Even the word person must by no means be understood in the sense in which it is used for humans. This word was conceived [*inventum*] and applied to God, because it was necessary for talking about ineffable things.

When examining other dogmas brought together [*conferantur*] by [69] omnipotence, justice, mercy, providence, and other attributes of the supreme God [*summi Dei*], it will become clear that, although they sometimes transcend the limits of a created and finite intelligence, they are not in conflict with right reason. Up to this point we have seen how much moderation of the mind a person [*ingenii moderatio hominem*] must exercise who has not yet embraced the true religion. Now, however, we must consider how the minds [*ingenia*] of those should behave, who already profess the Christian religion. After all, capriciousness of the mind [*libido ingeniorum*] is just as dangerous and sometimes even more dangerous for a person who has already accepted the true religion than for one who is still seeking. For it does not matter whether one is shipwrecked [*naufragium*] in the middle of the sea or in the middle of the harbor, if in both cases the shipwrecked are doomed to certain death.

Chapter 8

On Recognizing Christianity as the Only True Faith

The Recognition of the True Religion of Christ among a Multitude of Sects

[69] There are two categories [*eorum genus*] of those who accept and believe in the Christian religion as revealed by God. To the first belong all those who have been taught that divine and blissful faith since their earliest youth. To the other, those who arrive at the faith in their adulthood, through the prevenient grace of God and arguments from credibility, by which they realize the falsity of all other religions and the singular truth [*veritatem unius*] of the Christian Law [*Christianae Legis*]. Often, however, they are unable to calm their minds [*ingenia*], since this religion is fragmented and divided into so many sects [*in tot sectas divisa*], each of which claims to be the true heir of Christ, rejects the others, and declares them to be false. On one side stands the Catholic religion, which has its churches in all parts of the world, especially in Europe. On the other side, apart from the schismatic Greeks, we find in the Orient Nestorians, Eutychians, Monothelites, and many other, partly older, partly newer, heretics. In the Occident we find Lutherans, Calvinists, Socinians, Anabaptists, the descendants of the Bohemian and English [70] sectarians,[1] and a thousand other Christian sects

---

1. [By "Bohemian and English sectarians," Muratori means Hussites and Anglicans. U.L.]

without proper names, which are found in the Abyssinian[2] Empire in Africa. Among all these people the Gospel reigns, and the name of Jesus is pronounced with reverence. Nevertheless, it is astonishing how many different opinions about the teachings [*opinionum varietate*] of Christ exist among them, and how much discord and conflict [*dissensione inter se digladientur*]! What should a seeker then do? Where should human reason turn to search for truth and to avoid error? Since we have already established that this religion has been established by God [*a Deo profectam*], and since God could not reveal disharmonious and contradicting doctrines, it must not only be impossible for all these views to be false, but also certain that only one can be true. Whoever therefore desires to embrace a Christian sect, or has already done so, must remain undecided in his mind [*anceps animi*] until he realizes [*intelligat*] on which side there is light and truth, and on which there is darkness and error. In this endeavor one must make good use of one's reason, remember its weakness and thus never boast [*intumescere*], but instead be guided by beneficial rules that will lead most safely [*tutissime*] to the truth. Now then, let us see what these rules are.

Scripture as the First Repository of Truth

Among all the different Christian sects [*sectis*], there is almost none that does not accept the Holy Scriptures of the Old and New Testament. All agree that they are the highest guide of truth [*primum veritatis canonem*], that they contain the fundamental dogmas of revealed religion (or at least the most essential ones), that they teach what one must believe and do to be called a true follower [*sectator*] of Christ. Therefore, I think, one must start from here. For how could one hope to rise to the truth [*assurrecturum*] and to avoid error better than through the divine voice and light [*voce et lumine*] in Holy Scripture? From this voice, human reason [*rationis*] receives both help and hindrance [*fraenum*]. Through Scripture the intellect [*intellectus*] can make enormous progress [*profiscere*] when in the moment it is commanded [*jubetur*] to believe the revealed truths [*revelatis illic*], understands that what

---

2. [Abyssinia signifies the Ethiopian Empire. U.L.]

they contain is certain [*dum certa illic se habere intelligit*], and as a consequence submits [*substerne*re] all vain thoughts to the obvious truth of the revealing God. Therefore, here originates the first general rule: *All that is truly and obviously contained in Scripture must be held with the strongest belief. Moreover, nothing must be believed which evidently contradicts* [*adversatur*] *these teachings.*[3]

The Difficulty of Recognizing True Doctrine through Human Powers

Consequently, reason inquires further what is really contained in Holy Scripture and what contradicts it. [71] Yet here the weakness of reason begins to set in and the mind recognizes great difficulties. Unless a person is carried away by blind audacity [*caeca temeritate*] and rejects all admonitions of prudence, then he must stand still at this point [*subsistat*]. For how does he know, first, with certainty that the books of Holy Scripture are of divine origin, since some doubt or dispute their authenticity? Second, how can he be convinced of ever finding the true meaning of the entirety of Holy Scripture [*in legitimos omnes sacrorum librorum sensus*] if he does not speak all the languages in which the Old and New Testaments were—according to divine decree—written down? What should be done if there is no translation that can be fully trusted? What is to be done with the many obscure passages or the many apparent contradictions [*in speciem contraria*], which one so easily misunderstands? Should one perhaps suspend one's judgment? Even St. Peter testifies in his second epistle (2 Pt 3, 16) that many had misinterpreted St. Paul's epistles, because "[I]n them there are some things hard to understand that the ignorant and unstable distort to their own destruction, just as they do the other scriptures." The reason [*ratio*] of all uncultivated [*rudium*] and uneducated people will sooner or later encounter these problems. Even astute and learned men cannot expect much from their own faculties in this regard, unless they are familiar with the study of Oriental languages [*Orientalium Linguarum peritia*], the principles of criticism, and are equipped with all kinds of other

---

3. [Muratori's italics.]

scholarly aids [*artium et scientiarum subsudiis*]. For if they are truly learned and humble, they will nowhere become more clearly aware of the weakness of the human intellect [*humani intellectus aegritudo*] and the bottomless pit of difficult and sublime questions [*ardua quaestionum copia atque sublimitas*] than here! Nonetheless, if arrogant [*ambitiosi*] people undertake such inquiries, their disputes and difficulties will never end. They are easily biased toward their own views, carried away by their preconceived opinions [*opinionibus anteceptis in transversum rapitur*], their craving for innovation [*novitati*] or other desires, or imprudently champion their own cause rather than defending the truth. Experience proves this point fully. For it is clear as the midday sun that highly distinguished scholars trained in the interpretation of Scripture have, since the beginning of the Christian religion, strenuously disagreed with each other [*toto inter se coelo dissensisse*] and still disagree today [*adhuc dissentire*] about the most important doctrines [*gravissimis ... dogmatibus*] of the Christian faith. In fact, there is not one ungodly doctrine [*sententiam*] that heretics did not derive from their interpretation of Sacred Scripture or at least confirm through it. This danger therefore exists also for those minds [*reliqua ingenia*] [72] that excel in talent and scholarly education. Therefore, everybody who does not want to appear vain and silly [*superbus aut imperitus*] must confess: *It is extremely difficult to comprehend with the powers of human reason alone, which dogmas are really contained in Sacred Scripture, and which contradict them.* This, then, is our second rule—which, if reason ponders it, will not only protect it from exaggerated self-confidence, but also assist it in taking another, more convenient and safer way [*commodiorem tutioremque*] to the understanding of the divine books.

The existence of such a way in this world is in full harmony with God's clemency, and even necessary because of human weakness. If the most astute men have not only disagreed for centuries about the true teaching of the sacred books but also even which of these should be contained in the Canon of Scripture [*in Canonem Hagiographorum referendi*], then what should the uneducated and weak [*rudibus et infirmis*] who have neither strong mind nor copious learning [*mentis vigor et eruditionis copia*] do? What can they and others hope for after they have examined so many difficult biblical passages, compared them with each other, and consulted different interpreters, for which not only much time but also an enormous amount of resources was needed, if the specialist scholars themselves, after they have done all this, continue to doubt or to insist on contradictory views? If one follows this path, people will either too late or never at all—but definitely always without complete certainty—be convinced of the true teachings of Scripture and the errors that contradict them. Christian truth would be in a miserable situation if it could not be recognized within the many diverse Christian sects other than through this difficult, uncertain, and sometimes even dangerous study [*quandoque periculosum*] of Scripture. Yet is it really feasible that, since God *wants all humans to be saved and come to the knowledge of the truth* (1 Tm 2:4) and commanded the Gospel to be preached to everyone, he established the Christian religion in a way that makes it so difficult to recognize among the many false sects?

It follows that the good and merciful God has indeed provided a shorter and more comfortable way for us mortals. This can be no other way [73] than the one prescribed to humans above, through which they can distinguish the truth of the Christian religion from the falsehood of the non-Christian religions with ease and certainty. Therefore, they must make use of the *extrinsic arguments of credibility* [*extrinseca argumenta credibilitatis*] to determine with certainty which of the many Christian sects rightly claims to be the heir and legitimate church [*hereditas et ecclesia*] of Christ. Just as one can reasonably embrace [*prudenter amplectenda*] the Christian religion and reject all others, once one has recognized its holiness, just so one can most reasonably [*prudentissime*] believe what it teaches as necessary elements of the faith, even if it is not offering intrinsic reasons for them and even if these transcend the capability of the human mind [*superare captum humanae mentis*]. Evidently, we must proceed with the same method when we have found the true church of Christ. We can then reasonably flee to her bosom [*in hujus unius sinum ... prudenter confugere*], even must do so, reject all other Christian churches as false, and most firmly [*firmissime*] believe all that she teaches, even if it is disputed by heretics. In order to reach this goal properly and prudently, however, human reason must fulfill two tasks (and these, I dare say, are not difficult to recognize): first, we must ask what this true church is, and second, why we can and even must be intellectually satisfied [*acquiescere prudenter*] after accepting the teachings of this church,[4] even if we have not explored all obscure biblical texts and did not ponder the many questions debated by Christian sects. We will speak first about the latter.

The Need for a Divinely Appointed, Visible Interpreter of the True Religion

By the true church, founded by Christ, we understand an association [*congregatio*] of people who are united by the confession of the same Christian faith, the same true doctrine, by the same communion of the sacraments and the bond of love [*vinculo caritatis*] under Christ as its only head, in which exists a lawful hierarchy [*legitimus ordo*], which is he authority of bishops [*regimen pastorum*].[5] That this church will exist until the end of time will not be denied by any Christian and is clearly taught by Holy Scripture and reason. Such truth cannot be changed or annihilated [*mutari ... destruive*] by God. Consequently, the truths that have been revealed by God must exist for all eternity. Likewise, what God promises must necessarily come to pass, for God cannot lie, and nothing created can prevent him from fulfilling his promise. God has revealed his religion, his Church, his true doctrines through Moses, through the prophets, and finally through Christ, who

---

4. [Once one has found the true church, the mind can rest and does no longer have to doubt. It is this resting (*acquiescere*) of the mind from doubt and insecurity that Muratori alludes to. U.L.]

5. [St. Robert Bellarmine defines the Church slightly differently, namely as a "community of persons bound together by the profession of the same Christian faith and by communion of the same sacraments, under the direction of legitimate pastors, and especially under the Roman Pontiff, the one vicar of Christ on earth" (Robert Bellarmine, *De controversiis Christianae fidei adversus huius temporis haereticos* (Venice: 1721), vol. 2, controversy 2, bk. 3, ch. 2, 53 D, cited by Eric Demeuse, *Unity and Catholicity in Christ: The Ecclesiology of Francisco Suarez* (Oxford: Oxford University Press, 2022), 4). While Bellarmine does not posit internal virtue as a membership criterion, Muratori seems to insist on one, namely the "bond of love" [*vinculo caritatis*]. Moreover, he not only leaves out Bellarmine's emphasis on the role of the pope, but also qualifies episcopal authority [*regimen*] by first mentioning its sacramental character [*ordo*]. U.L.]

has promised that this religion, this Church, [74] should reign forever on earth, because it was instituted for the purpose of leading humanity to know and believe the truths that lead to salvation, and to a virtuous life. The sins of humanity, however, have never exhausted God's mercy, or frustrated his will or promises by destroying his holy religion and church. "Upon this rock," says Christ (Mt 16:18), "I will build my church, and the gates of the netherworld shall not prevail against it." And in Matthew, in the last chapter (Mt 28:18) it is said: "And behold, I am with you always, until the end of the age." If, therefore, the Church as the guardian [*custos*] of that most holy religion will continue to exist until the end of time, it follows that the truth in her will continue forever, and that she proclaims only true and not false doctrines. For if the Church accepted an error in matters of faith and taught this error to others, she would cease being the true Church of the true Christ [*jam vera Christi veracis*], which cannot happen.

Furthermore, if the Church allowed a doctrinal error to enter and even approved of it, both the uneducated masses as well as the community of scholars [*doctorum Respublica*] would no longer know whom to trust [*fidat*]. Nobody would be able to state he is proclaiming the true religion or calling his community [*coetum*] truly orthodox if one can perpetually question[6] [*dubium suboriri perpetuo*] whether this community, since it is fallible, could have accepted errors and taught them. Nobody would be able to presume that the Church interprets Holy Scripture correctly or correctly understands the divine word, if the Church herself (to whom Christ, as testified in John 14:16, has given his Spirit) is fallible and can adopt errors. Certainly, one could reply that it is up to human reason to recognize in the end whether the Church has erred or not, and whether she has properly interpreted Scripture or not, but by doing so one appeals to the weakest possible judge or at least a completely unqualified one [*infirmissimum ... aut saltem non satis fidum tribunal*]. Moreover, if everybody claims reason is on his side, will there ever be an end to strife? Yet, all Christian sects claim

6. [The verb Muratori uses here is "to doubt" to show the lack of certainty in a fallible community. The never-ending doubt, however, leads to never-ending questions. To the editor, "questioning" seemed to render Muratori's meaning better than "doubting." U.L.]

that reason is on their side. God must therefore have provided for the needs of humanity another safer way and appointed another reliable and visible arbitrator [*visibile tribunal*], who faithfully interprets the mysteries of Holy Scripture and the Christian faith, but also perpetually preserves [*perpetuo custodiatur*] the orthodox truth. This arbitrator can be none other than the Church herself, [75] which will continue forever, and which, as St. Paul writes to the Ephesians (Eph 4:11–13): "And he gave some as Apostles, others as prophets, others as evangelists, others as pastors and teachers to equip the holy ones for the work of ministry, for building up the body of Christ, until we all attain to the unity of faith and knowledge of the Son of God, to mature manhood, to the extent of the full stature of Christ." The same apostle, in the first letter to Timothy (1 Tm 3:15) wants us to submit to the true church, because it is the "pillar and foundation of truth."

The Catholic Church as the Only True and Infallible Church

The first and most certain reason for the Church's infallibility [*non errandi ratio*] is therefore based on the truthfulness [*veracitate*] of the revealing God and on the eternal truth of Holy Scripture. Additionally, God has provided and ordained another visible help, through which humans can securely know whether what is proclaimed to us as a belief [*nobis credenda proponuntur*] was really revealed by God, and whether his divine word is correctly explained. This is based on the truthfulness and stability of Church teaching [*stabilitate proponentis Ecclesiae situm*]. Once these foundations have been laid, nothing remains for human reason but to investigate where this true church of Christ can be found. Everybody, even those without a great mind [*ingenio magno*], can do this easily with the help of certain signs or characteristics [*notae ac signa*] that distinguish the true Church from false and deceptive ones. These notes are unity in doctrine, in faith, in charity, in the liturgy; holiness and efficacy of the doctrine of faith; purity of morals, splendor of miracles, age, expansion, apostolic origin, uninterrupted succession of bishops in their churches (especially in the Apostolic See, who is the teacher of all others), and several other such characteristics, which are listed by both the Church Fathers and newer theologians. These attributes convince us most reliably [*certissimos*] where the true church of Christ is found. Since none of these characteristics, or at least not all of them, can be found [*coeant*] and confirmed [*verificentur*] for any particular Christian community [*in nullo Christianorum ordine*] except the Roman Catholic Church, one can easily understand why she must obviously be the only true Church of Christ and no other. If she is the true church of Christ, then she has always been the true church of Christ. Consequently, everything she has ever taught was true, and everything she will teach will be true. Therefore, it would be an audacious and intolerable act of human reason [*ratio*] to doubt [*titubare*] or contradict [*contraire*] her. Instead, reason must be justly and intellectually satisfied [*jure conquiescere debet*] that whatever the true, [76] visible, and perennial church teaches about the holiest religion has to believed.

Chapter 9

On the Necessity of an Infallible Church

Heretics Unjustly Deny the Catholic Church the Gift of Infallibility

[76] I think [*puto*] that intelligent people [*ingenio*] who prudently seek the truth would approve of the method [*iter*] for inquiring about the true religion. Yet, what cannot be expected from imprudent minds, since they want to know more *than one ought to know* [*plus sapere*]! They presume more than is due to human weakness! They let themselves be carried away by the excited and unbridled passions of their souls! First, some thought they had discovered errors in the teachings of the Church [*ecclesiae dogmatibus*] and denied her immunity from errors. Consequently, since the teachings [*dogmata*] that were taught or held in the Roman Catholic Church, their mother, seemed in their opinion [*ipsorum ingenio*] to deviate from the truth, they asserted that this Church had ceased to be the preserver of true religion and had fallen away from the true creed. Finally, they claimed that the *Holy Scriptures were the only rule* [*regulam*] *of Christian truth*, and that therein, they said, was clearly contained everything that the Christian people had to believe, and that nothing else should be believed than what was obviously confirmed in them. These teachings were received very favorably by other minds, some of which were addicted to novelty while others hoped to reach the truth more safely in this way, and—which tends to happen easily—even the ignorant people were won over to this view. This view, which they imbibed with their mother's milk

[*cum lacte hausta*], has taken such deep roots in their minds that they find themselves too biased to hear the truth, and judge everything according to these prejudiced opinions.

I cannot repeat here what has been written by very many and very learned Catholic writers, and by whom it has been clearly demonstrated that such a view is baseless and can be easily refuted as a fable. [77] It is clear from their writings that the Church cannot be accused of error, nor can she even be thought to have fallen into error without thereby admitting that Christ made false promises and that his apostles taught falsities, which truly would be deranged for Christians to suspect [*quod sane dementis est vel suspicari inter Christianos*]. Then, among the doctrines that Protestants ascribe to the Catholic Church, there are some that they ascribe to her falsely; but the rest are not erroneous at all. We have only to examine whether the path taken by the Protestants to arrive at the truth is safe. All Catholics think it is obviously not. The Protestants would also have to consider this if they examined the truth impartially and seriously.

The Truth of the Matter

The Protestant method [*methodus*] is this: The truth of the Christian religion is contained only in the Holy Scriptures of the Old and New Testaments, from which all dogmas are drawn [*haurienda*]. The decrees of the Church must not be accepted if they do not agree with the Holy Scriptures, they say. Who, however, can state with certainty what the correct meaning [*germanus divinorum verborum sensus*] of the Sacred Scriptures is? Who can determine with certainty when the Church agrees with the Holy Scriptures, or deviates (which God forbid!) from them? Only human reason, they must answer. Some of them, for example the Calvinists and the Quakers, have indeed assumed a special divine light of grace, under whose guidance the correct sense of Scripture would become apparent to each individual Christian. Yet this insane view [*insanam opinionem*] has long been rejected by reasonable judges, and more than one new sect of fanatics has emerged from it. That such divine light of grace was audaciously invented is proved by the great diversity of sects and the fierce battles among them. These could not take place if all humans had received the heavenly gift of understanding the meaning of the Holy Scriptures. And who will decide in the end what is error and what is truth, if everyone claims that their thoughts are inspired by God? We expose God himself to ridicule if we give room to the opinion that he gives people contradictory ideas. The least prudent among the Protestants even felt compelled to assign the supreme right of making decisions [*supremum sive postremum tribuant decernendi jus*] about the questions and disputes in matters of the Christian religion to reason itself. Yet, in order to avoid the impression that the power of human reason exceeds its ability, they maintain that the words and the meaning of the Holy Scriptures [78] are so clear, so obvious in themselves, that reason, if it does not wish to be willfully blind, must understand them.

The Audacity of the Protestant Method and How It Leads to a Myriad of Heresies

There are two sources from which the great audacity and imprudence of this doctrine emerge. One is the already explored weakness of human reason, and the other is the lack of clarity in the words and meaning of Holy Scripture [*minime aperta ... sensa et verba*]. As far as human reason is concerned, we have already seen above how feeble its power is and how dangerous it is to trust in it, unless it is fortified by God's celestial light and powers. Yet, as far as the Holy Scriptures are concerned, there is nobody who does not know that there are many difficult and obscure passages in them, even apparent contradictions, which cause even the sharpest minds problems of comprehension [*quae justissimas haerendi causas, vel acutisssimis viris ingerant*], and whose meaning and interpretation are extremely difficult to determine. Indeed, it seems that God, by a tangible decree of His goodness, has decided to disgrace the opinion of those who pretend that the Holy Scriptures are so universally intelligible, and who attach such great importance to reason. After all, they disagree so completely among themselves, quarreling with each other over so many Christian dogmas. Each of them appeals to the books of the Old and New Testament; each is convinced that reason is on his side, and yet each has a different opinion; they are even at odds with each other over the attributes of God, the doctrines of the Trinity, the divinity of the Son and the Holy Spirit, over grace and free will, over the necessity of baptism, over the sacrament of the altar and the like. Moreover, it is also striking how often one and the same group [*secta*] has changed its view and taught quite differently about one and the same dogma. They boast in vain about the bright light of reason and the apparent comprehensibility of Holy Scripture, since neither the uneducated people nor the greatest scholars can be sure that they will reach the truth on this path that leads so easily into error.

Praise of the Catholic Method

On the other hand, the Catholic method is safe, and does not let unlearned or learned to fall into error [*errare non sinit*]. For as soon as one has clearly understood from a clear scriptural passage that the Church was founded by Christ, that the gates of Hell will not prevail against her, that she is a *pillar and foundation of truth* [*columnam et firmamentum veritatis*],[1] and that she will always enjoy the assistance of the Holy Spirit—if one then decides to have faith in Christ, one will immediately understand that one will find the truth more safely [79] if one closely embraces the doctrine of this church. This does not in the least harm the rights of reason, since it entails the most compelling reason of all: *One must firmly believe without any hesitation the one who cannot deceive and does not want to deceive, which is apparently true of the true Church of Christ, when she testifies to the teachings of Christian truth.* The Protestants therefore unjustly accuse us of reasoning like slaves [*veluti mancipia arbitrentur*] and of having renounced the use of reason. For apart from the innumerable cogent reasons by which the individual dogmas of Catholics are proved even without the authority of the Church, namely by being based either on the testimony of Holy Scripture or the testimony of ancient tradition, reason itself teaches us that we never demonstrate a greater intellectual achievement and never judge more reasonably than when submitting to the judgment of the Church [*se judiciis ecclesiae accomodat*] instituted by God, in

---

1. Cf. 1 Tm 3:15.

order to be safe from any error in doctrine. To prove and accept their doctrine of faith, Catholics use reason and Holy Scripture just as well as Protestants. But the difference between the two is this: Protestants determine the meaning of the divine word and the doctrines of faith according to each one's private insight [*privato ingenio*], according to that person's convictions [*uti ratio in consilium adhibita inicuique persuaserit*]. Thus, in such an important matter, as witnessed by daily experience and amply demonstrated by the many disputes still existing among them, they accept a weak and unreliable counselor and arbitrator. Catholics, on the other hand, examine and determine the meaning of Holy Scripture according to their own reason as well as according to the judgment of the Church. If they find that their view differs from the judgment of the Church, they do not assert it, but submit to hers. They do well not to trust an uncertain counselor, but rather the most reliable judge, who was appointed by Christ to settle faith disputes. After all, no prudent Protestant would ever boast of being certain of the Holy Spirit's presence [*sibi certo adesse jactet*], who would absolutely protect him from all error. No individual Catholic will want to ascribe such a great gift from Heaven to himself either. Yet, if we hear the Church and follow her, and if we consider the promise she received from Christ according to the Apostle John (Jn 14:17), that the Holy Spirit, the Spirit of truth, will always be with her until the end of time—must not everyone admit that we have taken the surest means to remain protected from error? Everyone must then realize [80] that those who are not in union with the Church of God [*ab Ecclesia Dei discordes*] must be uncertain at least about controversial doctrines of faith; according to our argument [*sententia*], they are certainly in error in doctrines in which they disagree with us [*dissentiunt*].

The Inadequacy of Reason for the Interpretation of Scripture and the Doctrines of Faith

But since Protestants realize that they cannot hold their ground on this side, they turn to another and come back to reason [*ingenium*]. They have formed in their mind [*animo*] the opinion that their mother, the Catholic Church, is full of false opinions and is practicing idolatry—

an opinion they constantly reiterate. Thus, they infer from the effects a cause and claim that since the Church has erred in the past, she cannot possess any God-given infallibility. Here, however, I must appeal to their love of truth and ask them to set aside their prejudices and their emotions [*praejudiciis et affectibus*] and to listen more carefully to the voice of reason, which they themselves accept as judge over the sacred writings. We, however, not only do not abhor such a judge, but gladly and earnestly desire its verdict. What is it that gives Protestants certainty about the errors of the Catholic Church? Holy Scripture, they will say. But Catholics, too, cite Holy Scripture, and are not only convinced that it demonstrates their claims, but also believe that it is stubbornness that prevents Protestants from seeing this. Yet, if it is uncertain which of the two parties interprets Holy Scripture correctly, who will then decide the dispute and pronounce the verdict? Right reasoning [*recta ratio*], they will say, aided by the sciences [*disciplinarum*], criticism, and philology. The sciences, criticism, and philology can, however, also be used to support the Catholic position. After all, Catholics have a lively desire for truth and eternal life, and no Protestant will deny that they have reason, too. Who, then, is the ultimate judge if the dispute cannot be settled this way? I think none other than God, whose judgment we will hear only after we have left this temporal life. If, however, following our argument, sincere Protestants must remain undecided whether the Catholic Church has erred, how can they even desire to overturn the doctrine of an infallible church, which is clearly stated in Holy Scripture and thoroughly approved by reason, by invoking uncertain accusations [*incertis criminibus*]? Why do they not themselves begin to regard this doctrine as certain, since nothing else stands in the way of their acceptance other than the preconceived opinion [*anterecepta persuasio*] that the Church [81] has fallen into certain errors? Reason [*ratio profecto monet*] teaches that what is certain must not be rejected on account of something uncertain or doubtful. It is reason [*ipsamet ratio*] itself that grants Catholics courage and acknowledges their possession of the truth. For they find in the Holy Scriptures the unmistakable promise that the Church of God will never deviate from the truth and will always remain the teacher of truth. Furthermore, they know quite reliably that the Church teaches nothing that contradicts the Holy

Scriptures or is not lucidly proved by them. Thus, they are convinced they cannot be mistaken in relying on the authority of the Catholic Church, an authority in which reason finds both support and restraint; a support so that reason may walk along that middle road on which truth is found; a restraint so that reason may be kept from going astray.

God's Commandment to Listen to the True Voice of the Church

Furthermore, I have said that one can see from the effects of what value the Protestant view is, whether it pleases God, who wants his religion to be always united and consistent, and whether it deserves the assent of reason, which abhors error. Luther (not to mention the old heretics) rebelled in anger [*irarum plenus*] against the Catholic Church, his mother, whom he accused of fornication. Whatever seemed to his mind [*ingenio*]—or, if you prefer, to his reasoning—in accordance with Scripture, he approved; what deviated from it, he rejected and condemned. He taught through his example as well as his loud voice [*grandi voce*] that the voice of the Church had to be rejected, and only Holy Scripture be listened to. Yet he concealed the necessary consequence of making reason the judge over the divine word and not the voice of the Church—as if the Church would not use reason herself! This most deceptive method [*fallacissima*] has given rise to Zwinglians, Oecolampadians, Karlstadtians, Anabaptists, and innumerable other religious teachers [*religionis doctores*],[2] who, if they may be believed, had nothing so dear to their hearts as to cling to the divine books: that is, to interpret the sacred writings according to their own ingenuity [*ingenio*] and private judgment [*privatae rationis consilio*], and furthermore stand united in their fight [*collatis viribus oppugnare*] against the Catholic Church. Thus, a thousand absurd opinions and a thousand sectarians have come to light, whose views are no less in conflict with each other than with those of the Catholic Church. The same age also

---

2. [Zwinglians followed the teachings of Ulrich Zwingli (1484–1531), Oecolampadians those of Johannes Oecolampadius (1482–1531), Karlstadtians those of Andreas Karlstadt (1486–1541), while Anabaptists comprised many different groups all of whom propagated adult baptism.]

brought forth another torch [*facem*] for Europe: Calvin. The same evil flame [*male ardor*] [82] that had torn apart the North into so many factions, now also seized England. Hereupon followed the Socinians and, I would have almost said their bedfellows,[3] namely the Arminians, the Syncretists, the Quakers and other enthusiasts [*fanatici*],[4] the Independents or Puritans, the Preadamites,[5] and, to say it with one expression, an almost innumerable variety of other sects. If you asked these sects, which teach such mutually exclusive and diverse opinions, they will tell you that Holy Scripture, truth, and reason are on their side, while their opponents' teachings were false and erroneous. And yet not even one of these sects [*sectis*] that have renounced the Catholic religion can cite for itself any proofs of credibility—such as antiquity, unity of doctrine, the succession of bishops from the apostles, the power to perform miracles, or anything like it.

It is therefore not at all difficult to see how great the disadvantages are that arise from the method used by Protestants. Firstly, it is difficult even for learned and perceptive men to recognize in such a great diversity of views the one that reliably leads to the truth, since both sides appeal to Holy Scripture and to the consistency of the evidence—and each party stubbornly asserts and believes that reason and the power of evidence speak in its favor. Secondly, uneducated people will have even greater problems, partly because they are unable to make a correct judgment about the controversial questions among Protestants, and partly because there are no overwhelming arguments of credibility

---

3. [Literally, Muratori calls Arminians and others *gregales* and thus members of the same herd. The phrase *paene dixi* ("I would have almost said") functions as an apology before the "insult" of grouping the antitrinitarian Socinians together with the Arminians. After all, no denomination wanted to be associated with the Socinians.]

4. [All kinds of dissenters, usually propagating some kind of spiritualism, were labeled "enthusiasts." See, for example, John D. Roth et al., eds., *A Companion to Anabaptism and Spiritualism, 1521–1700* (Leiden: Brill, 2007); Ronald Knox, *Enthusiasm: A Chapter in the History of Religion* (Notre Dame, IN: University of Notre Dame Press, [1947] 1994).]

5. [Preadamites believed that there were humans before the creation of Adam. The Calvinist theologian Isaac La Peyrère (1596–1676) was widely known for this position; see, for example, David N. Livingstone, *Adam's Ancestors: Race, Religion, and the Politics of Human Origins* (Baltimore: Johns Hopkins University Press, 2008).]

that could draw the mind of the uneducated to one or the other side. Thirdly, daily founders of new sects, new doctrines, and new delirious opinions will arise, if everybody is permitted to interpret Holy Scripture according to one's opinion [*ingenio*] and does not acknowledge limits for the use of reason. The other sects, however, cannot accuse anyone of audacity, since they do nothing different than what Luther, Calvin, and the other Protestants did and only claim the same right and the same liberty these other innovators once asserted. Thus, people can introduce insane ideas [*insania*] and perverse opinions [*perversa opinio*] as the teaching of Christ. It will also happen that one can no longer persuade them to acknowledge their errors, because they do not want to subject their opinion [*ingenio*] to that of another person. The Christian world has already seen what pernicious opinions this highly praised light of reason [83] has tempted people to embrace. There is not a single Christian dogma that has not been denied or disputed by a sect or an individual. This unrestricted freedom [*ista opiniandi licentia*] of thought leads in the end quite naturally to atheism and skepticism. Finally, the Lutherans have never succeeded in defeating the Calvinists; the Remonstrants[6] have despised nothing so much as the synods of the Calvinists; and we see that among all these sects exists until this day a deadly hatred, or an equally detestable syncretism.

Therefore, I ask them: What does reason [*ratio*] tell sincere and truth-loving men when they seriously and dispassionately consider this and other points that can be said about our question? To all of them reason would obviously have to say that with this perilous method it is not possible to arrive with certainty at the truth. Reason would furthermore state that it is not possible that Christ, who not only wanted his teachings to continue among humanity until the end of time, but also commanded them to be disseminated and recognized over the whole earth without hindrance, should have given only such a fallible rule [*fallacem regulam*] to use in determining the true meaning of

---

6. [*Remonstrants* disagreed with the Dutch Reformed Church over the question of freedom and predestination and largely accepted the views of Jacob Arminius, wherefore they were often called *Arminians*. See, for example, *Arminius, Arminianism and Europe: Jacobus Arminius (1559–1609)*, ed. Theodoor Marius van Leeuwen et al. (Leiden: Brill, 2009).]

Holy Scripture. If Christ had not provided for his religion in any other way than by the weakness of human reason, then—one can boldly claim—he would have never achieved his intention, nor would he ever achieve it. Yes, it even follows from this that the Christian religion and its author, God, are exposed to the ridicule of unbelievers by those who teach that God, apart from human reason, has not appointed any other arbiter to settle the disputes that arise daily in the interpretation of Holy Scripture, and that can determine with certainty what to believe and what not to believe, and has not through such arbiters put up limits for audacious minds [*fraenum temerariis ingeniis*]. Finally, the followers of Luther and Calvin will not be able to cite a single reason against Socinus,[7] whom they condemn just as much as we do, that could not also be used against themselves! And precisely where they believe they can refute and reject Socinus, they themselves are refuted and rightly rejected by the Catholic Church. Indeed, it seems that God has given rise to the Socinian plague [*pestis*] and other such monsters, in order to show the Lutherans and Calvinists how foolhardy they have been in setting an example by separating themselves from the Catholic Church, since it is precisely their method that has given birth to Socinus, Spinoza, and a thousand other heretical parties, which has supplied them daily with new weapons [*armavit, novasque in dies singulos parere & armare potest*], but has not been able to disarm and defeat any of them.

7. [Fausto Socinus or Sozzini (1539–1604) was, together with his uncle Laelio, one of the founding members of the Anti-Trinitarians, which were later named Socinians. See Sarah Mortimer, "Early Modern Socinianism and Unitarianism," in *The Oxford Handbook of Early Modern Theology, 1600–1800*, ed. Ulrich L. Lehner et al. (Oxford: Oxford University Press, 2016): 361–72. For the philosophical presumptions of Socinianism see Sascha Salatowsky, *Die Philosophie der Sozinianer: Transformationen zwischen Renaissance-Aristotelismus und Frühaufklärung* (Stuttgart-Bad Cannstatt: Frommann-Holzboog, 2015).]

Chapter 10

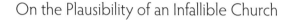

On the Plausibility of an Infallible Church

Justification of the Authority of the Catholic Church in Matters of Doctrine against the Objections of Phereponus

[84] Heretical sects are invincible as long as they fight each other but are easily defeated by the Catholic Church if one calmly compares [*placidissimis mentibus*] their principles with the Catholic method of teaching [*Catholicorum methodus*] as well as the quite contrary consequences drawn from them. Since it has been established how deceptive, how dangerous, and how deviant from the order of God is the method of teaching [*illorum methodus*] of those who declare reason or intellect [*rationis seu ingenii*] as the true and sole interpreters of Holy Scripture and Christian doctrine, it remains for me to prove that we cannot attribute infallibility [*infallibilitatem*] to an individual person, but only to the true—that is, the universal—Church, which, according to the promise of Jesus, the Holy Spirit will always assist as the true interpreter of Holy Scripture. That such authority was necessary and therefore granted by God to the Catholic Church to prevent so many absurd problems [*tot absurda evitentur*], we have already mentioned. Moreover, such [authority] is also explicitly testified, as we have seen, by Holy Scripture, by the Church Fathers, and by the oldest tradition and usage through the centuries [*usus tot saeculorum*].

If such an authority is established, then scholars as well as unlearned people must calm their minds even if they have not examined the controversial issues, since they can be certain to be protected from error if they believe what the Catholic Church under the guidance of the Holy Spirit has proclaimed as worthy of belief. Augustine says exactly the same in the seventh chapter of his book *De quantitate animae*: "To take something on authority is a great timesaver and involves no toil ... and for the unlearned ... [85] it is a decided advantage to trust a most reliable authority and to shape their conduct according to it."[1] Phereponus,[2] of course, perverts [*vellicebat*] the meaning of these words in his commentary: "One has to examine every authority before one trusts her, so that one believes her in every way, because it is undoubtedly clear that she is not deceived and does not herself deceive. Otherwise, it would be foolish to trust her [*credulitatem suam addicere*], since one could not be certain that she teaches the truth. Moreover, one would have to claim that all barbarian people, who believed their priests or their forefathers blindly [*temere*], acted correctly. Certainly, they took the short and easy path, but only arrived at errors from which they could never escape."[3] This statement contains some truth if one does not read into it that the Catholic Church can err and mislead, and that Augustine opined one must believe a Catholic clergyman merely on his authority, without examination or reason. After all, Augustine's view on this subject is, as we have seen, expressed in other passages. Nevertheless, we cannot leave the following words of our critic [*censor*] without comment: "Accordingly," Phereponus says, "everyone who deeply cares for the Christian religion must be cautious not to give it a foundation on which the greatest and most infamous errors can be built [*maximi et turpissimi quique errores nituntur*]."[4]

---

1. Augustine, *De quantitae animae*, ch. 7, FC 4:71–72.

2. [Pseudonym for Jean Leclerc or Le Clerc (1657–1736), a Calvinist Biblical scholar and historian from Geneva, who later joined the Arminians. Muratori and others accused him of Socinianism (anti-Trinitarianism). See Martin I. Klauber, "Between Protestant Orthodoxy and Rationalism: Fundamental Articles in the Early Career of Jean LeClerc," *Journal of the History of Ideas* 54 (1993): 611–36; M. C. Pitassi, *Entre croire et savoir: Le probleme de la methode critique chez Jean Le Clerc* (Leiden: Brill, 1987).]

3. Jean Leclerc, *Variorum exercitationes in S. Augustini opera in Patrologia Latina*, vol. 47, ed. Migne (Paris: 1877), 225.

4. Leclerc, *Variorum*, 225.

Believing the Church with Reasons

If Phereponus, as we must assume, criticizes here the teaching and procedure [*sententiam et usum*] of the Catholic Church, then he has obviously placed his best argument in a terrible place. For Catholics, as we have already shown, believe in the authority of the Church because they are convinced by indubitable evidence that she is neither deceived nor does she lead others astray. Moreover, they are ready to give reasons for this authority to anyone who demands them before they request that somebody embraces the Catholic doctrine. It is so far from being true that Catholics, having accepted this principle [*fundamento*], run the risk of falling into error, because nobody can ever attain certainty or escape the danger of error without it! Should, however, Phereponus have his fellow believers in mind [*animus*] with these lines, since nobody needs this advice more than the followers of Luther and Calvin, then his zeal and wisdom are indeed praiseworthy. For although many of them claim that one must completely renounce the authority of other human beings—even their preachers—in matters of religion, and believe only in the word of Holy Scripture, in fact they rely mostly on the authority and the confidence of [86] their founder [*institutoris*] and their preachers. After all, who among the common and uneducated people or (to say it less harshly) among the semi-educated [*semieruditis*] possesses enough scholarly education, knowledge of the Oriental languages and of criticism, and enough erudition to competently judge not only all the controversies between them and Catholics, but also between them and other heretics? If they are not in possession of this knowledge (which, I hope, every unbiased person will admit), then their reason enjoys no certainty that it has avoided error and is in possession of the truth. Since they furthermore do value authority, reason demands that everyone examines the individual dogmas in question, and carefully examines the reasons that are offered in favor or against them. It is, however, impossible to say how many resources, how many years, and what intellectual acuity is needed for this endeavor. Catholics do not have to undergo this travail since they can easily convince themselves of the truth and truthfulness of their Church, because they know that with her [*cum qua*] they cannot err.

While most non-Catholic Christians reject [*contemtores*] authority and only praise [*praecones*] reason, they foolishly accept being guided [*insonsulto duci*] in the business of religion by the authority of their preachers, who interpret Holy Scripture according to their individual views [*suo ingenio interpretantium*]. Phereponus did well to admonish them not to trust any principle [*fundamento fidant*] that is doubtful according to their doctrine [*sententia*] and serves both truth as well as error.[5] Therefore, it is in my opinion extremely disingenuous [*fallacissimum*] not to believe the authority of the Catholic Church, which, as we have shown, has and will always have the support of the Holy Spirit.

The Protestant Assumption of an Unreliable Authority

Nevertheless, Phereponus should be allowed to also reprimand his peers—that is, the people who have rebelled against the Catholic Church—and he should be granted freedom to save the Remonstrants[6] from the authority of the Calvinist Synod of Dordt.[7] He may even praise the rights of reason and may describe the dangers that threaten those who credulously believe in authority. Then, however, he who commends reason at every opportunity must also suffer it if we return his words to him, only with a few slight [*paucis mutatis*] changes. Thus, reason and its power must be examined before we trust it in questions of faith, so that we afterwards believe all things, because we are convinced by indubitable arguments [*indubitatis argumentis*] that our reason cannot be deceived. For it would be foolish to regard reason as a reliable teacher of truth, if it had not already been established that it is, [87] or if it was certain that reason is often mistaken and falls into the most abominable errors. However, all Christian sects that deviate from the Catholic religion acknowledge individual reason [*rationem suam*

---

5. [Muratori accuses Lutherans and Calvinists on the one hand of condemning authority, but on the other of reintroducing it through a backdoor. He therefore thinks their followers build their faith on a contradiction.]

6. [Leclerc belonged to the Remonstrants and thus had an interest in arguing against the authority of the Synod of Dordt.]

7. [The Synod of Dordt had condemned Arminian or Remonstrant teachings about salvation, free will, and predestination. See Aza Goudriaan et al., eds., *Revisiting the Synod of Dordt, 1618–1619* (Leiden: Brill, 2011).]

privatam] as the most reliable interpreter of Holy Scripture and believe in making safe progress [*tuto se progredi*] on this path. In reality, however, they only progress in committing more errors, from which they can never free themselves. Therefore, everyone who cares about the Christian religion must be cautious not to rely on the principle of individual judgment of reason [*privatum consilium rationis*], since it is a principle on which the greatest and most abominable errors and the many foolish assertions of heretics are based. Moreover, one must not reject the Catholic rock [*catholicam petram*], whose stability alone gives human reason hope for freedom from error [*a lapsu immune*m] if it only clings closely to it. As for Catholics, they have shown in their writings—and they do so still today—that Phereponus's remarks do not at all apply to the infallible [*minime fallacem*] authority of the Catholic Church. For we do not believe in this authority without reason, nor do we exclude reason, but rather desire reason and authority to be conjoined [*conjunctam*]. It is therefore the harmony [*concordia*] of both that gives reason its greatest [*robustissimam*] strength and guides it safely to the truth. Yet as far as the Protestants are concerned, Phereponus will have to show that they did not abuse the light of reason, and that all diverse and opposing heretical sects, all the monstrous errors and opinions, did not originate in presumptuous [*superbia*] reason like in a Trojan horse.

Their Uncertain Way to Truth

The reason of Catholics [*Catholicorum ratio*] will be fortified when they consider that the truth they have recognized and embraced is confirmed through many signs that clearly teach that none of the countless heretical sects existing today deserves the name of true or a truthful church. For it is not only evident that their origin and doctrines are new, but also that this new doctrine [*nova doctrina*] was established through a great deal of turmoil and human sophistry [*turbas et humanas artes*]. They cannot claim any miracles or other necessary signs that could prove that the truth of their novelty [*veritatem suae novitiae*] came from Heaven or which could justify their rejection of the Catholic Church and her authority. Likewise, they will realize that these founders (since they were never sent by God or legitimate ecclesiastical pastors) lacked a legitimate vocation [*defuisse legitimam vocationem*], a legitimate authority for teaching, which not only the apostles, but also good order and reason [88] demand for the Church of God. After all, only such a legitimate vocation prevents people from spreading errors under the pretense of truth, from constantly establishing new religions [*novas condere religiones*], and from imposing these on careless [*incautis*] people under the pretense that the old religion has deviated from law and truth. Therefore, the fickleness [*inconstantiam*] of doctrine among Protestants has nothing in common with the true religion of Christ. One could add the following, which is a reassurance for Catholics and an encouragement for non-Catholics to accept the only true Catholic religion: however fierce the hatred of the most distinguished heretics against this Church may be, they have nevertheless confessed and still confess that even the followers of this Catholic Church can attain eternal salvation, if they only arrange their lives according to the rule and the precepts of the Gospel. This can be read in the writings of Lutherans, Calvinists, Syncretists,[8] and Socinians. While the enemies agree that one can reach truth and salvation in the Catholic Church, Catholics teach—and the voices [*voces*] of the apostles, the Church Fathers and of the whole ancient tradition consent—that heretics, whether they profess Luther, Calvin, or Socinus, cannot obtain salvation [*aeternam salutem obtineri non posse*]. Therefore, reason teaches most clearly that one must accept the authority of the Catholic Church [*auctoritati standum*], must not persist in a heretical community, and must enter the bosom [*in sinum esse volandum*] of that Church in whose communion alone salvation can be hoped for. Since eternal salvation is a matter of highest importance (if Catholic doctrine is true), one must not expose oneself to danger in a group of heretics [*haereticorum castris*], if one can be free from such danger in a Catholic school [*schola*].[9]

8. [By *Syncretists*, Muratori seems to understand groups that mix different belief systems, such as Judaism and Christianity.]

9. [Either *schola* is to be understood metaphorically as the opposite to *haereticorum castris,* and means then something like community, or Muratori uses the noun deliberately to remind the reader that the attendance at Protestant schools can be a

But let us return to Phereponus and see what he brings up in another place. Augustine in his book *De utilitate credendi* had said of Christ: "Therefore, applying the medicine which was to heal the most corrupt customs, through his miracles he gained authority, through his authority he won faith." So far Phereponus agrees, but not in what follows: "through faith he drew the multitude, through the multitude he got possession of antiquity, and through antiquity he strengthened religion."[10] "Although," says our critic, "Christ had, after he found faith among the people, founded his Church and later enlarged her, [89] never intended [*spectavit*] to support his religion by old age [*vetustate*] as if the age of arguments could become the proof for its truth in the future. We therefore do not agree with those who confess the doctrine of Christ because their faith is old, but because it corresponds to the heavenly truth which Christ authenticated through his miracles."[11] Phereponus bravely defends his cause in this examination of the proof from antiquity [*argumentum a vetustate*], because he undoubtedly remembers that the novelty of the Arminian doctrine has been criticized by Catholics as well as Calvinists. Truly, the old age of opinions, even if they are always to be treated with reverence, is never a certain proof of their truth in the fields of physics, astronomy, and the other sciences. I am nevertheless astonished that a master of logic and criticism [such as Leclerc, U.L.], does not want to see or does not want to admit the weight of age in theological and historical matters! Certainly, if opinions of the first kind are concerned, they cannot be considered true, even if they have been accepted for a long time, for the ancients had no infallible teachers who could have indubitably demonstrated to them the truth of these views. Each one was guided by his own insight [*ingenium suum*]. Even the more recent philosophers have no reason to yield to the old ones, for they even surpass them at times, as they have applied greater efforts and possess better scientific aids. Who, then, does not see that the views of the more recent thinkers can be just as true as those of the older ones, and that our ancestors, as far as the

---

danger to Catholic children who might lose their faith there and who should therefore be sent to "safe" Catholic schools.]

10. Augustine, *De utlitate credendi*, ch. 14, FC 4:435.
11. Leclerc, *Variorum*, 513.

investigation of such truths is concerned, did not surpass us apart from the fact that they have investigated before us and paved the way for us to arrive at the truth?

The Age of Christian Doctrine and the Number of Believers as Evidence for the Truth

It is, however, quite different with views of the second kind. When the question arises, which of two historians—to whom, by the way, one must attribute the same credibility, judgment, and erudition, and equally probable narratives—one must believe because they differ from each other on a certain point, there is no critic who does not teach that one must believe the older rather than the more recent, even more so if one compares the oldest with a quite recent writer. This is also true in theological matters. Christians argue about which is the true Church of Christ, and whether certain doctrines are true or false. This dispute cannot be settled, since both sides affirm that their doctrines are true [90] because they are in accordance with the heavenly truth [*caelesti*] that Christ has authenticated by his miracles. Yet, there is a compelling reason [*potentissima ratio*] to cast judgment in favor of those who trace the antiquity of their doctrine and church back to the apostles and even to Christ, and to assume that the others, who can be reproached [*exprobari*] for novelty in both their church and their doctrine, have retreated far from the truth. For, who better than the ancients, the contemporaries of the apostles or their disciples, could hear or know what Christ's mind and doctrine [*Christi mens et doctrina*] was, what he commanded to believe and to do, since these are all things that depend not on human ingenuity [*ingenio hominum*] but on the revelation of God and Christ?

This argument is also valid, as everyone will understand, if there is a dispute about a dogma, or about the meaning of a scriptural passage [*scripturarum sensu*], between certain recent people [*quosdam recentiores*] who are fifteen to sixteen hundred years removed [*dissitos*] from the times of the apostles, and others who are only one or two or three centuries removed from that time, and when the entire Church, the consensus of the Church Fathers, and immemorable tradition are set against the small number and the novelty of these recent writers [*contra paucitatem et novitatem recentiorum*]. For this is not about establishing a religion according to our arbitrariness [*secundum arbitrium nostrum*], nor is it about understanding and explaining the teachings of Christ and Holy Scripture according to our own insight [*ingenio nostro*], which I think not even Phereponus would want, despite the fact that his words and deeds seem to indicate just that. It is rather a matter of upholding the religion [*de retinenda religione*] that Christ, the infallible [*certissimus*] teacher of truth, has revealed, and to understand and interpret the sacred books as they were understood and interpreted by Christ and the apostles. One must assume that nobody knew better [*magis scire*] what was false and what was true, had better access to this knowledge and was by necessity privy to it [*probe callere potuerunt atque debuerunt*], than those who heard either the apostles themselves or their successors preach. On the contrary, in such controversies anybody who is so many centuries removed from the times of the apostles and makes his own ingenuity the judge [*suum ingenium judicem faciunt*] in such important affairs and demands as a newcomer to be believed [*nuperis potius credi*] more than the ancients, with whom the Catholic Church has agreed and will always agree, least deserves to be heard [*minus audiendus*]. Of course, something is not true because it is old, but in the disputes that take place among Christians, antiquity is a weighty argument for the truth [*robustum veritatis argumentum*] or, to speak more correctly, a strong characteristic [*indicium*] of truth. [91] If one furthermore adds other characteristics of truth, which only the Catholic Church can offer, people can and must be convinced [*certos homines efficere potest*] of the truth of her teaching. A sign and proof of falsehood, on the other hand, is novelty [*novitas*]. Therefore, one must take caution to avoid it most carefully. Moreover, the apostles had already warned that it is a characteristic of heretics and false prophets. This is so obvious that all those who in the last two centuries have preached harmful and utterly false teachings, felt the need to present them [*persuadere necessum duxerit*] not as new but as old, as if they had been approved by the apostles and their successors. On this point, however, their erudition fails miserably, as many Catholic books prove. Therefore, Phereponus is wrong when he claims that antiquity has as little value and authority in theology as it has in philosophy. This arrow is, as everyone will admit, certainly one of the sharpest [*telum ... acutissimum*], yet only in the hands of Catholics does it display its power. Phereponus had even less reason to disagree with Augustine's claim that Christ had strengthened his religion through antiquity. After all, Augustine defended the truth of the same doctrine and the same Church against heretics, which also we commend and defend. This means that he argued against Christians who preferred novelty in origin, doctrine, and church, and were refuted by the antiquity that supports the Catholic Church and her doctrine. Therefore, he says of Christ: "Through antiquity he strengthened religion. And this in no way can be torn asunder, either by the most foolish novelty of heretics, working through fraud, or even by the inveterate error of nations, violently struggling against it."[12]

Novelty and a Small Number of Believers as a Sign of Error Outside the Church

Phereponus even admits this, and then continues: "Augustine used such proofs against heretics and schismatics, who he often reproached for their novelty and small number just as the pagans [*ethnici*] had done before to Christians."[13] We have already determined how valid the argument from antiquity is against heretics and innovators. Yet, I do not understand why Phereponus refers here to the pagans and contradicts Augustine. If there had been no difference between the cause of the Christians and the cause of the pagans [*gentilium et Christianorum causa*]—that is, if one had fought [*pugnatum*] on both sides with equally weighty reasons, and if the Christians had otherwise no evident proof of truth on their side—then the people at the time would have been excused in their judgment [*excusatione dignum fuisset hominum judicium*] for [92] preferring paganism over Christianity, since, after all, the opposing party [*adversae partis*] would not have produced any convincing evidence against them, and since antiquity and the great number of pagans [*vetustas ac amplitudo*] would have favored their

---

12. Augustine, *De utilitate credendi*, ch. 14, 32, FC 4:435.
13. Leclerc, *Variorum*, 513.

cause rather than the belief in Christ. The splendor of miracles, the fulfilled predictions of the prophets, and the holiness of the Christian law weighed much heavier than the idolatrous piety and foolishness of pagans, which both pagan commoners and scholars had recognized. All this strengthened [*roboris addebant*] the reasons of Christians, while it weakened [*detrahebant*] pagan religion to an extent that, despite its novelty and small number [*ut ipsa novitas et paucitas*], Christianity deterred neither unlearned nor learned from embracing her creed [*ad castra Christianorum transiret*].[14] Still, when Catholics and heretics argued with each other, both parties gave reasons and biblical texts for their views. As far as the reasons are concerned, Catholics were certainly superior. Nonetheless the opponents [*adversariis*] denied this, so it could have appeared to some that both parties had equally good arguments. The outcome [*exitus*] of the conflict would have remained ambiguous [*anceps*] had not the old age of their teachings and their worldwide diffusion [*amplitudo*] buttressed Catholic arguments. Now, one had to legitimately call Catholics the winners of this battle [*jure ergo ad Catholicos inclinare debuit victoria*], for one had to assume that those who came closest to the apostles and Christ also knew the mind of Christ [*mentem*] and the correct meaning [*verumque sensum*] of Holy Scripture best and most reliably [*melius ac certius*]. Yet, what does Phereponus say about the novelty of Christianity in contrast to the old age of pagan superstition? After all, the pagans could not even claim this argument in their fight with Christians and were even defeated on this point. It could not go unnoticed by Phereponus, because all scholars know that the Christian religion is essentially linked to the Jewish religion, which descended from Adam and thus surpasses all others in age. One only needs to recall what Clement of Alexandria, Eusebius of Caesarea, Augustine and other Church Fathers, as well as recent writers, have written about this subject. It is therefore both inopportune and unwise of Phereponus to cite the example of pagans to defeat the prerogative of age to disarm Catholic doctrine [*Catholicorum arma retundat*].

14. [The previous two sentences are one in the original Latin. For the sake of readability, it was broken up.]

Yet, not only in this passage but also in others, Phereponus mocks Augustine, because he contrasts the large number of Catholic Christians with the small number of heretics. This, he says, is [93] not a proof of truth. Otherwise, one would have to declare the Christian religion false if compared to the large number of pagans. It must certainly be admitted that the number of pagans used to be far greater than that of Christians, and still is. Yet, we argue with other plausible reasons against pagans, and show them that it would not do any good if they referred to the large number of their followers in their case against us. In a dispute between Catholics and heretics, however, we maintain that the large number of believers, in combination with other proofs and characteristics, has always been and will remain a very strong mark of truth. From the earliest origin of our holy religion down to our own times, there have arisen, as the apostle foretold, "ravenous wolves and false prophets" (Mt 7:15). Also many schisms and heresies have come into being. Therefore, the question has been raised whether the true doctrine and the true Church of Christ are to be found among Catholics or their opponents. The view has always been [*perpetuo sententia*] that it can be found nowhere else than among those who have proved the age and constancy of their doctrine and their Church, who have the greater number of followers [*multitudine*], and who can claim the succession and unanimity of the faithful [*successione, & concordia credentium*].[15] All this, however, could in the past—and even today—only be said of Catholics. Therefore, at the Council of Nicaea it was determined that the true Church of God was the church which, in addition to other characteristics, was called catholic or universal. This designation was not used for the first time then but had been attached to the true Church by the successors of the apostles themselves, since both the Smyrnians, in the letter about the martyrdom of Polycarp, and Ignatius, in his letter to the Smyrnians, call the holy Catholic Church, τῆς ἁγίας καθολικῆς ἐκκλεσίας. "But what does this do to the truth?," someone might object.

---

15. [One would have expected Muratori to say succession of bishops instead, but he only mentions succession.]

Refutation of the Objections of Phereponus

First, there are certain prophecies in both the Old and New Testaments according to which the Christian religion would *be preached to all nations, starting from Jerusalem, and that the preaching of the apostles would spread to all countries, to the ends of the world.*[16] This was not predicted about a false religion, but the true religion of Christ, and history [*effectus*] confirmed the prophecy. Therefore, the spread of the Catholic Church in connection with its antiquity, the harmony of its witnesses [*concordia opinionum*] and the succession of bishops [*successione episcoporum*] has been rightly established as a characteristic of the true Church and orthodox doctrine. Christ has promised this privilege to the true Church and to true doctrine, but by no means to the assembly of the churches of the wicked [*ecclesiis malignantium*] and the errors of heretics. [94] Second, the true religion of Christ has been proclaimed far and wide, innumerable churches have been founded in all parts of the world and in the most remote countries, which have learned about and from the teaching of the apostles that nothing is to be added to the doctrine of Christ, and that what has been handed on is to be held onto most tenaciously. Such universality [*amplitudo*] is not only exceptionally suitable for the preservation of [*custodiendae*] true teaching, but also to signify [*indicandae*] it. After all, it would have been possible that one or even many [*una aut plures*] churches had erred and violated the teachings[17] of Christ through novelties [*illata novitiate documenta Christi*]. Nevertheless, it would have been impossible that a neighboring [*proximae*] church and innumerable other churches would not have noticed such an offense (especially if the bishops would have neglected their obligations to the true religion), would have kept silent and turned a blind eye to them [*silere omnes et connivere voluisse*]. On the contrary, it is quite clear from ecclesiastical history that in such cases they would not have remained silent. Therefore, reason demands [*quare postulat ratio*] that one should give more credence to such a large, uninterruptedly continuing multitude of believers and churches, which have preserved since antiquity in harmony the deposit

---

16. [The italics are Muratori's.]

17. [*Documenta* means not only documents, but also teachings, instructions.]

of faith [*tot Ecclesiis sacri depositi custodibus, & antiquis, & concordibus, potius adhibeatur fides*], than to a single innovator [*uni novatori*] or his small number of followers, who only recently—one does not know from which corner—came forth interpreting the heavenly teachings according to their own whim [*ingenio suo*], but can neither offer signs to prove their divine mission nor show how the Church has deviated from right teaching [*recta opinione descivisse*], nor demonstrate that their new sect, although smaller than the Catholic Church, surpasses her in health of doctrine [*doctrinae vero sanitate*]. Consequently, one can see now that the large number of Catholics and the universality of the Catholic Church really contributes to proving her truth in a dispute with heretical sects.

Chapter 11

On Reason, Tradition, and Authority

The Pernicious Heresies of Socinianism

[94] The widely extended right [*jus*] to investigate the truth and the desire [*libido*] of the human mind [*mentis*] has boundaries. The first [95] and most important boundary [*fraenum*] for the human mind [*ingeniorum*] is Holy Scripture, the second is the voice and authority of the true—that is the Catholic—Church. These we must follow if we want to be sure of our faith and stand invincibly strong in our religion. For if we have and accept the one true and infallible [*minime fallacem*] church, we are in a good position to fight all pernicious, heretical doctrines. If we do not accept her, we will remain embroiled in eternal warfare with such doctrines, and victory will never be decided for either party. The old heretics and the recent innovators have transgressed these boundaries. That is why, after Luther broke the lock, the floodgates were opened for countless schisms that wound the church. We would, however, not be surprised if daily new evils came to light in the land of the heretics [*haereticorum tellus*], such as most recently the godless teachings of Spinoza. For among them the cause of truth is left to the weakness of reason and audacious judgment [*infirmae ac judicio temerario*], which for two centuries have boasted of creating novelties and becoming leaders instead of followers [*ducem non sectatorem*]. Among those who enjoy being called Christians, there is no group that has committed more deplorable, harmful, and sacrilegious errors than the Socinians. These have subjected God and his religion to human

reason so that they neither believe nor teach anything that transcends human reason [*humanae rationi captum superet*]. For such doctrines, they say, are contrary to sound reasoning [*rectae rationi*]—as if all other Christians did not love reason! Whether our [*noster*] Phereponus belongs to this arrogant group of people, as many suspect and think, is not my business. It is, however, certain that nothing is found as often in his books as the immoderate praise of reason [*immodica rationis ecomia*]. That is why he complains so often that Catholics and the rest of Christians renounced and dismissed reason to elevate [*extollatur*] divine revelation. Unfortunately, Calvinists, too, are gradually falling into Socinianism, although this should not surprise us in the least. For it must be admitted that the doctrines of Socinus, however detestable, are precisely related to and logically derived from the same principles the other heretics [*arctius et ingeniosus iisdem ipsius insistere et superaedificare principiis*], especially Calvin, chose as the foundation of their sects when they defected from the Catholic Church. Since the Calvinists and the other heretics have no useful weapons [*arma valida*] to fight Socinianism, except those borrowed from the Catholic armory, [96] and since there is perhaps no heresy that flatters the ambition of human reason more, how can one be surprised if Calvin is abandoned, and Socinus embraced?

On the other hand, one must wonder why those Protestants who condemn the opinions of Socinus just as we do, do not at the same time see their own condemnation in the rejection of his doctrine. I am surprised that [*mirum*] they can still not see how the stability, the infallibility, and the authority of the Catholic Church are in necessary and full agreement with the entire message [*aequitati et Christi verbis consona*] of Christ. But on the other hand, they have also not realized how reprehensible the plot [*conspiratio*] of Luther and Calvin is, who had no other secret reason for their defection from the Catholic Church than Socinus, Arminius, and so many other sectarian parties had for defecting from Luther and Calvin. Moreover, if the audacious method of Socinianism were embraced, religion would cease to exist in a short time. For what monstrous ideas [*monstra*] have not been approved by human ingenuity [*ingenio humano*]? Which revealed truth will not be disliked, if only that is called true or false, which either pleases or upsets the feeble, constantly changing and often contradictory human mind [*hominum ingeniis*]? And who will determine with certainty where human reason [*ratio*] errs and where not, when Holy Scripture is correctly interpreted and when not? Could not new sects arise daily, each claiming reason to be on their side? Could not texts be expunged from the list of canonical books [*explodi quaedam a scripturis canonicis*]? Nothing is more intolerable than the desire to believe God only with what we can grasp [*intelligere possumus*] according to our reason and intelligence [*rationique seu ingenio nostro accomodatum*]. I must repeat here the remark that the heretics quite often equate sound reason [*rectae rationis*] with the power, insight, and peculiar ideas of their own ingenuity [*ideas particulares ingenii sui*]. True religion, however, cannot be dependent on human understanding. For we have not made it, but God has created and revealed it. In natural science one may devise a system. Trying to do the same in religion is of the greatest audacity—it is a work of insanity [*summae temeritatis est, immo insaniae*]!

If God Teaches Us, We Must Believe What He Teaches Even if It Transcends Reason

This is no longer sound reason [*recta ratio*], since it rejects any boundaries of the human mind [*nullis ingenium fraenis teneri*] in religion and the explanation of divine dogmas, and does not recognize that there is much in God and with God [*multa in Deo et apud Deo esse*]— that he could have done many things and will do some, that he could have wanted many things and still wants some that transcend human intelligence, which is imprisoned in the darkness of a body [*humani intellectus corporeis tenebris obsiti*]. [97] Therefore, the celebrated and very perceptive philosopher Descartes established the rule: *God and his works should not be measured by human standards*. Those who used to deny that antipodes existed were wrong, because they could not understand that people whose feet were turned against ours should be able to walk. A blind man would make himself ridiculous if he denied that there are colors or magnetism only because he cannot perceive their appearance or power. Likewise, it would be foolish if someone, because he finds something superfluous or inconvenient or defective in the construction of the human body or the world that he cannot comprehend, wanted to deny the divine wisdom by which all this was created and the providence that guides it. Besides, it would be extremely stupid [*dementissimus*] if someone would not believe what God has revealed about his nature, his will, and his power because it does not correspond perfectly to the ordinary concepts of his understanding [*vulgaribus humani intellectus ideis*]. After all, these are things that one must worship with downcast eyes, but not reject with impious sacrilege! For God has revealed it, God has made it, the all-truthful, all-powerful God, whose judgments, whose secrets, whose actions, although they may at times seem incomprehensible to us, are for that reason no less true, no less wise. Therefore, Augustine says in the ninth book, first chapter of *De trinitate*: "Let us not doubt with unbelief about things to be believed, and let us affirm without rashness about things to be understood; in the former case, authority is to be upheld; in the latter, the truth is to be sought."[1] Cassian also writes beautifully in the fourth book, sixth chapter of *De incarnatione*: "But do you ask the reason of what is said? However, I do not give it to you. God has said this. God has spoken this to me: His Word is the best reason. I get rid of my arguments and discussions. The Person of the Speaker alone is enough to make me believe. I may not debate about the trustworthiness of what is said, nor discuss it. Why should I question whether what God has said is true, since I ought not to doubt what God says is true?"[2] Other Church Fathers and Christian writers, some older and some more recent, say the same. And indeed, the faith of Christians, according to the apostles, is nothing other than "the realization of what is hoped for and evidence of things not seen" (Heb 11:1), because "we see indistinctly, as in a mirror" (1 Cor 13:12) and "walk by faith, not by sight" (2 Cor 5:7). Thus, our faith, by its very nature, is not possible without some obscurity. Therefore, to speak with the same apostle, [98] we must destroy "every pretension raising itself against the knowledge of God and take every thought captive in obedience to Christ" (2 Cor 10:5). In the first

---

1. Augustine, *De trinitate*, bk. 9, ch. 1, FC 45:270.
2. John Cassian, *De incarnatione*, bk. 4, ch. 6, in *A Select Library of Nicene and Post-Nicene Fathers: Second Series*, vol. 9, ed. Philipp Schaff and Henry Wace (New York: 1894), 576.

letter to the Corinthians, the same apostle rightly calls Jews and Greeks fools because their wisdom and reason would not agree with Christ's humility and death. He said: "For since in the wisdom of God the world did not come to know God through wisdom, it was the will of God through the foolishness of the proclamation to save those who have faith." (1 Cor 1:21–24). After this, he continues to mock the wisdom of this world, in whose eyes all which is wisdom in the sight of God is regarded as foolishness.

The Punishable Presumptuousness of Reason

Therefore, we must lament the audacity of those who cite as a reason for their rejection of a Christian or Catholic dogma its incompatibility with their reason; that is, with peculiar concepts of their mind [*ingenii sui peculiaribus ideis*]. This is all the more deplorable because, in order to explain Holy Scripture according to their views, they are forced to circumvent, to twist, to distort [*eludere, invertere, subvertere*] the words of the canonical books against their clear literal meaning, against the consistent explanation of so many centuries [*tot saeculorum consensu*], and against the view [*ratione*] of so many Christians. If their ingenuity and hypotheses do not agree [*ingenium et hypothesis conformari*] with Holy Scripture, they must adapt [*accomodari ad illorum*] it in a way that fits their ingenuity and hypotheses. All those who read their books will know this, but they will also know that the ancient view and practice of the Catholic Church, as can be seen from her oldest writers, plainly contradicts Socinus. This is especially evident from an ancient author who wrote an interpretation of the Creed, which is attributed to Justin the Martyr, in which it is said that one must make every effort to come into the possession of the knowledge of divine things: "But if we cannot attain it because of weakness, then we must regard it with reverence as something that exceeds our comprehension, lest our faith suffers shipwreck."[3] Nonetheless, if the question arises whether one can fully comprehend [*perspiciatur*] whether the dogmas of the

---

3. [Pseudo-Justin Martyr, *Expositio rectae fidei*, possibly a work of Theoderet of Cyrrhus. See Vasilije Vranic, *The Constancy and Development in the Christology of Theodoret of Cyrrhus: Vigiliae Christianae, Suppl. 129* (Leiden: Brill, 2015), 71–128.]

Catholic Church, which are to be believed even if they transcend the capabilities of human reason [*humanae rationis captum excedant*], are revealed by God or not, one must respond that our reason alone [*per unum ingenium nostrum*], as we have already shown, cannot indubitably and securely comprehend them [*certo atque indubitanter perspici non posse*]. It is therefore necessary and prudent to consult the tradition [*traditio*] and the authority of the Church if one desires to acquiesce the mind. [99]

The Sources from Which the Truth of Christian Doctrine Is Drawn

Now we must go a step further, for the person who investigates the truth of Christianity may or even must ask what the dogmas of the true Church are, how they are constituted and from what sources they are reliably drawn. On this point, many of the older heretics as well as the more recent ones have been mistaken. They did not doubt that the tradition [*traditio*] and authority of the Church should be accepted and that in case of disputes they should be decisive. Yet, since they believed that this tradition fought [*militare*] for their side, they confidently asserted and stubbornly defended a doctrine that was in contradiction with the tradition of the Church itself. Even among Catholics there were some in earlier times (and there will most likely be some in the future) who made certain absurd claims [*sententias absurdas*] because they believed that they agreed with the teaching of the true Church, or at least that their opinions did not contradict it. Therefore, to find the truth with certainty and to avoid error, one must know the sources [*loca*] from which the Catholic dogmas are drawn [*haurire*], proven, and confirmed and how the opposing views are refuted. Moreover, one must also get to know the boundaries [*fines*] that for human reason [*ingenio humano*] to transgress is either illicit or quite dangerous. In addition to Holy Scripture and tradition, the councils (especially the ecumenical councils), the letters and decrees of the Roman pontiffs, the writings of the Church Fathers, credible testimonies of history, and the writings of theologians and other orthodox authors, are the sources from which Catholic doctrine is to be drawn. We might also add human reason and the authority of the philosophers, so that nobody opines that among Catholics the aforementioned sources would be accepted without the help of reason. Nevertheless, one must not draw from all these sources indiscriminately [*promiscue*] since they do not all have the same authority or credibility. First, as far as the councils among Catholics [*Catholicorum Concilia*] are concerned, they authenticate orthodox doctrine by divine decree. This is executed by general councils and, if they are lawful, by provincial and diocesan councils if their declarations in matters of faith have been accepted by the whole Church. Secondly, the Roman pontiffs are also reliable judges of Catholic doctrine. Thirdly, no single individual holy Church Father [100] can define or judge Catholic doctrine with divine authority and certainty. The common consensus [*communis ... consensus*] of the Fathers, however, when they define the dogmas of Holy Scripture [*in exponendis sacrae Scripture dogmatibus*], gives us a secure proof of the truth, because they express the belief of the entire Church, which God did not allow to fall into error. The proofs that are taken from the other sources are probable, but not certain and unshakeable.

The Authority of Tradition and Its Necessity in the Church of God

While Catholics accept these sources, Protestants find much to disagree about therein. They accept, as they say, the revealed teachings recorded in Holy Scripture, but reject traditions [*traditiones*]—that is, those doctrines which, as we contend, were handed down by Christ and the apostles through oral teaching.[4] They say that the Church, the Roman pontiffs, and the Church Fathers are subject to error and thus are unreliable witnesses of the truth [*infidos veritatis testes*]. Prudent men will, however, soon see how to discern [*decernendum*] between opinions that are so far apart! Regarding traditions, two questions can be raised. The first is: Did the apostles transmit anything only orally [*viva tantum voce*] about the Christian religion, which was not recorded, or

---

4. [For the history of the Catholic understanding of oral tradition, see Johannes Beumer, *Die mündliche Überlieferung als Glaubensquelle* (Freiburg: Herder, 1962). Translated into French under the title *La tradition orale* (Paris: Éditions du Cerf, 1967).]

did they write everything down that they proclaimed orally or through their example or in another way? The second: Do those teachings that Catholics call traditions and believe to have been handed down from the apostles, have the same power [*vim*] and authority—if they were indeed transmitted—as the teachings of Holy Scripture? No Christian or reasonable person will ever raise the latter question because it exemplifies an exceedingly great desire to argue. After all, if we believe the apostles when they write on behalf of Christ, why should we not believe them when they speak on his behalf? Moreover, it is known that what was recorded by the apostles in writing had previously been proclaimed orally [*eadem antea ab ipsis viva tantum voce tradita fuisse constat*] and received with equal obedience by the faithful [*pari obsequio a fidelibus accepta*].[5]

The first question is not answered any better by heretics. Everyone knows the famous passage from the second letter to the Thessalonians (2 Thes 2:15), where Paul says: "Therefore, brothers, stand firm and hold fast to the traditions that you were taught, either by an oral statement or by a letter of ours." Just as well known is the other passage from the second letter to Timothy (2 Tm 2:2) where he says: "And what you heard from me through many witnesses entrust to faithful [101] people who will have the ability to teach others as well." From this follows clearly that the Church of God must receive, care for, and serve [*suscipiendam, colendam et servandam*] the teachings of the apostles with the same reverence as Holy Scripture, regardless of whether they were given in writing or orally. Even if it cannot be determined with the same certainty what an apostle has taught only orally, and which was later recorded by the other apostles themselves or by others (for it is at least known that the Apostle John did not publish or make known his writings until after the death of Paul), one can nevertheless become convinced of its [truth, U.L.] by the mere testimony [*testimonio*] of the Church, and can due to her decision resolve such a dispute. Do not the heretics themselves know with certainty due to the mere testimony of the Church and tradition [*traditione*] which writings either

---

5. [The Council of Trent stated instead that Scripture and Tradition are to be accepted in "equal affection of piety" (*pari pietatis affectu*). See Council of Trent, session IV (1546), decree on Canonical Scriptures, DH 1501.]

originate from the apostles or were approved by them, which are genuine writings of the apostles, and which are falsely ascribed to them? Why should we not believe the Church, since we believe her when she testifies to the authenticity of the writings of the apostles, when she testifies to other teachings? Moreover, even most heretics themselves accept some doctrines and customs [*plerique sententias nonnullas aut ritus*] or even defend them, which only the tradition [*traditio*] of the Catholic Church commands. Consequently, ecclesiastical traditions must not, as even they admit, be held in contempt but in veneration. And if it is evident that the other dogmas or customs are derived from the most ancient traditions, and that they have been celebrated and observed [*celebrata ac servata*] by the Christian Church in the fullest harmony with all other Christians, then it would stubborn and unjust [*pervicax et injustus*] to reject [tradition] for no other reason than that it was not mentioned in the writings of the apostles.

We have so far discussed in detail that the authority of the Church is approved and buttressed by Holy Scripture, and how much the orthodox religion needs this authority. Based on this, one can comprehend the necessity of tradition [*traditionis*]. When the Church interprets Holy Scripture, when it explains a dogma [*explicat*], when it settles disputes that have arisen over Christian doctrine—what else does she do than present and explain what she has previously known [*antea sibi innotuerant*] from tradition [*traditione*], or demonstrate what follows consequentially from it [*consequentia*] and what is necessarily connected [*necessario connexa*] with it, or expose what contradicts [*repugnantia aperire*] it? For neither the Church nor the councils can teach anything new in dogmatic canons but profess and proclaim only what she has received from her ancestors [*majoribus*], only that which has been handed down from the apostles and their successors until today, and only that which is in agreement [102] with tradition [*traditioni consentaneum*]. Hence, whenever there was a dispute about the scheduling of Easter, the Nicene Fathers wrote, as we can see from the beginning of the letter of St. Athanasius about the Synods of Rimini and Seleucia in volume one: "It seemed to us and to the Holy Spirit," but when they wrote about the doctrine of faith, they proclaimed instead: "The Catholic Church believes," in order to indicate that they were not expressing their own opinions, but the doctrine of the apostles.[6] Therefore, it has always been held by the Church [*semper fuit ecclesiae consuetudo*] that when a dispute arose over the doctrine of Christ, they would refer to Holy Scripture and the unanimous tradition [*concordem traditionem*] of the ancient Christian saints and Church Fathers. She had their witness always close at hand and could invoke it against the heretics, who tried to assert their innovations. The latter argued with reasons [*rationibus isti contendebant*] and cited sources [*loca*] from Holy Scripture that seemed to be favorable to their new teaching. The Catholic Church, however, used first and foremost arguments [*rationibus*] for her defense, but her strength and the reason for her victory was founded on the fact that she had the oldest tradition [*antiquissimam traditionem*] on her side, and that she knew what had always been believed to be the true meaning [*sensus verus*] of the scriptural passage in question. This strategy [*consuetudo*] is based on certain unshakeable principles, which would be easy to prove in detail, but with which I will content myself with a few comments.

The Principles of Tradition and Authority

The first principle is that Christ communicated or revealed to the apostles everything that was necessary and useful to believe and to do in his holy religion to attain salvation. Christ sent the apostles to orally proclaim [*viva voce praedicanda*] this message everywhere, and some of them to write down the life of Christ and many other things. The apostles, who proclaimed these things on the explicit command of Christ [*ex Christi praecepto*], presented them unadulterated, clear, and without ambiguity. For example, when they invoked "the Word" as God, when they called the Spirit "holy," when they transmitted Christ's words over the bread, the listeners clearly understood them, but also comprehended [*intelligerent probeque perciperent*] what was signified by these words and as dogma.

The second principle is this: this teaching has been made known

---

6. Athanasius, *De synodis*, in *A Select Library of Nicene and Post Nicene Fathers of the Christian Church: Second Series*, vol. 4: *St Athanasius*, ed. Philipp Schaff and Henry Wace (New York: 1892), pt. 1, ch. 5, 452–53.

not only to a small number of people, but to the whole world [*toti terrarium orbi*] and countless churches through the apostles and disciples of [103] Christ and their successors. The faithful, as Paul testifies, have become rich in words and salvific science [*scientia salutari*]. Especially the apostolic churches, which were founded by the apostles themselves and were cared for and taught by them, have understood these teachings more fruitfully [*uberius*] and clearly than all the others.

The third principle is this: the apostles have tirelessly [*saepius et enixus*] recommended and taught that believers should hold steadfastly to the doctrines that they had originally accepted, and should not give credence to any man, even to an angel, if he proclaimed a doctrine contrary to or other than what had already been proclaimed by them.

The fourth principle is this: the believers of all Christian congregations, especially the pastors [*pastores*] of the churches, knew above all that they could neither add nor take away from the teaching that the apostles had transmitted [*traditae*], and that a person who dared to do so would be guilty of the greatest crime [*summi scleleris*] and worthy of gravest ecclesiastical punishments unless he reconsidered after proper admonition. After all, such action would accuse Christ or the apostles of ignorance or jealousy [*invidentiae*], as if they had withheld from mankind something necessary or useful for salvation.

The fifth principle is this: the bishops and the pastors of the churches have known it to be their duty to oppose such changes or errors [*mutationibus atque erroribus*], to condemn or refute them, even to endure [*tolerando*] persecution for the sake of the truth, or even to flee from the authors and promoters of such errors. They have always known that in such cases it was never permitted to dissimulate[7] [*neque dissimulare in his casibus licuisse*], either out of love for peace or out of fear, or out of obedience owed to their superiors.

---

7. [*Dissimulation* is the concealment of one's convictions. In this context, the words could also be translated as "never permitted to fall silent," indicating the duty to stand up against heresy and error. Muratori's choice of words is, however, interesting because dissimulation was a key element of Jesuit probabilistic moral theology. Its use could therefore indicate an opaque criticism of Jesuit theology. See Stefania Tutino, "Jesuit Accommodation, Dissimulation, Mental Reservation," in *The Oxford Handbook of the Jesuits*, ed. Ines Županov (New York: Oxford University Press, 2019), 216–40.]

The sixth principle is: every novelty or change in the teaching of Christ has been opposed by the Roman pontiffs, other bishops, ecclesiastical writers, the Church Fathers, and even the faithful people. Whenever necessary, even the entire church rose in opposition against the innovators and the despisers of the old tradition. All synods and bishops, especially the Roman pontiffs and the Church Fathers, whose lineage begins with Ignatius, Polycarp, and Irenaeus, have praised from the earliest centuries of the Christian faith down to our days nothing more than the adherence to the received ancestral, ancient, and unanimous tradition [*traditioni majorum receptae, antiquae, et concordi*]. Therefore, they have condemned all heresies [104] primarily on the grounds that they smacked of innovation [*novitatem saperent*] and conflicted with this tradition. It is therefore highly improbable that so many great men, so many great churches, which were resolutely opposed to innovation and change [*novitati et mutationi*] in the teaching of Christ, should have transmitted and taught something other than the old tradition. On the other side, it is certain that no heretic has ever been able to defend his teaching [*sententiam*] by invoking the antiquity of tradition. I might even add that among the ancient heretics only a few did not recognize the power [*vim*] and authority of tradition. Instead, they claimed that tradition stood on their side. Those, however, who rejected the tradition, were even in the first centuries of the Church considered rash and foolish [*temeritatis ac insaniae*]. I will only mention here what Irenaeus writes in his book *On the Gnostics*: "For there is not one of them, but is so entirely perverted, as without shame to preach himself, utterly spoiling the rule of truth. But when on the other hand we challenge them to that tradition, which is of the apostles, which is guarded by the successions of presbyters in the churches, they oppose tradition saying that themselves, being wiser not only than presbyters, but even the apostles, have discovered the genuine truth."[8]

These have been the foundations of the Church's manner [*consuetudo*] of condemning heretical teachings. She always considered it her main duty to discern [*perspicere*] when newly proposed teachings deviated from the perennial tradition of the ancestors [*traditione constanti*

---

8. Irenaeus, *Adversus haereses*, bk. 3, ch. 2.1, in Irenaeus, *Five Books against Heresies*, trans. John Keble (London: 1872), bk. 3, ch. 2, 205. Capitalization adapted.

majorum] and the oldest consensus of the universal church [*antiquissimo ecclesiaee universae consensus*]. If they did, they were immediately rejected as reprehensible, according to the command of the Apostle Paul, who taught us to discard innovation in doctrine and instead preserve diligently the traditional teaching. It was utterly sufficient to condemn a new doctrine or a new interpretation of Holy Scripture only because it was in contradiction with the interpretation and doctrine that had been unanimously accepted in the universal Church of God since the earliest times and therefore originated in the apostolic tradition. The whole Church of Christ, however, had been promised by the founder to never err in her teaching! Since she could easily show that her decisions in controversial questions always perfectly aligned with what had been believed in earlier centuries and especially throughout all antiquity, she was able to refute any suspicion that she could err. After all, it is not up to us to interpret the teachings of Christ according to our own liking [*pro arbitratu nostro effingere*], to [105] reform or invert them [*reformare, atque invertere*], and to adapt them to the uncertain concept of our intellect [*incertis intellectus nostri ideis*], but to accept them with the same reverence as they were revealed by Christ to the apostles, as they have come down to us through the unanimous tradition [*per unanimen tot saeculorum traditionem*] of so many centuries, through the testimonies of so many churches, so many councils, so many bishops, and the witness of the Church Fathers. For it is not at all credible to assume that all of these had conspired [*simul conspirasse*] either out of ignorance, dishonesty, fear, or indifference to destroy the holy religion, either by falsifying it through innovations or by tolerating distortions. It follows, therefore, for every good critic and anyone with good sense [*homines cordatos*] that the sources [*fontes*] of tradition—that is, the councils of Catholics, the decrees of the Roman pontiffs, and the harmony [*concordia*] of the Church Fathers in faith and morals—provide ample proof of her truth. There is hardly anything that has been brought forward in the course of the last two centuries by presumptuous or ignorant men that has not already long ago been rejected by the Church, by the councils and by the Church Fathers, or at least declared reprehensible, as soon as it was shown to be an innovation and thus incompatible with the ancient Catholic tradition, with the existing dogmas and with the explanation of Holy Scripture as it is accepted by the Catholic Church.

Praise of Dogmatic Theology and of Petavius, Whom Phereponus Should Have Held in Higher Esteem

This is also the place to speak at length in favor of that branch of theology that we call dogmatics. Its value is apparent. Dogmatics has the task of drawing [*colligere*] the dogmas of the Catholic Church from the writings of the councils and the Church Fathers, and to bring to light what the universal Church has approved and what she has rejected. It is therefore evident that neither reason nor human ingenuity [*rationi seu ingeniis humanis*] have the right to investigate these propositions as potentially false and subject them to their judgment. For everybody who loves [*amat*] to be a Christian, and who has examined the principles that I have presented so far, this is obvious. Yet, Phereponus has demonstrated that he does not understand what the characteristic of a Catholic is [*Catholici hominis indoles*] when he denigrates the merits of the incomparable Dionysius Petavius[9] and his outstanding *Dogmatic Theology*. For him the man was a careful collector of ancient views but criticizes his weak and unsatisfactory interpretations of difficult theological and philosophical controversies in which reason must have the right to decide and is in need of conceptual [106] clarity. It seems that for Phereponus, Petavius was only a well-read man but not an excellent theologian. Nevertheless, there is probably no real scholar who does not know that this famous man was not only gifted in intellect and judgment [*ingenio et judicio*] but also in [historical, U.L.] erudition. As proof of how excellent his mind was, I could cite, of course, no better witness than his own works. Moreover, even if I admitted that Petavius was parsimonious with philosophical proofs [*a rationum usu*] in his

---

9. [Denis Pétau or Dionysius Petavius, SJ (1583–1652), was one of the most prominent Catholic theologians of the seventeenth century. The French Jesuit excelled especially in the history of doctrine. See John P. Donnelly, "Petau, Denis," in *Diccionario Historico de la Compania de Jesus: Biografico-Tematico*, ed. Charles E. O'Neill and Joaquín M. a Domínguez (Madrid: Universidad Pontificia Comillas, 2001), 3113–14.]

dogmatic theology or, to put it more correctly, that he did not engage in arguments to prove the dogmas of the Church, his achievement was nevertheless magnificent. After all, it is the primary task of the dogmatic theologian to discover [*detegat*] what the Catholic dogmas have been and still are, and what the Church has believed about them and still believes. This was his main task. If he therefore uncovers only the teaching of the true and universal Church, he has also found the most certain teaching of Christ [*invenisse certissimum dogma Christi*] and the truth that leads to salvation. There is, however, still another task that is fulfilled especially by the followers [*cultores*] of scholastic and polemical theology. They prove the articles of faith with arguments from natural reason and philosophy [*a ratione quoque naturali et a philosophia*] and defend them both against infidels and heretics. Careless theologians [*incauti homines*], however, at times commit mistakes in this area. Trusting too much in their reason and dialectical skills, they set up proofs and explanations for the greatest divine mysteries that transcend the acuity of our intellect. Although they consider them suitable for such sublime objects, they have in reality no weight [*nullius sunt ponderis*] at all [*excelsae materiae*]. Sometimes they even gradually abandon the faith [*credere dediscunt*] in established dogmas because they seem to be incompatible with their individual and presumptuous reason [*ista privatae ac temerariae rationi*]. A dogmatic theologian, however, who correctly undertakes his task, will be as far from such misconceptions as the true Church is from the danger of erring in her teaching, since her doctrine is certain even without philosophical arguments and intrinsic proofs [*intimis argumentationibus*], because it has been revealed by a reliable teacher—by God himself—and has been transmitted to us through reliable channels [*fidos canales*].

Chapter 12

On the Freedom of Thought

The Desire for Freedom of Thought

[107] So far, we have dealt with the beneficial limitations [*fraenis salutaribus*] and the necessary moderation of the human mind in matters of religion [*necessaria ingeniorum moderatione in religionis negotio*]. There are still some things that should be said about this topic, but I will [*duco*] first say something about the laudable idea of freedom of thought [*ingeniorum libertate*].[1] This subject is no less useful than the one treated before,[2] but will appear much sweeter [*dulcius*][3] to the readers. After all, the proud human mind [*superba hominis mens*] and nature seek, both in thought and in action, to elude all alien domination, because they love only their own commands. Therefore, we listen to nothing so happily as the song [*cantus*] of those who promise to

---

1. [Even the two German translations (Muratori, *Abhandlung*, 228; Muratori, *Über den rechten Gebrauch*, 151) use "Denkfreiheit," freedom of thought, which they did not use for any other occurrence of *libertas* and *ingenium* in the previous chapters.]

2. [Chapter 9 dealt with the infallibility of the Catholic Church, chapter 10 with the authority of the Catholic Church, chapter 11 with the heresies of the Socinians and excessive use of reason.]

3. [Since freedom was often associated in classical literature with being "sweet," particularly in the works of Cicero, the editor decided to use this more literal translation instead of "more pleasant" or "more attractive." See, for example, Cicero, *De re publica*, bk. I, 47, cf. Chaim Wirszubski, *Libertas as a Political Idea at Rome during the Late Republic and Early Principate* (Cambridge: Cambridge University Press, 1968), 7–30; 9, 25 on the "sweetness" of freedom.]

procure for our mind [*mentem nostram*] the unrestricted freedom to act and opine [*libertatem agenda atque opiniandi*] as we desire. Not just once but on several occasions has Phereponus done this. Yet, just as sound reason [*recta ratio*] denies a reasonable [*ratione praedito*] human being unrestrained [*effraenem*] freedom, so the religion of Christ does not permit a Christian immodest [*immodica*] freedom to opine [*opinionum*] whatever one finds pleasing. In our argument we [*nos*] shall therefore grant to the human mind [*ingenio*] a freedom that suits sound reason and the laws of the Christian faith, in a way that it does not feel coerced [*coerceri*] either by unjust barriers [*finibus iniquis*] or by excessive burdens [*nimiis compedibus*], but is at the same time not permitted [*sinatur*] to transgress [*evagari*] the limits [*metas*] that were set by reason and the most holy faith. Excessive freedom of speech [*nimia opiniandi licentia*][4] gives rise to heresies, and violates faith and reason, while a slavish mind [*ingeniorum servitus*] leads to superstition, which is a terrible evil and must be abhorred just like [*et aeque*] heresies in the true religion. Reason and the Catholic Church admonish to avoid both [*utraque cavendum*]. We have already seen that the first danger can be avoided by agreeing with the Church [*cum ecclesia consentiamus*] in what has to be believed [*credenda*] regarding divine revelation. Nevertheless, it is also worth [*pretium est*] inquiring how the second [danger, U.L.] can be avoided.

The Threefold Structure of Christian Doctrine

First, then, we must know what doctrines relate to the human person [*ad hominem*] and can relate to it insofar as that person is a Christian. There are three classes. The first class concerns all doctrines that have been revealed by God (they may refer to discipline or to doctrine, [108] necessary or merely useful, commandments or counsels), so that a person may know the true religion and faithfully embrace what it teaches, so that one loves [*diligat*] and serves God and attains from him one day blessed immortality [*beatam demum immortalitatem*]. The second class covers all doctrines that are not revealed by God;

---

4. [Literally, *excessive permission to opine*. Since opinions can only become heresies if they are shared publicly, Muratori seems to mean here freedom of speech.]

for example, all that relates to the history of the Church and is of great value for erudition in the Church and its members as Christians. The third class includes all profane arts and sciences—namely physics, mathematics, secular history, and other knowledge that is useful to a person who strives for the earthly happiness of body, mind, and reason. The latter seem to have no relation to religion and the business of a Christian as such, but since it can lead us away from the true goal of a Christian, or can lead us to it, it is necessary to investigate it as well.

For all these three classes of doctrine, it can be asked whether a doctrine has been revealed by God or not, whether it is up to the authority in the Catholic Church to declare a doctrine as revealed by God or congruous with right reason and unobjectionable. From this consideration follows another—namely, when and under which circumstances honorable obedience [*honesta servitus*] or moderation, and in which circumstances honorable freedom of the Christian's mind [*honesta libertas Christianis ingeniis*] is appropriate. In the case of a divinely revealed doctrine, a case the Church has had the right to decide and has really decided, sound reason [*recta ratio*] commands us to reject the deceptive subtleties [*fallaces argutias*] of our mind and instead listen to the infinitely more trustworthy [*fidissima*] edicts of God and the Church. Yet, in cases in which no divine revelation is concerned or in which the Church has no right [*jus*] to make a pronouncement or has hitherto not made one, the mind is free to think [*liberum erit ingenio nostro iis in rebus sentire*] what seems to come closest to the truth.

One Must Always Ask Whether a Doctrine Has Been Revealed by God

Having said this, now we will consider the truths of the first class, namely those about dogma and discipline. Dogma tells us what we are to believe about the nature of God and his will, or about the Incarnation of the Word, other mysteries, and doctrines of the Christian religion, but it also tells us how to act as Christians [*quae agenda sunt*]; that is, it gives us the laws of rules and duties [*morum et officiorum leges*] that are necessary or [109] useful for the attainment of salvation. Discipline, however, teaches us the rites used in the sacraments, the external worship of God, and other Christian practices. Yet, it also makes us acquainted with the laws on which the hierarchy and the government of the Church, its ministers, and its members are based, which in a few cases can also be counted as dogmas. The most superior erudition a Christian can obtain is therefore knowledge of the dogmas. For what does religion demand of us other than to believe what we are supposed to believe, that we live an honest life [*inculpatam vitam*] according to the rule of the Gospel [*Evangelii normam*], and love God and virtue? It is therefore necessary to examine whether these precepts of morality and what must be believed [*credenda*] came to us from the revealing God or from the light of sound reason [*rectae ratione lumine*], or from the arguments of individual human beings [*privatorum ingeniorum argumentibus*]. If they came from God or from sound reason, then it is obvious that they are true and correct. In this case the mind must surrender and may not presumptuously [*temere*] fight against such authorities, although something may be taught by God that we do not fully understand and cannot grasp with certainty. Dogmas derived from individual ingenuity [*privatis ingeniis dogmata prodeunt*] we may assent to only if we have examined them according to the laws of reason and logic [*rationis et logicae leges*] and have fully grasped [*evidenter*] that they are free from error. For what can move us to agree with the doctrine of another person's mind [*ingenium alienum*] if not reasons? If we find these reasons to be weak and are convinced that ours are better, why should we believe another person more than ourselves? Moreover, since, as we have seen, we can only reliably know which teachings God has revealed through His Son, the prophets, and the apostles, when they are confirmed by the testimony of the true Church, we must permanently keep this rule in mind [*ob oculos semper*]: *the authority of the mind* [*auctoritatem ingenii*] *must recede, where the authority of the Church steps in* [*intercedit*], *but can continue where this does not occur.*[5] For there are many things that the Church has no right to decide; there are also many things that fall under ecclesial jurisdiction but which have not yet been decided. In both cases there is a lot of freedom for the mind [*magna est ingeniis libertas*]. Consequently,

---

5. [Italics in the original.]

a person who does not tolerate such freedom or wants to take it away [*adimere velit*], acts unjustly.

The Existence of a Dogma, Its Meaning, and Its Evidence Must Be Distinguished

To proceed in our investigation with certainty and correctness, we must first consider three points about dogmas, namely [110]: the existence of a dogma [*existentia dogmatis*]; the way in which the dogma is explained [*modus explicandi dogmatis*], or the clarification and interpretation of doctrine [*interpretatio et significatio*]; and the proofs [*rationes*] that verify either a true dogma or falsify a phony doctrine. These things are very different from each other and must not be mixed up. There are many dogmas that, as far as their existence is concerned, are already confirmed by the authority and decisions of the Catholic Church. Yet these dogmas can be explained [*explicari*] in different ways. Since such explanations are sometimes neither accepted nor rejected [*nondum receperit, rejeceritque*] by the Church, the truth of these explanations does not have the same strength and power [*robur et vis*] as the existence of an already confirmed dogma. Finally, the dogmas whose existence is established and whose interpretation or explanation is unanimously accepted [*consensus explorata significatio sive explicatio*], can be proved in manifold ways. However, single proofs are neither irrefutable nor certain if they do not have the full approval of the Church. After this consideration, then, a threefold question may be raised: whether there is a dogma; what God or the Church intends to say with a dogma or by the words of such a dogma; and finally, how a dogma is proved.

We recognize the existence of a dogma if we are certain that according to the definition of the Church [*ecclesia definiente*], God has revealed and established [*revelasse et constituisse*] a dogma through the mouth of Christ, the prophets, and the apostles. Holy Scripture teaches that God is omnipotent, omniscient, and eternal. It also teaches us that at the end of time Christ will judge the whole human race: the righteous will be rewarded in the kingdom of God with eternal bliss, while the wicked will be thrown with the devils into eternal fire and punished together with never-ending unhappiness. Every Christian knows that such dogmas exist in the Christian religion and cannot deny it. It belongs, however, to the existence of a dogma that we also clarify its content [*substantiam*] as well as the conclusions that can be drawn from it or are attached to it [*consectaria et annexa*]. The latter two are often also regarded as dogmas although one can question how they were instituted [*de ipsis institui*]—namely, whether they were revealed and whether they were established by the Church [*constituta per ecclesiam*]. Consequently, there are many disputes among Catholics [*inter Catholicos intercedunt controversiae*] between those who affirm and those who deny that certain dogmas are revealed by God or whether certain conclusions from established dogmas follow or not, which one must believe or not. [111] Those who firmly hold onto this principle will not remain undecided in such disputes nor be content with some conjectures: *the Church has always been preserved from error and will always be if she interprets Holy Scripture and defines a dogma.* Without great effort one can find out whether the Catholic Church has already decided this or that doctrine, and since everybody can find out what she proclaims as doctrine, a Catholic mind [*Catholico ingenio*] will easily realize what opinion one must embrace and where the truth most certainly dwells [*habitet*].

There are, however, theological disputes between Catholics and Protestants, even among Catholics themselves, in which the Church remained neutral [*neutram partem hucusque*] and declined to make a definitive statement. The writings of the so-called scholastic theologians are full of questions about these. Both sides argue, both sides cite scriptural passages and reasons as proof, and sometimes one or both parties try to claim the authority of the Church Fathers and the Church for their view. It is, however, hitherto uncertain which of these theological opinions is supported by Holy Scripture or reason [*firma ratio*] or which the Church favors or agrees with. Everybody will recognize the right of the mind [*ingenium*] in such cases. For it is its right [*fas ipsius*] to examine the different opinions of the disputing parties and their reasons, to refute them or to agree with those that seem to come closest to the truth [*ad veritatem propius*], or to accept other, more preferable opinions. After all, these propositions do not at all [*minime*] belong to the category of dogmas and are properly called "opinions." The mind [*liberum sit ingeniis*] is free to show and exercise its powers (if only there is no danger of violating established dogmas) in this field. Such a person, however, will avoid admonition and receive much praise, if he presents his findings [*inventa*] with intellectual sharpness [*ingeniosius et acutius*] not only according to the rules of logic and a better criticism [*criticaeque melioris*], but also according to the mind [*ad ... mentem*] of Holy Scripture and the Church. This, however, is the general rule, or freedom in general. Yet since many people abuse this rule, and can abuse it, it is necessary to point out some necessary rules and exceptions that force [*coerceatur*] restraints upon the excessive freedom [*nimia licentia*] of precipitous and all too curious minds [*temerariis et supra modum curiosis mentibus*].

What Is Allowed to the Human Mind and What Is Not

[112] We have said that after one has become convinced of the existence of a dogma that one can ask about its authentic meaning [*germano sensu*] or about the intention [*mente*] God's Church [*dei ecclesiae*] had when she proclaimed it as such. Many dogmas are written in such clear terms [*manifestis verbis*] and in complete harmony with the light of reason and the other teachings of the Church, that no Christian dares to raise a doubt about their meaning or interpretation [*sensu et modo explicandi*]. There are, however, others whose meaning [*significatio*] is disputed and can rightly [*merito*] be disputed. This is the case when the dogmas are formulated in somewhat obscure and ambiguous terms [*subobscuris aut aequivocis verbis*] or when they do not seem to be in harmony [*non satis commode congruere*] with other established, certain, and clear dogmas of the Catholic religion. Even Holy Scripture, even the decisions of the conciliar bodies, even the sayings of the Church Fathers are subject to different explanations [*diversis obnoxia interpretationibus*]. This is the source [*fonte*] from which most of the heresies and heretics sprang: since everybody wants to interpret Holy Scripture, councils, and Church Fathers according to their own strengths, individual judgments, and ideas [*secundum privatas ingenii sui vires atque ideas*], human ambition and human weakness are often

drawn to various divisive [*distracta*] views and into the most pernicious errors. When some read in Holy Scripture that Christ was called inferior to the Father, they claimed that he was a mere man, or they denied that he was of the same nature and substance as the Father. Others, examining the meaning of the words spoken by Christ about the bread at the Last Supper, found in them what was most agreeable to their understanding [*ingenio suo magis accomodatum*]. Others believed that in Christ the divine and human natures were mixed, because they knew from a decision of the universal Church that these two natures were united in the One Christ.

The human mind [*ingenia*] , however, does not need to waste its energies [*fatigentur*] on inquiring about the meaning or explanation of certain dogmas. The Church has taken this burden from us by most lucidly explaining the authentic meaning [*sensum germanum lucidissime*] of her decisions and of Holy Scripture. Since these explanations are readily accessible [*facile colligi*], one can easily avoid error. In such a case, our minds [*nostris ingeniis*] are only free to examine and interpret those passages and words [*loca et verba*] of Holy Scripture or the councils and the opinions of the Church Fathers that seem hitherto to be unexplained [*ancipiti adhuc esse videntur*] according to sound reason [*recta ratio*] [113] and the Church, and likewise [to understand] the meaning of these scriptural passages through already established dogmas and the tradition of the Church Fathers [*clarissimis dogmatibus et traditione patrum*]. Apart from this, however, freedom is also permitted in another case. After all, there are certain dogmas among Catholics whose meaning and interpretation are not up for dispute, but whose mode of explanation is not defined [*nondum constat modus*]—that is, how they bring about or have brought about what they proclaim [*quo fiant aut facta sint*]. Faith teaches us, for example, that the damned in Hell are tormented by fire, but faith does not teach us *how*[6] this happens. In such cases there is no general law forbidding us to state our opinion and our reasonable thoughts [*sententiam nostrum dicere et verisimilia afferre*], and one can dissent [*dissidere*] from another's explanation without doing harm to the Church. Yet, this freedom

---

6. [Editor's italics.]

still requires certain restrictions and exceptions, and these will be discussed below.

Thirdly, one must consider the proofs [*rationes*] by which the doctrines of Catholics [*dogmata Catholicorum*] are confirmed and those of the unbelievers and heretics are refuted. These are taken either from Holy Scripture, or from tradition [*traditione*], or from the authority of the Church. Many other proofs are deduced from sound reason [*recta ratio*] and philosophy. Among so many proofs are some that are extremely certain and invincible [*certissimae ... invictae*], and these exist for every dogma. Nevertheless, it can be the case that some proofs are weak, useless, or even false, even if the dogma itself is absolutely true [*verissimum*]. Therefore, the human mind has great freedom in this respect [*ex hac parte ingeniorum libertas*]. For it is not only permitted to conceive better arguments and new proofs, but also permitted to reject the inappropriate and meaningless ones [*aliena quoque elumbia repudiare*]. After all, the truth does not need a lie for its defense [*mendacio non indiget*]. For the truth refuses to rely on unsteady crutches [*nutantibus fulcris*], since it has due to its own weight enough stability [*suo pondere jam stabilis*] and is grounded upon indubitable foundations. Therefore, no theologian of any school will consider it unlawful to argue with new proofs [*rationibus novis*] against the errors of the heretics or defend the true dogmas of the faith, or even to attack [*bellum indicere*] proofs of other Catholics if they are inappropriate and unworthy [*minus opportunae aut indignae*] for the defense of the truth. The famous theologian Gregory of Valentia[7] has shown that some of the proofs used by Thomas Aquinas for the existence of God were invalid, and other respected and pious divine scholars have done the same. Nevertheless, there are some dangers for immoderate minds [*immoderatis ingeniis*], for the Church has through her decision obviously positioned some proofs beyond our critique [*supra nostram censuram*]. For this reason, we establish in the next chapter some general rules that keep this freedom within honorable boundaries.

---

7. [The Jesuit Gregory of Valentia (1549–1603) was arguably one of the most gifted theologians of the sixteenth century. He also had tremendous influence on the nineteenth-century theologian Matthias Scheeben.]

Chapter 13

On the Limits of Freedom in Theology

The Danger of Writing about Authority

[114] The Church's authority is nowhere stronger and more venerable than in the proclamation of a dogma [*in dogmatibus sanciendis*]. That this is really the case can be seen from our previous proof that the Church can never deviate from the truth in the doctrine of salvation. The eternity of religion as well as the weakness of human reason makes this a necessity [*necessitas postulat*]. Christ has promised this to her, and the Church of God has always and everywhere and harmoniously believed this [*id ubique et semper et concorditer*]. Moreover, the councils have taught it as well as the Church Fathers. Her authority extends to all three kinds of dogmas, which we have already discussed. However, even this authority is circumscribed by limits [*limitibus constringitur haec ipsa facultas*] and must be handled with great care, as I will explain in more detail. However, before I proceed to this, I have to say a few things that relate to the authority of the Church and the freedom of thought [*ingeniorum libertate*]. Authority is one of the most delicate of all things [*delicatissimum*], as everybody knows. It is therefore always an unpleasant business to write about authority because one thereby attracts fierce attacks from opponents, but also the suspicion and hatred [*suspicionibus et odiis*] of those whose authority is investigated. There is a desire to rule [*dominationis*] and a desire for distinction [*praecellentiae*] innate in almost all human beings. Our mind, however, is impelled to embrace it [*concitatius in illud mens nostra fertur*], [115] the stronger

it realizes or believes [*sentimus aut credimus*] that the defense and amplification of this authority is in the interest of general welfare. No authority that God bestowed upon humans, however, can be equated [*aequanda*] with that of the Church. For the various kinds of authority in human affairs are certainly of great use to the state. They serve a noble purpose which is, however—like all earthly happiness—of short duration. The authority of the Church, on the other hand, is alone about the noblest and eternal object, because it leads humans not only to happiness on earth, but also to eternal happiness in Heaven. Therefore, people who are suspected of even slightly discrediting such a necessary and useful authority, or even desire to eliminate the Church [*tollere*] or treat her without the necessary respect [*aut non satis venerari*], cannot be tolerated, because this would open the floodgates [*claustra referare*] for countless heresies and errors.

The Consequences of Unreasonable Zeal, and the Usefulness of Moderation

Nevertheless, sometimes such religious authority is excessively honored. Precisely therein lies the reason that some expand it immoderately, and what is even worse, are immoderately furious [*succenseatur*] with those who defend moderation. I call such undue veneration [*nimiam religionem*] an exuberant zeal without reason, and thus a zeal, as the apostle said, that is not grounded in understanding [*scientiam*] but comes close to superstition [*zelum superstitionem affinem*]. Indeed, those who opine that the Church's authority has no limits, and who therefore defend ferociously what they find in the writings of the councils, the breviaries, the papal charters, or the Church Fathers as if it were a battle for their own hearth and home, are caught in what can best be called imprudent zeal [*inconsultus ardor*]. This kind of people [*genus hominum*] believes that all these should be accepted indiscriminately [*sine ullo discrimine*] as main parts [*capita fidei*] of the faith. Since the Church never errs and can never err—and should anyone contradict this opinion, they will immediately consider him a heretic, who should be punished to the fullest extent of the law and condemned by everybody [*gravisbusque poenis, et omnium odio mulctandum*].

I confess that the goodwill [*proba voluntas*] of these people is praiseworthy, but one cannot deny that they sometimes lack knowledge and prudence. They are far too suspicious and too fastidious, and therefore tremble with fear where there is nothing to fear. If they just helped the holy Church flourish as much as they inflict harm on her with their clamor, their threats, and their scandals! For since there is much in Church history [*in ecclesiastica eruditione*][1] that is either probable, doubtful, contradictory or—according to the opinion of all [116] Catholics—false, it would endanger the dignity, sanctity, and truth of the most excellent religion not only among heretics and unbelievers, but also among Catholics, if all of this had to be embraced indiscriminately [*indiscriminatim*]. Moreover, a person who forces others to believe something that is not to be believed at all, is a tyrant [*ad tyrannidem accedet*], and a person who declares all kinds of fables as truths, is a teacher of lies [*erroris magistrum*]. The Church of God, however, must be free from both such extremes as well as the remotest suspicion of such error, and indeed she is. Nevertheless, she does not like pious flatterers [*pios assentatores*] but knows very well [which will be explained later] how far her authority extends and does not usurp more rights than those given to her by Christ and accredited to her by public welfare and the consensus of all reasonable human beings.

All reasonable [*cordati*] people, especially the Catholic bishops, and in general all those who have studied true theology and ecclesiastical scholarship, neither want the Church's authority diminished nor extended beyond the boundaries of what is proper [*aequitatis*]. It is, after all, very easy to go too far in both cases, but both extremes are wrong [*utrumque vitiosum*]. Among commoners, those who diminish the rights of the Church seem to be seen as sinners, while those who exaggerate Church authority beyond good measure as pious. Yet, according to the judgment of reasonable Catholics, those who exaggerate

---

1. [Muratori only says "much" [*multa*] but seems to avoid specifying it with a noun such as "propositions," "opinions," or "doctrines" [*sententiae, opiniones, doctrinae, propositiones*]. He therefore seemingly leaves it open whether only opinions can be doubtful, contradictory, etc., or in fact also official teachings [*doctrinae*]. The editor therefore decided to avoid adding a qualification as the German translation did (Muratori, *Abhandlung*, 247).]

the authority of the Church improperly, who are hostile [*irasci*] to those who disagree with them [*contraria sentientibus*] and who abuse [*abuti*] this authority to favor their private opinions or affects, harm the Church just as much. Their work [*horum facinus*] appears to be pious, but it is a pernicious piety [*perniciosam pietatem*] they display, because it surrenders the victory of the Catholic cause to the enemies of the faith. For who does not see that if ecclesiastical judges have erred in a case in which the Church really had authority, that one must also admit that the Church could also be subject to error in everything else? Therefore, it is of the greatest importance, both for the Church herself and all her theologians, to investigate and know exactly where the prescribed limits of Church authority are [*quinam auctoritati ecclesiae limites praescripti*], so that we do not attribute to the holy shepherds [*sacris pastoribus*]² uncertain and unwarranted rights and thereby endanger certain and warranted rights. [117] Just as it is the duty of a modest and virtuous person [*modesti et non vulgaris animi*], who controls his passions and inclinations, to never claim anything [*sibi arrogare*] for himself than what augments the common good, protects justice, and preserves truth, so it is the duty of a pious and prudent theologian not to grant anything to the Church, which ultimately disgraces our mother [*tributum in ipsius matris nostrae contumeliam*] and harms the common good [*publicumque incommodum recidat*]. The Church is best served not by zeal and piety alone [*non solus zelus, non sola pietas consulenda*], but only when they are combined with science, logic, criticism, knowledge of history, and above all, prudence. Nevertheless, if after an academically serious [*accurata*] dispute it remains doubtful whether the Church has the alleged authority or not, it might be commendable to attribute it piously to her rather than to deny it harshly. These remarks are certainly not necessary for the sophisticated, but for the weaker people [*infirmiores*], so they do not suspect me of having an audacious mind [*temeraria ingenia*]. Now, however, I will proceed to the solution of my main task.

---

2. [That is, the bishops.]

Chapter 13

The Infallibility of the Church in the Proclamation of a Dogma—under Two Conditions

If it is asked how far the authority of the Catholic Church extends to the definition of dogmas, we will follow this general rule: *the Church may decide, without suspicion of error, which dogmas are necessary and useful for the faithful to know, as long as it can be shown by means of a correct interpretation or by means of a correct demonstration that they already existed [praeexistenti] within the dogmas revealed of Scripture, or that they have come down to us through unanimous [concordem] and ancient tradition.*[3] There are, however, as it seems to me, two conditions that must be met so that the Church can define dogmas without the danger of error. The first is that they are necessary and useful for the faithful, and the second is that they are founded on the written divine word as it appears in Holy Scripture or the tradition [*divinorum verborum, sive scripto, sive per traditionem*] that has been handed down to us. The first of these conditions refers to the authority to make such a decision, the second to being unable to err in such decisions. For ecclesiastical decisions both must always be kept in mind, which is what tends to happen. As for the latter condition, the view of Vincent of Lérins is known, who writes the following about the Church: "She does not establish new dogmas, but brings to light the old ones."[4] For the doctrine that Christ proclaimed was perfect and complete, and without committing a sin we cannot add anything to it, because we would thereby falsely and carelessly declare it to be defective or incomplete. "I know," said the Samaritan woman, "that the Messiah is coming. When he comes, he will tell us everything."[5] And Christ himself has made known [*nota facere*] to us all that he has heard from the Father [118], and he has commanded his apostles to proclaim to all the nations all that he has taught

---

3. [Muratori's italics.]

4. [This sentence is not found verbatim in Vincent of Lérins, *The Commonitorium of Vincentius of Lerins* (Cambridge: Cambridge University Press, 1915), ch. 23 and ch. 27, a fifth-century work against heresies, but was widely attributed to him in the seventeenth and eighteenth centuries. See, for example, Henrico Marcellio, *Ars Interpretandi Scripturas Divinas: Pars Secunda* (Cologne: 1659), pref. nu. 8.]

5. Jn 4:2.

them. The Church therefore does not produce new dogmas, but only repeats the old ones, explains the obscure, and defends those that Christ himself proclaimed and taught. Thus, the Church cannot teach that something must be categorically [*certissime*] believed *divina fide* [*divina fide credendum*] other than what is contained in the words of Christ, whether written or unwritten, and what can be deduced from them by means of a correct interpretation and proof [*per rectam interpretationem et argumentationem deducere*]. The Holy Spirit has always been present [*adfuit*], as Christ has promised it, and will be so [*adfuturus*]—not in order to proclaim through the mouth of the Church [*per ipsius ecclesiae vocem*] new revelations [*revelationes*] or new dogmas [*nova ... dogmata*] but in order to assist her in the task of diligently consulting Holy Scripture and ancient tradition, so that through the Church the right interpretation and the right proof [*interpretatio recta, rectaque argumentatio*] are infallibly established [*nullusque error in easdem subrepat*].

In the following section we will examine in more detail what kind of things are necessary and useful for the faithful, and in what cases the Church is authorized to offer authoritative interpretations and proofs. Some things are absolutely necessary for the faithful, others only partially. By the former we understand [truths] whose ignorance exclude an adult and reasonable person from the kingdom of God. We understand by [truths] that are only partially [*ex parte*] necessary for believers those a person can be ignorant about but cannot deny them or be in error about them [*negare aut in eis errare*] without committing a great injustice. Useful are all those proclamations that help a Christian person to attain Heaven with greater certainty and to avoid the punishments of Hell. These dogmas, however, are divided into two classes: some consist merely in contemplation and demand to be believed, while others, in addition to contemplation and belief, also demand works, which are in religion teachings about morality. But "as we await the blessed hope, the appearance of the glory of the great God and of our savior Jesus Christ," nothing is so necessary, nothing so useful as to know which attitudes and actions are pleasing to God and which are displeasing to him, so that "one may renounce ungodliness and worldly desires and live righteously and piously in this world."⁶ The rules for the conduct of our lives, at least the most noble moral precepts, are clearly described in Holy Scripture, and since from them as sources all other special precepts can be deduced, it is easy for the Church and often also necessary to decide with certainty what is permissible [*quae liceant*] and what is not. It would therefore be a grave crime [*grave crimen*] to not accept her decision, and an even [119] graver one to contradict it. The words of Christ in Mt 23:2 clearly refer to this: "The scribes and the Pharisees have taken their seat on the chair of Moses. Therefore, do and observe all things whatsoever they tell you."⁷ Accordingly, for a Catholic nothing is more certain than that all is indubitably permitted or forbidden that the Church declared either permitted or forbidden.

Which Dogmas for Contemplation Can or Cannot Require Actions, and Which Can Be Freely Explained?

Some of the dogmas for contemplation [*in sola contemplatione sita*] must be known by every believer. Whoever does not know and does not believe that there is only one God, is lost forever, as the apostle confirms. Also, a Christian must also know that there is only one God and three persons in the one Godhead; that the Word became flesh, that Christ died and rose again for the redemption of the human race. There are, however, also some that one does not need to know to be saved, but nevertheless must be embraced when they are proclaimed [*annuntiantur*]. For even if one does not need to know them under certain circumstances, one is never free to reject them or err in them once one has realized [their truth]. Therefore, they are in a certain sense also necessary for believers to know, because if one denies them after learning them or distorts them through error, one is turned away from virtue, provoked to do evil, or believes something that is unworthy of God

---

6. Ti 2:13–14.

7. [Muratori leaves out the second part of Mt 23:3: "but do not follow their example. For they preach but they do not practice." Or as the *Vulgate* states: "secundum opera vero eorum nolite facere: dicunt enim, et non faciunt." This is all the more remarkable since he insinuates that the teaching Church takes the place of the Pharisees.]

and in contradiction with his revelation. For example, the Calvinist heresy contains many things that, if accepted, can lead a person who otherwise reasons well [*probe argumentetur*] to vices and away from the virtues, although such a person would not believe that he has lost eternal life because of it. Here also belongs the doctrine that justification and sanctifying grace cannot be lost by any sin, so that he who has once obtained this grace from God can never lose it, even if he sins gravely. According to this teaching, every righteous person must firmly believe that even grave sins cannot exclude one from the kingdom of God [*justum ... ne a peccatis quidem gravibus eripiendum*], that it is impossible for the righteous to fulfill the divine commandments, and that the good works of believers are sins before God, and the like. Both older and newer heretics have taught in contradiction to the dignity and nature of God, when they claimed that he predestined those he did not elect to glory to everlasting punishment or when they incautiously called him the original author of sin, and other presumptuous teachings [*aliis sententiis temere*].

Countless ideas have been produced in the workshop [*officina*] of the human mind and might be created there in the future, [120] which are—despite the fact that it was illuminated by the light of the Gospel—in contradiction to divine revelation. There are only few Christians who, after assuming that Holy Scripture was inspired by God, still opine [*arbitrati*] or suspect [*suspicentur*] that they contain something false. The number of those is also not easy to determine, who have labeled individual doctrines revealed by God as not revealed, or consider doctrines to be revealed that have never been revealed. This will soon become apparent when we shed light on individual heresies. Whenever such questions are raised [*quaestiones excitentur*], there can be no doubt that it is necessary for every Christian and for the Christian Commonwealth [*Christianorum Reipublicae*] to listen to the Church's decision [*definitionem*] about these matters, so that no one goes astray and contradicts virtues or the divine nature [*naturae divinae*] or divine revelation. In these cases, therefore, the Church can and must exercise her right of interpreting and verifying [*argumentationis*], "so that," as the Apostle Paul writes to the Ephesians (Eph 4:15) "we may no longer be infants, tossed by waves and swept along by every wind of teaching." The former right is exercised when she teaches what the venerable tradition [*revera traditio*] teaches about the doctrine of Christ and the meaning of ambiguous and obscure words in Holy Scripture. The latter is exercised when she approves or rejects dogmas, which are deduced from Holy Scripture or from other established dogmas. That Christ is true God and at the same time true and perfect man has always been believed by the orthodox church, since Holy Scripture obviously agrees with tradition [*apertissime consentientibus*]. From this one has rightly concluded that Christ did not only take on human form [*non in speciem tantum*], but really took on human flesh [*veram humanam carnem induisse*], and insofar as he was human, he consisted of a human body and a human soul [*ex corpore animaque humana constare*], but also two unmixed natures and two wills. These dogmas, which have been derived with the help of a correct proof from Holy Scripture (in which they were hidden and embedded) [*ubi abdita atque involuta errant*], have been confirmed by the constant tradition of the Church in opposition to the heresies of Marcion, Apollinarius, Eutyches, and the Monothelites. Thereby they have completely defeated these latter errors and lifted up the truth. In the same way, the opinion of innovators [*novatorum opinio*] has been refuted, who denied that it is necessary or permitted to worship Christ in the sacrament of the altar.[8] The Catholic Church believes that Christ is present in it as true God in a peculiar way [*peculiari modo praesentem esse*]. Assuming this, it necessarily follows that he must also be worshipped in it. Consequently, nothing seems [121] more unreasonable than to accuse Catholics of idolatry when they worship something whose worship is not a crime [*adorantibus id, quod non adorare sit crimen*].

Some necessary proofs are being deduced from what we have hitherto demonstrated. First, since the pronouncements of the Catholic Church must always be based on divine revelation in order to be regarded as decisive proof of the truth [*certissimum veritatis argumentum*], it follows that where this condition is not met, the authority with which God has endowed the Church does not exist. Second, that everything which has been established and approved or not approved and

---

8. [A classical study of the Protestant accusation of "idolatry" is Carlos Eire, *War against the Idols: The Reformation of Worship from Erasmus to Calvin* (Cambridge: Cambridge University Press, 1986).]

rejected by the Church, the councils, and the Church Fathers, must be accepted with the same obedience and reverence [*eodem obsequii venerationisque genere*]. Moreover, what the Church proclaims publicly in her interpretation and proof to be contained in Holy Scripture and the apostolic tradition, demands from us the same divine faith [*fidem divinam*] and is therefore licitly counted as dogma. Whatever rests on the foundation of human reason and human experience [*humanis experimentis*] alone, however, can only demand human faith [*fidem humanam*], never divine faith, and can never be counted among the dogmas of faith. Consequently, a person who does not want to believe in these things mentioned might be considered foolish or audacious [*temerarius*], and could, I might add, be suspected of heresy and deserve a sharp rebuke [*gravi castigatione*]. Nevertheless, such a person never deserves to be called a heretic and must therefore not be punished as such. About this, however, we must deal in more detail in another place.

Third, there are also other questions relating to dogma that the Church could decide without any danger of error but must out of prudence abstain from a decision. There are in fact many but they can be found predominantly among the scholastics [*apud scholasticos*], where they can multiply enormously [*enormem adhuc in numerum excrescere posset*]. We have said that the Church has the right to make a decision because such disputes touch upon divine revelation, and because a decision is deduced and grounded in it. Nevertheless, the Church usually does not decide such questions because the acceptance or rejection of such a teaching [*sententia*] by Christians does not negatively impact the moral doctrine [*scientiae morum*] established by Christ, does not keep somebody from pursuing the virtues or tacitly incites vices, but it also in no way [122] fights against or violently distorts [*nulla vis infertur, nullaque ex parte repugnatur*] the most important, pronounced, and accepted [*praecipuis, expressis, ac receptis*] teachings and principles of Holy Scripture and tradition [*scripturarum traditionisque documentis, atque principiis*]. For if the Church were to put an end to every dispute that has arisen or may arise in the future through her irrevocable decision, she would impose upon herself a superfluous and indescribable burden [*supervacaneam incredibilemque crearet molestiam*] and render a poor service to immoderately inquisitive minds [*ingeniis immoderate curiosis*]. And when could she be absolved from dealing with such work? Why even take on such tremendous work proclaiming such a vast number of new doctrinal decrees? I would almost call such behavior evidence of presumption [*ambitionis*] or at least of intemperance rather than of necessity. And yet, it would not prevent people who delight in arguing, who feed on quarrels, from inciting new controversies. Moreover, many of the disputed questions are quite insignificant, while others can only be reconciled with great difficulty [*difficile referre*], either with the obvious meaning of Holy Scripture or the antiquity of tradition [*traditionis antiquitatem*], so that it is more advisable to consider them probable [*verisimilia*] than to declare them either true or false. As we have already said, special consideration must be given whether the views of the contending parties lead either straightforwardly or indirectly to the overthrow of an existing dogma and of a truth expressed in both Testaments that relates to the salvation of humanity or salvific faith. Wherever and whenever something deserves to be immediately rejected or approved, to be tolerated in the interest of the Christian Commonwealth, to be overlooked or condemned, it must be left to the prudence of the Church and the popes.

Fourth, among those teachings that the Church can most certainly decide are not only—as we have said—doctrines that have not yet been included among the dogmas of faith. After all, there are views, which although they are contained in the texts of the councils and Church Fathers, were never officially approved or rejected. This is the case with texts in which the councils or Church Fathers did not deal explicitly [*non ex professo*] with some doctrines [*sententias*], but rather in passing [*obiter dicta*]. Nevertheless, what councils or some Church Fathers only reference in passing [*in transitu*], can be found in other documents of the tradition as absolutely certain [*certissime*]. Such doctrines will then be held with the strength of a dogma even if they were not the main point of the text [*praeter propositum dicta*]. [123] It is, however, true that the mere mentioning of a sentence, which otherwise is not firmly grounded and accepted, in passing [*ab ore aliud agentis exciderint*] alone does not endow it with the nature of a dogma [*e vestigio naturam dogmatis induunt*]. On the contrary, it would be no crime to oppose such a view in a dispute. After all, among Catholics nobody denies that the councils when they decide about matters of faith and shape them into dogmas of faith, have to diligently consult Holy Scripture and tradition. Yet, how can one comprehend that this has really happened if the Church Fathers only mention a teaching in passing on an unrelated occasion [*obiter atque alio intenti*]?

Whether the Question of the Angels as Corporeal or Incorporeal Beings Has Been Decided by the Councils

At the seventh Ecumenical Council Act. V,[9] Tarasios of Constantinople, one of the leaders at that synod, citing the words of John of Thessalonica, asserted that the angels had a light, ethereal or fiery body. The universal synod does not seem to have disagreed at all on this point, and—why should we hide this fact—a few Church Fathers seem to have been inclined to accept this opinion. During the Lateran Council,[10] Pope Innocent III called the angels *spiritual* beings and distinguished them from corporeal beings. Other Fathers thought the angels were completely immaterial [*plane esse materiae expertes*]. There is, however, an easy way to resolve this contradiction [*antilogiae*]. Neither of these opinions was ever defined [*definita*] at either of the two councils nor included [*adscripta*] among the dogmas of faith. After all, this idea was only mentioned in passing at both councils, during the deliberation of another doctrine. The Nicene Council had only the intention of declaring that it was permitted to paint the angels and the souls of the saints, but it did not want to determine whether the angels were in fact corporeal beings. In the same way, the Lateran Council was concerned with the reawakened heresy of the Manichaeans, who put forward the ungodly proposition that not everything was created by God. Rightly, the Fathers defined [*sanciunt*] the contrary position as

---

9. [The Seventh Ecumenical Council is better known as the Second Council of Nicaea of 786/787. The texts of its decrees can be found in *Conciliorum Oecumenicorum Generaliumque Decreta, Editio critica, Volume I: The Oecumenical Councils from Nicaea I to Nicaea II (325–787)*, ed. Giuseppe Alberigo et al. [Corpus Christianorum] (Turnhout: Brepols, 2006).]

10. [Muratori means the Fourth Lateran Council of 1215.]

dogma[11] [*contrarium dogma*] by approving the profession of faith issued by Pope Innocent III. Whether the angels were utterly immaterial beings [*omnino materiae sint expertes*] was, however, not at all a topic of its deliberations and the Church Fathers certainly did not intend to determine anything about it. Both views are therefore mentioned in the conciliar texts not as dogmas, but merely as opinions.

Some but Not All Proofs for Dogmas Always Belong to the Faith

One thing, however, must nevertheless be mentioned here. If opinions are expressed casually during an ecumenical council [124] and are not rejected, such sentences do not gain immediately the certainty of dogmas, but it does follow that they have either nothing in common with the faith or that they do not contradict it. Then they belong to that part of doctrine that the Church cannot sanction [*sancire*] with an absolutely certain decision [*sententiam certissimam*] and which we have already mentioned above but will nevertheless give below a few more examples, or they belong to the part of doctrine that can be defined by the Church's decision, in which case then the silence of the council can be cited as supporting evidence that such opinions do not contradict the faith. Since the Church obviously did not approve these opinions verbatim [*ex professo*], she did not include them among the decrees of the faith. Nevertheless, since she did not reject them either, she tacitly taught [*tacite docuit*] that they were by no means [*minime*] in contradiction with the doctrine of the faith. For the councils could certainly pass over in silence what did not belong to the faith [*dissimulare Conciliis licet*], but certainly never over opinions contradicting it. After all, the Church must know what is in conflict with the teachings handed down by the apostles and Church Fathers, and therefore it would be contrary to the duty of the Church if she were to tacitly witness and permit the violation of her doctrine [*sinere hanc doctrinam, se audiente, & dissimulante, violari*]. For "error" [as it is said in Canon Law, Dist. 83, canon on error[12]] that is not contradicted is "approved," unless, on that

11. [Namely, that God is the creator of everything.]
12. ["Error cui non restitur, approbatur" is a legal principle found in medieval

account, one is silent about it, because the disputed question is reserved for a future, more careful examination.

Therefore, the controversial question about the angels (as quite a few would agree) either belongs to the realm of doctrine that cannot be decided from Holy Scripture or tradition, and consequently everyone has the right [*fas est*] to think about it what one considers probable [*veri videtur similius*] or, if it is within the authority of the Church to decide it, one has to wrestle with the fact that neither [*neutra*] of the two views has been rejected by a council. From the silence of the councils, one may only deduce that neither view is contrary to the doctrine of the faith. Thus, it could happen that someone inquires how both propositions could be true, namely that angels are both material beings and at the same time immaterial beings? I answer that they are most likely merely spiritual beings, but since at times they seem to have taken on sublime bodies [*tenuissima corpora*] in order to carry out their mission for the good of those to whom they appear visible, one could say that they are contingently corporeal beings [*per accidens*] and therefore paint them as such. It is, however, not certain whether they immediately discard this ethereal shell [*aetheream vestem*] or retain it, and thus a reasonable person should withhold judgment about this question. Finally, one should not rely too strongly on the words of these councils. After all, at the Council of Nicaea, [125] Tarasius merely emphasized from the speech of John of Thessalonica (and the other Church Fathers agreed with this), that the angels are limited beings [*circumscriptos*], unlike God, who is unlimited. Moreover, he said, that since they had been seen in human form, it was permissible to paint them as such. He did not even speak about their bodies. In Act. IV, he even calls them *incorporeal* [*incorporeos*]. And when Innocent III calls the angels spiritual [*spirituales*] at the Lateran Council, this expression [*ea vox*] by no means excludes a bodily connection [*corporis societatem*]. Other Church Fathers have called the angels incorporeal and spiritual beings [*spirituales*] because they do not consist of coarse matter [*crassa materia*]. Nevertheless, they opined that they consisted of extremely subtle, ethereal matter. But enough about this.

---

canon law, see Decretum Magistri Gratiani c. II, dist. 83, in *Corpus Iuris Canonici,* 2nd ed., vol. 1, ed. Aemilius Friedberg (Leipzig: 1879), 293–94.]

Let us now deal with the proofs of some dogmas; these laws [*leges*] also permit us to consider the controversy about angels. It seems clear that the Fathers of the Nicene Council decided for no other reason that it was permissible to represent the angels in painting, than because they considered the arguments of John of Thessalonica to be of critical [*gravissimae*] importance. Yet, if the Catholic Church is infallible [*nulli errori obnoxia*] in the establishment of dogmas, it must also possess this privilege [*praerogativam*] for finding and establishing the proofs of the dogmas [*dogmatum rationibus inveniendis atque edicendis*]. For are not the proofs the foundation for the dogmas? Therefore, if the proofs fall, do they not also tear down the dogmas? Accordingly, the proofs and the evidential grounds that were used by the councils and the Church Fathers to confirm the doctrines of faith but also to reject heresies, must be regarded with the same reverence, with the same faith [*pari veneration et fide*], as the dogmas themselves.

Still, great caution is necessary for such an inquiry. After all, whoever measures their proofs with the same yardstick, or thinks they have to be measured as such, will not be acquainted with the writings of the Church Fathers or councils, and also be inexperienced in logic and criticism. Thus, we maintain, *first*,[13] that no dogma has been established by the Church that was not based on irrefutable proof, and thus there is always an irrefutable proof for a dogma, which, like the dogma itself, belongs to the deposit of faith. We add *secondly*[14] that such proofs can not only be found in the writings of the holy[15] Church Fathers and the texts of theologians, but also in the acts of the councils, which must almost always be obeyed by moderate [*modestis*] people, [126] but never with divine faith [*fides divina*].[16] The heterodox might deny the first conclusion, but the same reasons that demonstrate the right and the infallibility of the Church to establish dogmas also prove quite obviously

---

13. [Italics of the editor.]

14. [Italics of the editor.]

15. [The editor chose to translate in this instance "sanctos," since it seems of importance for the argument.]

16. [Thus, every Catholic who respects the boundaries of reason and is moderate, will accept the proofs put forth by a council but does not have to hold them in the same esteem as a dogma.]

that the Church could never proceed to give a decision without having a proof for that faith, which has been infallibly derived from [*minime fallacibus deducta*] Holy Scripture and the documents of the tradition. These, however, can be called the most fundamental and powerful [*fundamentales et potissimae*] proofs of the dogmas.

The second conclusion—that not all proofs of the dogmas have the same weight—will at first sight perhaps not appeal to those who are ill-informed about the powers of the Church. However, no educated and truly learned theologian would contradict it, but only approve of it. Somebody who has a different opinion would face the resistance of experience and will only find a few arguments in his favor. For what is more obvious than that all truths, of whatever kind they may be, whether theological, philosophical, or moral, can be proved not only by so-called demonstrative evidence [*argumenta demonstrative*], but also by reasons that are plausible and probable [*argumenta probabilia et verisimilia*]? Thus, for many truths, although they are well established by revelation or the light of reason, one can also offer reasons from plausibility and probability. The truth of the dogma does not need them [*harum quidem ope non indiget veritas*] but loves them as aids for easier persuasion. That there is a God, that he is the creator of the world, that rational souls do not perish with their bodies, that there is punishment or reward after death—all this we recognize most reliably by the light of reason, and we firmly believe it also on the testimony of divine revelation. Consequently, nothing prevents us from elucidating and illustrating such clear truths by the means of probable arguments [*probabilius quoque rationibus*], so that they can easier convince others [*persuademus*].

This has sometimes been done at the councils, often by the Church Fathers, and daily by the most excellent theologians and writers, when they deal with other subjects of Christian doctrine. The faithful, however, cannot be required to accept such proofs from probability and plausibility [*argumenta verisimilia, rationesque dumtaxat probabiles*] with divine faith [*divinam a populis fidem*] because they are not unmistakably true. Everything that is merely backed by probability could, after one has thoroughly [127] examined it, be falsified. Thus, should we be surprised when we sometimes find among the interpreters of the divine things [*rerum divinarum interpretes*] and among the most beautiful lights [*praestantissima ecclesiae lumina*] of the Church, proofs [*rationes*] that substantiate little or nothing at all? Yet this does not diminish the reliability of the dogmas, and the decisions [*decreta*] of the Church must be accepted and believed with no less obedience of the mind [*mentis obsequio*]. The power of the fundamental proofs is sufficient for their steadfastness. Since there is no dogma that does not have such evidence on its side, it follows by necessity that the Christian people have a duty to recognize and embrace a proposed dogma.

On the Freedom of the Human Mind

Yet, how does one distinguish auxiliary [*subsidiariae*] from fundamental proofs? I must confess that this may not be as easy for everyone as it is for simultaneously pious and judicious people [*piis simul et judiciosis*]. Nevertheless, it is a matter of the greatest importance for every theologian to distinguish them in order to be safe from error [*discernendus ab errando*]. One should not think [*cogitandum non est*] that not only a person who dares to doubt and reject the main or fundamental proofs would harm the Church. It is of course an error, although a pardonable one, but still an error that can generate quite a few inconvenient problems if a person attaches not only more value to proofs from plausibility [*probabilia*] than they deserve but also demands their acceptance without the slightest doubt [*sine dubitatione credenda proponere*], as if they were the most recognized doctrines [*firmissima capita*] of faith. This is contrary to the advice of the Church [*ab ecclesiae ipsius consilio abhorret*], which uses these arguments from probability [*verisimilibus*] merely to make it easier to accept the truth and to confirm it all the more, but not to present doubtful doctrines [*dubia*] as quite certain [*certissima*] by means of such uncertain [*incertis*] proofs. But if we ask furthermore how one can distinguish subsidiary and probable proofs from the fundamental proofs, it seems to me that no other principle can be applied here than the one that teaches us how to discern [*discernere*] certain doctrines from those that are uncertain. Consequently, proofs belong to the faith and are called fundamental proofs, which either have been everywhere, always, and unanimously held by the Church Fathers to be reliable and plausible [*pro certis atque evidentius*], or which have been accepted and proclaimed as foundational proofs of the dogmas by the ecumenical councils and the Roman popes in creeds [*fidei formulis*], decrees, and decisions that have been unanimously received by the universal Church [*ab universa ecclesia ... concordi*]. If therefore one of the Church Fathers or a bishop in the acts of a general council presents proofs from his own ingenuity [*suopte ingenio rationes*] that are not embraced through the consent of the whole Church—that is, by the whole ecumenical council, or by the Roman pope, or by the consensus [128] of the other Church Fathers—it will be permitted to withhold our judgment [*cohibere judicium nostrum licebit*]. Moreover, in such a case, we are not obliged to believe these proofs because it is uncertain whether God speaks through a single bishop or writer [*per unum episcopum aut scriptorem*].

After this, it is necessary to notice that the main proofs of the dogmas must be contained in the very words [*verba ipsa*] of Holy Scripture or in indubitable documents of the tradition. Proofs conceived by human philosophical reasoning can add weight to the ecclesiastical decisions, but they cannot be the first and foremost foundation [*primum ac praecipuum fundamentum*] since they are not based [*innitantur*] on Holy Scripture and tradition. Even passages of Holy Scripture that are used by the councils, the Church Fathers, and the theologians to prove the dogmas, can by no means always be regarded as fundamental and most certain proofs. After all, these could be allegorical passages and texts, which are according to the consensus of scholars [*ex communi eruditorum voto*] quite obscure [*obscurissima*]. Certainly, one can add these to the clear testimonies [*clarissimis aliis*] of Holy Scripture and the legitimate tradition [*traditionis legitimae*], not in order to use them as foundational proofs of future dogmas, but in order to enhance and protect [*ornamento atque praesidio*] the already existing ones. Tradition, if it is correctly derived from ancient harmony [*antiquitate concordi*] and asserted according to the rules established by the theologians [*secundum regulas a theologis praescriptas adhibita*], always gives ecclesiastical decisions a most solid foundation [*solidissimum ... fundamentum*]. After all, even the passages [*loca*] of Holy Scripture require the consent of tradition [*consensione indigent*] if the Church is to build a secure judgment upon them. After all, the Catholic Commonwealth [*Catholicorum nempe Respublica*] knows very well that it neither may nor can establish a dogma whose truth does not flow [*effluat*] from tradition and Holy Scripture [*atque ex divinis Scripturarum oraculis*] as foundational proofs. Without these the Church has never declared a dogma, and never will, although if I may say so, sometimes she spoke or speaks with almost royal [*regia*] authority that urges us to believe the dogmas without any proofs [*minime propositis*]. Even in such a case, one can be certain that her dogmas always have their ground in the documents of tradition and Holy Scripture, and if these are the foundation, we have no reason to demand other proofs.

A famous example for this is Pope Stephen. A heated [*fervebat*] controversy had developed between the African and the other churches about the validity of baptism by heretics. [129] Cyprian, an otherwise exceedingly holy man, maintained that baptism must be repeated, and his new view had, to speak from Vincent of Lérins's chapter 6, "on its side such force of genius, such floods of eloquence, such a number of partisans, so close a resemblance to the truth, such textual support in Holy Scripture—only obviously interpreted in a novel and wrong sense—that it seems to me the whole of that combination could not have been destroyed."[17] Nevertheless, Stephen asserted to him that tradition was on his side; and relying on these weapons, he gained the victory, with the general approval and applause [*consentiente et plaudente*] of the Church. Long afterwards Augustine, the strongest fighter for the Catholic cause [*fortissimus Catholicorum pugil*], supported Stephen's view with so many reasons and proofs against the Donatists that even the uneducated [*rudibus*] realized that Cyprian had gone far from the truth. We must also state that the proofs human ingenuity [*humano ingenio*] invents—as smart and ingenious [*acutissimas ... ingeniosissimas*] they may be—are ultimately worthless [*nihil valere*] and always insufficient [*aliquo semper vitio laborare*] when they argue against a dogma that has been confirmed by the Church on the grounds of tradition and Scripture. Should they, however, defend this dogma, they

---

17. Vincent of Lérins, *Commonitorium*, bk. I, ch. 6, in *The Commonitory of St. Vincent of Lerins*, trans. T. Herbert Bindley (London: SPCK, 1914), 37.

should not all be judged by the same standard. Some proofs can be extremely certain [*certissimae*], others only plausible or only probable [*certissimae ... probabiles ... verisimilesque*], and others completely useless. Therefore, the human mind is free to choose among them or to reject them [*Quocirca et judicio in iis seligendis locus erit, et in quibusdam rejicendis libertas*].

Chapter 22

On the Exegesis of Scripture and the Copernican System

Whether the View of the Astronomers about the Daily Movement of the Earth Contradicts Holy Scripture

[221] We will now, since the matter demands it, examine according to principles we earlier established some new discoveries [*inventa*]—different opinions of physicists, historians, and everything that is taught in the mathematical, astronomical, and geographical studies in past and present. If we are, for example, confronted in astronomy with a system according to which the sun is stationary and the earth moves daily around it—a view that several passages of Holy Scripture seem to contradict—then it is the duty of a prudent theologian to investigate whether these passages [*loca*] of Holy Scripture are so clear [*ita perspicua*] and explicit [*evidentia*] that we would completely fail [*omnino peccetur*] the laws of sound criticism [*melioris criticae*] and reason itself [*ipsius rationis*] as well as the obvious rules of true interpretation, if we were to follow the view [*illa trahere velimus ad opinionem eorum*] of those astronomers about the movement of the Earth [*de telluris motu*]. The advocates of this view might, however, cite much evidence in its favor. For although in physics and astronomy there is nothing settled [*certi*] about the movement of the Earth, this view has not been condemned by the Church or by the Apostolic See, and all the learned

men, who in former times or in the last two centuries have publicly or silently paid homage to it, are by no means considered heretics. The Copernican hypothesis is, by the way, not completely new, as we can see from Aristotle, Cicero, and Plutarch. Moreover, eighty years before Copernicus it had already been asserted by the famous Cardinal Nicholas of Cusa in his book *De docta ignorantia*.[1] Yet Copernicus developed it in some parts, and it seems that the reformers of the Julian calendar followed in his footsteps [*eiusque vestigia*] in the Gregorian correction. The following passages of Holy Scripture that mention the movement of the sun and the standstill of the Earth seem to be in contradiction with this opinion. After all, in Genesis 29:32 it is said: "at sunrise" [*ortusque est ei statim sol*]. In Ecclesiastes we read (Eccl 1:5–6) "The sun rises and the sun sets; then it presses on to the place where it rises. Shifting south, then north, back and forth shifts the wind, constantly shifting its course." When Joshua commanded the sun and moon to stand still, "the sun stood still, the moon stayed, while the nation took vengeance on its foes.... The sun halted halfway across the Heavens; not for an entire day did it press on."[2] I will pass over other passages in Holy Scripture that are already known and have been explained by scholars and that state that the Earth stands still and that the sun moves. I must confess that it is an easy task [*parvo negotio*] to bring those passages of Holy Scripture that seem to speak of an immovable Earth [*immobilem*] to agree with the view of the astronomers. After all, these passages claim that the Earth will continue to exist, will always be, and will not be moved from its hinges [*neque a suis cardinibus umquam dimoveri*]. All this indicates permanence, continuity, and firmness [*consistentia, perduratio, ac firmitas*], which in no way exclude local movement [*locale motum nequaquam excludit*]. Therefore, the firmament is called "the Heavens" [*coeli*], and Proverbs 8:28 states that

---

1. [For Cusa's views of astronomy and their context, see Rivka Feldhay and F. Jamil Ragep, eds., *Before Copernicus: The Cultures and Contexts of Scientific Learning in the Fifteenth Century* (Montreal: McGill University Press, 2017); for the calendar reform see Charlotte Methuen, "Time Human or Time Divine? Theological Aspects in the Opposition to Gregorian Calendar Reform," *Reformation & Renaissance Review* 3 (2001): 36–50.]

2. Jos 10:12–13.

divine wisdom has fixed the ether or the Heavens on high, and yet the firmness [*firmitate*] of the Heavens by no means excludes their movement, as the Ptolemaic system teaches.

Holy Scripture Makes Use of Popular Sayings and Images to Express a Certain Truth

Far clearer are the passages of Holy Scripture that speak about the movement of the sun. However, it must be noted that Holy Scripture sometimes accommodates its expressions according to the common language of the people [*ad opinionem vulgi accomodare*] and maintains this expression so that the uneducated [*rudis populi*] can all the easier understand their meaning. For the uneducated people grasp and understand more easily that which is expressed in the usual rather than in an unusual manner of speaking [*dicendi formulis*], although the latter may be more accurate. This is most evident in those traditions [*tradendis*] that do not belong to the salvific faith and the truth of morals. As we have already explained, God, who speaks to us through Holy Scripture, did not intend to satisfy vain human curiosity [*hominum curiositatem pasceret*] for knowing unnecessary things, such as the elements and bodies of this world, but only to teach what is truly necessary to attain eternal happiness. God also does not speak in the learned vocabulary of human wisdom but condescends to use a language [*sese demittit ad earum locutionum usum*] that, although not very accurate and even inappropriate according to the rules of human wisdom, is useful to convey to the uneducated the salvific truth in an expedient [*commodius*] manner. The writers who were inspired by God did not scruple to attribute to God not only a body, but also body parts, human affects, and actions [*corpus, et membra, et animi perturbationes et operationes humanas*], [223] in order to signify the divine effects of his actions [*vero divinae operationis effectus*]. How much more could they use an even less precise form of speech in their narrative about physical and purely human things? They used figurative language [*figurate loqui*], which is in use among all peoples—even among scholars—and especially among poets and the Orientals. Yet, the truth does not suffer from this, for the truth that one intends to communicate is also communicated through such figurative expressions, albeit in a more elegant [*eleganter*] manner. In the traditions that are not necessary for salvation, scholars must decide what is to be understood literally [*proprie*] and what figuratively, but in matters that relate to faith and Christian doctrine, this decision belongs to the ecclesiastical judges.

What Do Expressions Like "the Whole World," "the Ends of the Heavens," "the Sun Becomes Warm" as Well as Other Expressions about the Heavens, the Stars, and the Sun Mean?

It has been the custom of the sacred writers to express themselves in more popular language [*secundum vulgi sententiam*], which can be proved with a great number of examples. When we speak of the *world*[3] [*terrarum orbem*] and especially when we add the adjective *entire*[4] [*universi*], then everyone knows that this means all peoples, all provinces and countries that are located on the surface of the entire globe. However, people have sometimes had and still have a different view and way of expressing themselves. After all, by the expression "entire world" [*orbis*] one can also understand the formerly known [*antea cogniti*] provinces and peoples, or a large part of the Earth, or a great empire like the Assyrian empire or the empire of Alexander the Great or the Roman empire. [The Evangelist, U.L.] Luke writes (Lk 2:1): "In those days a decree went out from Caesar Augustus that the whole world should be enrolled" [ἀπογραφέσθαι πᾶσαν τὴν οἰκουμένην]. The Evangelist obviously makes use of the ordinary conception [*vulgari opinione*] and expression. After all, the Romans thought highly of their realm. According to their opinion and their speech, they were nothing less than the masters of the whole Earth. A famous passage in Petronius in his book *De Bello Civili* exemplifies this:

> *The conquering Roman now held the whole world,*
> *Sea and land and the course of sun and moon.*[5]

---

3. [Muratori's italics.]
4. [Muratori's italics.]
5. ["Orbem jam totam Victor Romanus habebat, /Qua mare, qua terrae, qua sidus currit utrumque." Petronius, *Satyricon*, trans. Michael Heseltine (New York: Heinemann and Macmillan, 1913), 277, n.119.]

Also, Hegesippus says: "The whole world is regulated and defined by the Roman Empire."[6] Anyone who is only somewhat versed in history knows that the Romans, although they had subjugated a large part of the Earth [224] through their victorious weapons, were far from ruling the whole Earth. They possessed only a relatively small part if one compares their territory to the many countries that they did not subject to their rule. If, therefore, individual passages of Holy Scripture talk about the Earth [*terra*] or the whole world [*de toto orbe*], περὶ τῆς οἰκουμένης, then one must not understand these expressions as meaning all peoples and nations of the Earth. At times they mean the whole of Judea [*Judaea tota*] with all its tribes, sometimes the Roman Empire, and at other times only a small part of the then known world with which the Jews were acquainted through trade. This explanation fits the passage in the Letter to the Romans (Rom 10:18), where Paul applies the fifth verse of Psalm 19[7] to the proclamation of the Gospel: "But I ask, did they not hear? Certainly they did; for 'Their voice has gone forth to all the earth, and their words to the ends of the world.'" After all, it is not probable that at that time the Gospel and the apostles had already reached the farthest provinces of Scythia and the inhospitable regions of Tartary, the vast lands of America, and so many other barbarous countries between the two poles, since a large part of these lands has only been discovered in the last three centuries. Moreover, despite the best efforts of recent European discoverers, who are far superior to the older seafarers, there are still, undetected, great nations between the Arctic and Antarctic. There seems to be no doubt that before the consummation of all time the true rule [*verae ditionem*] of the Catholic Church and of the true faith will no longer be constricted [*nullo termino constringendam*] so that all nations will share in the inheritance of Christ. Yet in the times of Tertullian, Jerome, Augustine, and other Church Fathers this had not yet happened, although according to their expressions the Catholic Church "occupied the world, had taken hold of the whole globe, spread over the whole Earth, filled the Earth, was spread over the whole Earth." With these words, one meant the

---

6. Pseudo-Hegesip, *Antiquitates*, lib. 2, 9; Vincenzo Ussani, ed., *Hegesippi qui dicitur historiae libri V*, Part 1 (Vienna: Hoelder, 1932), 154, my own translation.

7. [In the *Vulgate*, which Muratori uses, this is Psalm 18.]

largest part of the whole Earth, especially frequented by Jews, Greeks, and Romans. This was the known Earth for the uneducated people, the whole world for the Church Fathers. Holy Scripture, however, used this popular phrase to designate that part of the Earth that was known to the common people [225]. After all, it was not God's intention to instruct people that there were still vast and unknown stretches of land outside the known world. Something similar can be said about the passage in which Daniel predicts that Alexander [the Great, U.L.] will rule over the whole world. Likewise in the words of Acts (Acts 2:5): "Now there were devout Jews," says Luke, "from every nation under heaven staying in Jerusalem." (The common people also seem to think that human thought and will originate in the heart [*in corde nasci*]. Yet, it is established that the brain and head are the place of mind and will. Nevertheless, there are countless passages in Holy Scripture that follow the view of the common people.)[8]

Here is also the place to mention another passage from the Acts of the Apostles (27:27): "Toward midnight the shipmen deemed[9] that they discovered land." The Greek texts do not say: *discovered* [*apparere*] but rather that the coasts neared *them*, using the word προσάγειν. From this we see that Luke expresses himself like the common people did. For to those who travel by sea, it seems as if the shores move, as if the remote objects come closer or move away. "Soon out of port we ran, and watched the hills and cities fading far," is a well-known verse from Virgil's *Aeneid*,[10] to which one could add without much trouble many similar ones. When the Apostle Paul states in the First Letter to the Corinthians (1 Cor 1:21), that "it was the will of God through the foolishness of the proclamation to save those who have faith," he

---

8. [This note must be understood in the context of the controversies about the Sacred Heart veneration, of which Muratori was critical. See, for example, Lauren G. Kilroy-Ewbank, *Holy Organ or Unholy Idol?: The Sacred Heart in the Art, Religion, and Politics of New Spain* (Leiden: Brill: 2019).]

9. [NABRE reads: "Toward midnight the sailors began to suspect *that they were nearing land.*" The *Vulgate*, which Muratori uses, reads: "Circa medium noctis suspicabuntur nautae apparere sibi aliquam regionem." He therefore emphasizes the verb *apparere* and contrasts it with the text of the Greek original.]

10. Virgil, *Aeneid*, trans. Theodore C. Williams (Boston: Houghton Mifflin, 1910), bk. 3, line 70, 78.

referred to the preaching of the truth and the Gospel, since Christian faith and doctrine seemed foolish to the wise men of this world and to human reason. The same apostle calls, however, in the Second Letter to the Corinthians (2 Cor 4:4) the devil "the god of this age" not because he really is, but because he is considered and worshipped by idolaters, and because he considers himself to be god, as Matthew (4:9) and Luke (4:6–7) indicate. I will not give more examples of this kind but will rather use ones better suited to the task at hand.

In fact, Holy Scripture follows nowhere more evidently the judgments and opinions of the uneducated masses as when it speaks about Heaven and heavenly bodies. Isaiah (13:4–5) says: "The Lord of hosts is mustering an army for battle. They come from a far-off country, from the [226] top of Heaven" [*de terra procul a summitate coeli*]. The Hebrew text, however, reads: *from far away, from the end of Heaven*. People who come from far away and from the farthest part of Heaven means nothing else than that they came from the remotest parts and from the borders of the Earth to invade the Babylonian empire. This expression, however, is borrowed from popular imagination [*ex opinione populari*]. To them the sky was not spherical but only hemispherical, and thus limited by the ends of the Earth. The same expression occurs in Exodus 4:32 and 30:4, in 2 Esdras 1:9, Matthew 24:31. One has to mention in this context also that these books call the mountains "the foundations of the Heavens." The royal bard David exclaims in 2 Samuel 22:8:[11] "The earth shook and trembled, the foundations of the mountains were moved and shaken."[12] Instead of the foundations of the mountains, the Hebrew text reads: the foundations of Heaven shook, מוסדות השמים ירגזו *Mosedoth hasciamaim irgazu* [*môsədôt haššāmayim yirggāzû*].[13] If we judge by the eyes and by popular imagination, the sky seems to end in the distance on the mountains, seems to touch them and to rest on them, as it were, like on a foundation. The mountains themselves are also called pillars [*columnae*] of Heaven (Job 26:11),

---

11. [Muratori initially referenced "2 Reg. 22:8," which is a citation from the *Vulgate* that referred to 1–2 Samuel as 1–2 Kings.]

12. *The Holy Bible Translated from the Latin Vulgate* (*Douay-Rheims*) (Baltimore: John Murphy, 1914), 345.

13. [Muratori's transliteration. In parenthesis the contemporary transliteration.]

because judging by their appearance, they seem to carry the sky like pillars. This expression is familiar to the poets of all peoples, and therefore it has been said of Atlas, Olympus, and other mountains that they carry the sky because it seemed to rest upon them. That is also how the term *horizon* [*finitoris seu horizontis*] came into being, because the sky in its hemispheric appearance seems to touch this region there.

I also find in Exodus (16:21) an obviously figurative expression: "Now every one of them gathered in the morning, as much (*manna*) as might suffice to eat; and after the sun grew hot, it melted."[14] How can one say that the sun becomes hot? If the sun alternates between being hot and cold, does it sometimes lose some of its power and heat, which it regains later? Certainly not. Holy Scripture uses the language of the people. In the morning, when the night cold is still in the atmosphere, and when the rays of the sun, because of their refraction on the dense layer of air opposite the atmosphere, [227] have not yet gained strength, the sun seems to have a lower degree of warmth. Now the people believed that the warmer the sun becomes, the higher it rises on the horizon, as if the heat in the sun itself increases and not in the air and in the person that are exposed to the action of the sun. The same expression occurs in the first book of Samuel (1 Sam 11:9) and in both passages the Hebrew editions use the word חמם *chamam*,[15] which has a passive meaning and means to become warm. Add to this the passage in Isaiah (Is 13:10) where it is said, "the sun shall be darkened in its rising."[16] Here Holy Scripture merely describes how it appears. When the sky is covered with clouds, or when the moon comes to stand between the sun and the earth, it seems as if the sun is eclipsed. Thus it seems to humans because the sun itself is not eclipsed nor its light diminished. Therefore Ezekiel (32:7) expresses the thought of Isaiah differently, saying: "I will cover the sun with a cloud."[17] But when it is said in Holy

---

14. [*The Holy Bible Translated from the Latin Vulgate*, Douay-Rheims Edition (New York: P. J. Kennedy & Sons, 1914), 79. Cited as *Douay-Rheims* with page numbers.]

15. [The modern scholarly edition, *Biblia Hebraica Stuttgartensia* (BHS), based on the Leningrad Codex, has here כחם *kəḥōm* (Qere) or בחם *bəḥōm* (Ketiv). Thanks to Ms. Noelle Johnson for this comment and the transliterations from the Hebrew text. Muratori's transliteration above.]

16. [*Douay-Rheims*, 769.]

17. [*Douay-Rheims*, 927.]

Scripture that stars would fall from Heaven, or that they have already fallen, the prophets only allude to what appears to happen, for several stars cannot fall upon the earth, since some of them are greater than the whole earth. Perhaps this is also true of the passage in the Epistle of Jude (Jd 1:13). What are called "wandering stars" [*stellae erraticae*] are not stars, but meteors and tail-like combustions of air, which look like shooting stars and are usually mistaken for such.

And what if the scribes of Holy Scripture preferred using popular terms for the daily movement of the sun, which are cited as contradicting the opinion of the astronomers, rather than more diligently chosen and accurate words from astronomy and physics? In the sixth verse of Psalm 19 (Ps 19:6[18]), where the prophet speaks of the glory of God, which is especially revealed through the sun, he says: "He has set his tabernacle in the sun and he, as a bridegroom coming out of his bride chamber, hath rejoiced as a giant to run the way. His going out is from the end of heaven, and his circuit even to the end thereof: and there is no one that can hide himself from his heat."[19] Here the rising sun is compared to a bridegroom emerging from his bridal chamber, and the expression alludes to the opinion of the people who believe that the sun, as long as it is out of our hemisphere, rests and sleeps; only with the dawn it emerges from its resting place as if it had slept, to begin anew its interrupted course [*interruptum cursum resumere*]. The following words are incorrectly interpreted by a famous astronomer, the author of the *Novi Almagesti*,[20] [228] for he says that in our passage "according to astronomical manner the beginning and the end are called the farthest end of the sky [*a summo et in summo caeli*], which is taken from the height of the meridian and from the highest point of the sun." Yet, one end of the sky [*summum caeli*], which is mentioned here, from where the sun begins its course, and the other end, where it ends

18. [In the *Vulgate*, which Muratori uses, this is Psalm 18.]

19. [*Douay-Rheims*, 589.]

20. [Giovanni B. Riccioli, *Almagestum novum astronomiam veterem novamque complectens observationibus aliorum* (Bologna: 1651), vol. 1/2, bk. 9, sect. 4, 480, ad 5. The author was the Jesuit astronomer Giovanni Battista Riccioli, SJ (1598–1671). For his theories see, for example, Christopher M. Graney, *Setting Aside All Authority: Giovanni Battista Riccioli and the Science against Copernicus in the Age of Galileo* (Notre Dame, IN: University of Notre Dame Press, 2015).]

its course, are nothing but the outermost ends of the sky, which present themselves to our eyes as our horizon, namely sunrise and sunset. Above, we have already seen that the *Vulgate* in Isaiah (Is 13) also mentions the ends of heaven. In the same way one reads in Deuteronomy (Dtn 4:32 and Dtn 30:4): "from one end of heaven to the other." Instead of "at the ends of heaven" the *Vulgate* reads "poles of heaven" [*cardines coeli*]. All these expressions mean the same thing, namely the outermost parts of heaven (an expression that is also used by the *Vulgate* in Neh 1:9) that are in Hebrew called קצה *katseh* [*qātseh*],[21] which always means the end, the outermost part of a thing. Consequently, in the quoted passage of Psalm 19 in its Hebrew text, Holy Scripture expresses the popular opinion: "The sun comes from one end of the Heavens and runs to the other end." Since the people do not grasp the circular shape of the sky [*rotunditatem minime aspiciens*], they imagine [*sibi fingit*] that the sky has two ends. This opinion is confirmed by their eyes, since they believe that one end is where the sun rises, and the other where the sun, tired of its course, withdraws at nightfall. Even some Church Fathers have shared this popular view and have attributed a hemispherical shape to the sky. The other words, which mention "no one can hide from its heat" explain that the sun's warmth penetrates everything, but they also function as a popular and unscientific expression, but I will not dwell on that.

Rather, I want to cite what is said in the abovementioned passage of Ecclesiastes (Eccl 1:5–6) according to the Hebrew text about the sun. For here we read: ואל מקומו שואף *veel me Komo scioeph* [*waʾel məqômô šôʾēp*].[22] This means: "the wind longs for its place or blows [*anhelat*] to its place." From this we see that the text does not describe literally [*proprie*], but figuratively—for example, as if the sun lived, as if it moved and hurried, panting from running, to a place determined as its goal. Therefore, Nicholas of Lyra comments about the words: "the sun rises and sets" thus: "as it appears to the eye." Likewise, the narration of the famous miracle [*prodigium*] of the sun that answered the prayer of Joshua, offers us expressions that the Holy Spirit has used—not to describe the real qualities of the event, but as they appear to our eyes

---

21. [Muratori's transliteration. In parenthesis the contemporary transliteration.]

22. [Muratori's transliteration. In parenthesis the contemporary transliteration.]

[*non qualia revera sunt, sed qualia oculis nostris apparent*]. [229] In Joshua 10:12, the words of this military leader are quoted: "Move not, o Sun, toward Gabaon, nor thou, o moon, toward the valley of Ajalon"[23] or, as others translate "above Gabaon and above the valley of Ajalon." Since the Earth is small in comparison with the sun, and since Gabaon and Ajalon valley are insignificant points on this globe, how could the sun be commanded not to move, or (according to the Hebrew) to remain silent and to stop above Gabaon and above Ajalon valley? Can the enormous solar sphere, which according to the assumption of the most distinguished astronomers is ten thousand times bigger than the whole Earth, even react to this tiny point [*huic puncto respondere potest immanis solis globus*]? Joshua seems to express himself in colloquial language, for to our eyes it appears as if the sun is a small disk that moves through a small space in the sky. Further, it is then said: "So the sun stood still in the midst of Heaven."[24] But the celestial orbits, if we want to express ourselves exactly, have neither a center nor an end; for how can one think of a real center and real ends in a spheric body or in a circular path or line? Therefore, one must also explain these words from popular imagination and colloquial language. To the eye, that place in the sky seems to be a center, which is equally far away from sunrise and the sunset. The narration is finally closed with these words: "There was not before nor after so long a day."[25] It would be ridiculous if one wanted to understand these words literally and claim that there has never been a longer day in the history of the world than this one. Those who have been in the polar regions know that the sun shines longer there, and that there are indeed longer days. Yet, Holy Scripture was based on the understanding and knowledge [*ad intellectum et scientiam*] of the Jewish people. To this uneducated people, the effects of the sun in the polar regions were unknown, and the Holy Spirit did not want to reveal it to them, since he is only concerned with what is useful and not with satisfying vain human curiosity.

According to what has been said, and since it is clear from so many examples that Holy Scripture not infrequently but preferably uses a

23. [*Douay-Rheims*, 234.]
24. [Jos 10:13; *Douay-Rheims*, 234.]
25. [Jos 10:14; *Douay-Rheims*, 234.]

language commonly known to the people when it describes celestial bodies, something already stated by Augustine in his *Questions on Genesis*,[26] and which also other Church Fathers thought: [230] It is neither imprudent nor unsophisticated [*neque temere, neque imperita*] to take passages of Holy Scripture which speak of a movement of the sun in a figurative [*figurate*] sense and to explain them metonymically [*per metonymiam*], so that Holy Scripture in these passages does not signify what things are [*non quae sint*], but how they appear to us [*sed quae appareant*], and that it expresses true facts [*vera facta*] in colloquial and imprecise idioms [*per improprias vulgi phrases*]. One should therefore not give these passages a forced, unusual, or absurd interpretation, as is suggested by as many reasons as examples. If then, by such a well-balanced method of interpretation [*aequam interpretationem*], Holy Scripture is freed from and preserved from all suspicion of error and falsehood, and the dignity and credibility of divine history are thereby secured, I do not see why we would want to dispute this view of the astronomers with uncertain passages that can easily be explained differently, or even accuse these scientists together with others of impiety [*impietatis*]. Certainly, this hypothesis is not certain; it is not established by any demonstrative evidence; perhaps it could even be in some parts replaced by the Tychonian[27] system; but it is nevertheless plausible [*verisimilis*] and according to general assumption quite suitable to explain the movements of the celestial bodies and to reject a lot of superfluous hypotheses. The explanations of Holy Scripture that contradict this hypothesis are neither certain nor obvious enough

---

26. [Muratori means Augustine, *Quaestionum in Heptateuchum Libri Septem* (PL 34), bk. 1, ch. 39 (available through www.augustinus.it) where he gives a summary of his view on accommodation: "Verba haec si non dubitantis quid duorum potius eventurum sit, sed irascentis et minantis accipiamus, nulla quaestio est. More quippe humano Deus in Scripturis ad homines loquitur, et eius iram noverunt sine perturbatione eius intellegere qui noverunt. Solemus autem etiam sic minaciter loqui: Videamus si non tibi facio, aut: Videamus si non illi fecero, et: Si non potuero tibi facere, vel: Sciam, id est, hoc ipsum experibor, utrum non possim; quod cum minando non ignorando dicitur, irati apparet affectus, sed perturbatio non cadit in Deum. Mos autem humanae locutionis et usitatus est, ut humanae infirmitati congruit, cui Deus coaptat locutionem suam." Source: https://www.augustinus.it/latino/questioni_ettateuco/index2.htm]

27. [The cosmological system of Tycho Brahe (1546–1601).]

to eliminate by their apparent truth the plausibility [*veritas nutantem istius verisimilitudinem suo pondere aperte prosternat*]. Although some have asserted that "every passage of Scripture must be understood in its literal and proper meaning as long as no contradiction arises from such an explanation, either with other teachings of Holy Scripture, which are just as certain or even more certain, or with a decision of the pope, or with a doctrine that derives clearly and distinctly from the light of reason,"[28] I confess I do not know how such a wide and general principle could be correctly applied. Certainly, we must, as much as possible, retain and seek to determine the literal meaning [*litteralem proprium Scripturae sensum*] of Holy Scripture. Yet, there are countless passages, expressions, and words that neither a doctrine of faith, nor a decision of the Church, nor the light of natural reason contradicts. Nevertheless, they are not understood in the literal and proper sense, neither by the Church Fathers, nor by other Catholic commentators. There is consequently good reason to explain things differently than they appear *prima facie*, but there must be a very probable and plausible reason [*probabilior ac verisimilior*] for this that can be taken from the liberal sciences [*liberalibus disciplinis*], from secular history, from the customs of peoples, and from other even less reliable [231] sources. Nevertheless, it is crucial that this interpretation does not do violence to the text [*sit non violenta*] but follows naturally and has been applied and approved also for other passages.

When Must We Accept the Proper, Literal Sense in Holy Scripture and When Are We Allowed to Use Another Way of Interpretation?

In order to clarify some of my remarks, I would like to remind theologians that the literal meaning of Holy Scripture, in so far as it is distinguished from the mystical meaning, is either proper or figurative.

---

28. [Muratori obscures the source for his quotation, possibly because it is from the standard astronomy textbook of the time, namely Giovanni Riccioli, *Almagestum novum astronomiam veterem novamque complectens*, vol. 2 (Bononiae: Haeredis Victorii, 1651), lib. IX, sect. 4, num. 9, 494. On Riccioli, see Alfredo Dinis, "Giovanni Battista Riccioli and the Science of His Time," in *Jesuit Science and the Republic of Letters*, ed. Mordechai Feingold (Boston: MIT Press, 2002), 195–224].

On the Exegesis of Scripture and the Copernican System 225

According to Augustine and several others, one and the same passage of Holy Scripture can have multiple literal meanings. Others, on the other hand, maintain that it can have only one. It seems, however, that both are right and that both views are easily reconcilable. It must be assumed that the Holy Spirit wanted to express only one literal meaning (not excluding the mystical meaning) in every passage of Holy Scripture, either in proper or figurative words. Yet because the words of Holy Scripture are sometimes obscure in relation to the literal sense and can be interpreted in different ways, and because it is not seldom uncertain whether they are to be understood literally or figuratively, one may also use various literal explanations for such a passage [*diversas propterea litterales interpretationes*]. Each of these explanations, if it is not artificial or forced, if it does not contradict other teachings of Holy Scripture, tradition, and the lights of reason, can be considered appropriate, can be approved, or even tolerated [*convenire et laudari, ac tolerari*]. For as long as it is not determined [*quamdiu non constet*] what meaning the Holy Spirit intended in such a passage and as long as its single meaning is not evident, how can it be forbidden for us to explain the same passage in several ways, if this is done with due diligence [*religiose*]? Moreover, we maintain that those passages of Holy Scripture that refer to the doctrine of faith and morals can only have one [*uno dumtaxat modo*] and not several different literal meanings [*neque plures pati posse litterales sensus*]. After all, the Church has come to know the correct meaning that God has inserted in those passages, from God Himself, and has transmitted to us through tradition and the unanimous consensus of the Church Fathers. Therefore, it is also forbidden to deviate in the explanation of such passages from the Church, tradition, and Church Fathers. However, in other passages of Holy Scripture that do not contain any doctrine of salvation, and whose meaning has not already been established or is obscure and allows several literal explanations, the view of St. Augustine can be applied: namely, that one and the same passage allows for several literal explanations that can and must be tolerated. Here the laws [232] of healthy [*sanioris*] criticism have to be applied. If, however, the *prima facie* meaning of a passage, although it does not violate a doctrine of faith and morals and does not contradict sound reason, does *not* harmonize well with other plausible [*verisimilibus sententiis*] teachings from experience, physics, geography, astronomy, history, logic, and other sciences, but can be brought easily into harmony with them by showing its figurative meaning [*vel figuram aliquam illi ostendendo*], supplying something lost, or providing an explanation of something obscure—then one can assume also other literal interpretations that are equally probable and tolerable.

We are therefore not obliged to stop at the proper, literal meaning of a scriptural passage and may instead prefer the figurative literal meaning of it, if there is an acceptable reason to prefer this rather than that meaning, if other similar passages allow a similar explanation, or even if such an explanation is not disputed by the Church Fathers and does not deviate from clearer passages of Holy Scripture, from the articles of faith, or from sound reason. For this does not mean to transform the historical, literal sense into allegories [*non in allegorias historicum litteralem sensum deflectere*], but to give Holy Scripture a true historical and literal meaning that suits the matter and manner of the prophets. I will give only one example. Of the fall of the city of Jerusalem, our divine master said beforehand that not one stone would be left upon another (Lk 19:44). Everybody must grasp immediately that the literal and proper meaning of these words is that the walls and buildings of this city will be destroyed and razed to the ground, so that no stone would be left connected with another. Nothing prohibits us assuming that this really happened after the famous war and victory of Titus. This meaning does not contradict other passages of Holy Scripture, nor the tradition of the Church Fathers, nor the decrees of the Roman popes or the councils. It also does not contradict the light of reason [*naturali lumini*]. After all, the Romans could have easily executed this plan had they desired it. Moreover, according to historical records and the Church Fathers, Jerusalem was so heavily destroyed, even razed to the ground, that not a trace of a habitable city was left. Christ had also predicted that in the temple in Jerusalem "there shall not be left a stone upon a stone that shall not be destroyed."[29] That this prophecy was fulfilled is testified by history. [233] The victorious army has destroyed the giant stones of this colossal building and stolen the iron and lead

---

29. Mt 24:2 (*Douai-Rheims*, 32) and Mk 13:2.

that kept these stones together. Not even a trace of this famous temple remained, for even the foundations were plowed over by Turnus Rufus so that nothing remained intact, and truly no stone was left upon the other (although this story is not very probable). It therefore does not contradict truth but comes close to it if one believes that the whole city suffered great devastation. Indeed, if one wants to follow the rules we have established above about the veracity of historical events, then we must believe this account without doubt.

Nevertheless, it is hard to believe that the Romans had enough time [*otii*] to utterly destroy such a great city with all its foundations. After all, Josephus Flavius reports in his book *De bello judaico* in bk. 7, ch. 1[30] that the towers that stood in front of the others and were a part of the western ring wall, were not destroyed. Accordingly, one can give up the proper literal meaning that was presented at first, and give the words of our Savior another meaning, namely a literal and historical and thus much more plausible meaning. He spoke according to the common usage and expressed himself hyperbolically in the words: "not one stone shall be left upon another," to indicate that the city would be destroyed from the ground up, that its devastation would be horrendous, unheard of, and terrible beyond all measure. This prediction was completely fulfilled and cannot be doubted. Therefore, we have to inquire why one could not permit astronomers to deviate in certain passages of Holy Scripture from the *prima facie* meaning, especially if a similar explanation of other, quite similar passages of Holy Scripture is not only not censored but approved. After all, according to the general assumption of the astronomers, more reasons speak in favor of the Copernican rather than the popular view [*vulgari sententiae*] and these more plausible arguments suggest that the explanation the astronomers gave of the scriptural passages should be preferred or at least tolerated. We must, however, see that through this method the integrity of the literal meaning of those scriptural passages is protected [*litteralem sensum in iis scripturae locis intactum custodiri*], through which also the miracle

---

30. [Muratori must mean ch. 1 since there is no ch. 18. Reporting that three towers were spared, see Flavius Josephus, *De bello judaico*, bk. 7, 1. Josephus, *The Jewish War, Volume III: Books 6–7*, trans. H. St. J. Thackeray, Loeb Classical Library 203 (Cambridge, MA: Harvard University Press, 1928), 307f.]

of Joshua can be explained. However this question may be decided, it is certain that the Church requires in these same matters [234] nothing more from exegetes than to keep every suspicion of error and fallacy [*omnis suspicio falsitatis ac erroris*] from Holy Scripture. This happens through reasonable and plausible interpretations [*commodas ac verisimiles interpretationes*] in which the more plausible explanation is always preferred to the less plausible, although the latter does not have to be rejected outright. All this, however, the followers of the Copernican system believe they have achieved. Whether this has in fact been done is for prudent scholars to judge until the Church—should the most holy religion consider it useful and necessary to do so [*sit tamen id facere aut utile sit, aut necessarium*]—finally decides this controversy.[31]

Nevertheless, one cannot object that it cannot be strictly demonstrated [*demonstrative ostenditur*] that the Earth really rotates daily, and that therefore this view should be rejected and instead the old and common view of the movement of the sun be maintained. For not all scriptural explanations may be rejected because there is no demonstrative evidence available. Otherwise, the commentaries of the Church Fathers and other writers would have to be rejected, since they often give different and completely contradictory explanations about such passages. Then, however, one can also keep with a good conscience the Ptolemaic or Tychonian view, but in such a way that one considers them not belonging to the faith [*ad fidem pertinere nondum dicatur*] and consequently considers their rejection not as heretical [*neque haeresis postuletur contraria sententia*]. Although the proofs for the Copernican system are not demonstrative, they are nevertheless of such a nature that they make the meaning of the abovementioned passages of Holy Scripture doubtful, and at the same time show by means of a plausible and probable [*ipsum verisimili ac probabili*] explanation that they are not contradicting them. Yet, what if this proof could be achieved one day by astronomers and philosophers? Would it not then be obvious that the explanation given is not only tolerable and suitable, but even necessary? Does one not see how extremely dangerous [*periculosissimum*] and alien it would be for the very foundation

---

31. [Muratori's view seems to be that the Church should not at all decide this question.]

[*institutione*] of the Church, if she today proclaimed something as part of the faith, but can no longer do it tomorrow [*velle id nun pertinere ad fidem, quod cras pertinere non possit*]? After all, faith and stability of doctrine in the Church of Christ cannot depend on human experience! Elsewhere we have already seen that, according to Augustine, even the ecumenical councils cannot decide with reliability things that can turn out differently by new experiences [*definire non posse, quae e novis experimentis aliter se habere deprehendere possint*]. Perhaps one will object that it will never be possible to invent a demonstrative proof for the Copernican view. Well, perhaps that is so. [235] Perhaps one will never find such a proof because of the difficulty of the matter, but by no means because a clear divine revelation has ruled out any hope for such a discovery. Also, the Ptolemaic and Tychonian systems have hitherto no demonstrative foundation and face even greater difficulties than the Copernican system. In the meantime, therefore, a reasonable person will suspend judgment and not force an interpretation upon the passages of Holy Scripture that accuses a contrary view of heresy or atheism [*impietatis insimules*]. For this is also against the spirit of the Church [*contra Ecclesiae ipsius mentem*], whose moderation in such controversies is proved by many ancient documents, which I will discuss in more detail in the following chapters.

INDEX

Abyssinia, 136
Adam, 30, 38
affections, 65, 67, 117
   disordered, 118
   as source of error, 116
Africa, 136
Alexander the Great, 215
ambiguity, 164, 189
Ambrose, Saint, 31
Ambrosiana Library, 2
Amsterdam, 42
Anabaptists, 135, 150
angels, 31, 118, 203, 205–6
Antarctic, 216
Antwerp, 42
Apollinarius, 200
arbitrariness
   in doctrine, 162, 170
arbitrator
   for Scripture interpretation, 142, 148–49
Arcesilaus, 58
Arctic, 216
Arianism, 95
Aristotle, 3, 16, 116, 213
Arminianism, 11, 23, 151
Arminius, Jacobus, 169
Asia, 95
astronomy, 212, 213, 220, 222–23, 227–28
asylum, 122
atheism, 152, 223
Atlas, 219
audacity, 137, 143, 146, 169, 195
Augustine, St., 11, 12, 28, 31, 42, 43, 44,
   45, 49, 55–57, 60, 86–109, 155, 160,
   163–65, 171, 210, 216, 229
authority, 157, 173, 192
   abuse of, 195
   of antiquity, 160–163, 179

assent to, 155
credibility of, 155, 158
deceptive human, 86
delicate nature of, 192
divine, 82, 90
extremism and, 194
false, 157
flattery and, 194
general welfare and, 193
harmony with reason, 158
limits of church, 192–94, 197–98, 200
of the mind, 186
of numbers, 165
principle of, 15, 18, 70, 71, 73, 76, 86, 93
reason and, 157
stability of, 169
to define a dogma, 196

Babylonian empire, 218
Bacchini, Benedetto, 2
barbarians, 155
Bayle, Pierre, 12
beauty, 59, 100
belief, 130, 137, 139, 144, 155, 184
   blind, 155
   explicit, 186, 198
   prudent, 98
   rational defense of, 87
   and trust in church teachings, 18
   without intrinsic proofs, 90
   without reason, 90
   without reasons, 86
Bellarmine, Robert, St., 140
Benedict XIV, Pope, 7, 9
Bignon, Jean Paul, 13
body, human, 60
   influence on mind, 113
   weakness of, 113

Brahe, Tycho, 223, 228–29
Brahmans, 125

Calvin, John, 104, 151–53, 169
Calvinism, 11, 19, 30, 103, 135, 145, 157, 159, 169, 199
Capri, 53
Carneades, 58
caution
  in search for truth, 66
celibacy, 31
Celsus, 102
censorship, 8, 13, 23, 27
Chaldeans, 125
Chinese, 125
Christocentrism, 9
church
  accused of defection from truth, 144
  arbiter of interpretation, 153
  arbitrator of interpretation, 142, 148, 149
  custodian of true doctrine, 175–76, 178–79, 192
  decision power to define dogma, 188
  decision power withheld, 188
  definition of, 140
  discernment of theological opinions, 179
  doctrinal error and, 141
  extension of decision power, 186
  infallibility, 18, 22
  limitations of her authority, 21, 22, 23, 25
  notes of, 142
  right to interpret revelation, 199
  as rock, 158
  stability of teachings, 142
  truthfulness of, 147
  universality of, 166
Church Fathers, 20, 23, 25, 27, 31, 32
church history
  church teachings, 19
  definitive, 20, 29
  as a theological discipline, 22
Cicero, 130, 183, 213
Clement of Alexandria, 125, 164
clergy
  authority of, 96
  common sense, 78
  pastors and shepherds, 85

Commonwealth, Catholic, 210
Commonwealth, Christian, 199, 202
concepts, darkness of, 124
concupiscence, 30, 117
confession, sacrament of, 56
conscience
  erring, 128
Constantinople, 203
Copernicanism
  plausibility of, 223
Copernicus, Nicolaus, 6, 13, 24, 25, 32, 37, 213, 220, 227–29
councils, 107
credibility, 76. *See also* faith; authority; clergy; doctrine; *motiva credibilitatis*; reason; revelation; trust; witnesses
credulity, 27
creeds, 107
criteria of truth, 65, 66
criticism, 14, 72, 97, 101–3, 189, 212, 225
curiosity, 189
Cusa, Nicholas of, 213

David, King, 129, 218
deception, 116
deism, 11
demonstration, 19
denunciation, 21
Descartes, Rene, 5, 15, 38, 63
development of doctrine. *See* dogma
devotio moderna, 4
discernment, 208
discipline, 22
dissimulation, 178
doctrine
  age of, 160–63
  arbitrary interpretation of, 180
  Catholic teachings, 191, 201
  certainty of, 148
  change of, 147
  classes of, 184
  comprehension of, 172
  contrary to tradition, 173
  credibility of, 180
  discipline and, 22
  obedience and, 185
  origin of, 158
  private interpretation, 148, 189

Index

stability of, 159, 162, 166, 169, 178
transcending reason, 173
doctrines. *See also* opinions, theological
   difference between
   certain and uncertain, 208
   mentioned in passing, 202
dogmas, 8
   ambiguous terminology, 189
   assent to, 186
   authentic interpretation of, 190
   auxiliary and fundamental proofs, 208–11
   church as custodian of apostolic faith, 197
   clarification of content, 188
   classification of, 187
   explanations of, 187
   interpretation of, 189
   irrefutable proof for, 206
   knowledge of, 186
   loci of, 173
   no invention of new, 197
   proofs can belong to faith, 204
   proofs for, 191
   proofs of different weight, 207
   as revealed, 187
   their reasonable explanation, 186
   unanimous tradition, 190, 196
Donatism, 28, 210
Dordt, Synod of, 106, 157
doubt, 63, 65–66, 68, 171
   aim of, 68
   cause of, 68
   comparison of Christianity with other religions, 80
   for illumination of faith, 81
   imprudent, 15, 67, 73, 79
   licit. *See* doubt, prudent
   limitation to learned people, 81
   limits of, 15, 65, 67, 69, 80
   obligation to doubt one's religion, 14–15, 70, 72–73
   obligation to refrain from doubting one's religion, 70, 79, 83
   of Christian religion, 79
   prudent, 1, 14, 15, 67–69, 72
   reasonable. *See* doubt, prudent
   for the sake of better insight, 68
Druids, 125
Drusius, John, 32

Egyptians, 125
enthusiasm, 21, 151
Epicurus, 16, 116
Erasmus, 1, 4
error, uncorrected, 204
eternal life, 53
Ethiopia, 136
Europe, 114
Eusebius of Caesarea, 164
Eutyches, 200
Eutychianism, 135
Eve, 30
evil
   acquired or natural, 57
   effects on will, 54
   seduction to, 55
Evodius, 57
exegesis, 26, 32, 75
   accommodation, 24
   and allegory, 31
   exegesis, biblical, 9, 83

facta dogmatica, 22
faith
   assent to, 16, 73, 97, 98
   blind, 3, 16
   credibility and, 91, 92, 93, 100
   explicit, 197, 198, 207
   gift, 81
   hiddenness of truth, 17
   humility and, 17
   intrinsic proofs and, 92
   in the person of Jesus Christ, 90, 99
   preceding rational insight, 106
   reason and, 14, 27
   reasonable, 130
   understanding and, 97without reasons, 95
fallibility. *See also* infallibility, ecclesial: fallible
fasting, 22
Feijoo, Benito, 3
fideism, 5
Fontanini, Giusto, 11
France, 13, 41, 125
freedom
   to doubt, 19, 70
   from error, 158

freedom (*cont.*)
  honest, 185
  immodest, 184
  limitations of, 26
  of the mind, 186
  reasonably restraining, 184
  religious, 27
  of research, 14, 20, 26, 51, 54, 63, 80
  restrained, 189
  as a right, 186
  to proclaim truth, 26
  of speech, 26
  of speech, excessive, 184
  in theology, 185, 186, 201
  of thought, 23, 183, 185, 191, 192
  tyranny and, 194
  unrestrained, 184
freedom of thought unrestricted, 152
freemasonry, 8

Gabaon, 222
Galilei, Galileo, 13, 25, 220
Genesis, book of, 213
genius, 125, 127
geography, 212
geometry, 119
grace, 17, 30–31
  prevenient, 135
Greece, 95, 172, 217
Greeks, 125
Gregory of Valentia, 191
Grotius, Hugo, 32

Hegesippus, 216
heliocentrism, 24
heresy, 56
heretics, treatment of, 26
hermeneutics
  allegorical meaning, 31
  of church documents, 20, 22, 31
  figurative meaning, 25
  literal meaning, 25
  of Scripture, 23, 25
  of suspicion, 23
hierarchy, 140
holiness
  of Christian teachings, 82
Horace, 41
Huet, Pierre-Daniel, 5, 36, 38–39

humans
  as rational beings, 61
humility, 5, 16–17

ideas, innate, 71, 111
idolatry, 148, 164, 200
Ignatius of Antioch, St., 165, 179
ignorance, 16, 53, 58, 111, 113, 119, 121
  as evil, 53
  due to bodily weakness, 113
  due to lack of education, 113
  innate, 112, 114
imprudence, 146
Indians, 125
infallibility, 141–45, 148–49, 154–56, 158, 168–69, 182, 188
  papal, 10
ingenium, 125, 127, 132, 135, 138, 142, 144, 148, 150, 154, 157, 160–62, 167–69, 172, 181, 183–84, 186, 188–92, 195, 209–10
Innocent III, pope, 203, 205
innovation, 138, 144, 152, 158, 160–62, 164, 168, 179–80, 199–200
Inquisition, 24, 29
intellect, 136
  progress of, 136
  slavery to perverse will, 117
  weakness of, 118, 138
Irenaeus, St., 179
Isaiah, prophet, 107
Islam, 15, 28, 69, 73, 76, 80–81

James, St., 128
Jansenism, 4, 22, 104
Jerome, St., 108, 216
Jerusalem, 226
Jesus, 135, 136, 139–43, 145, 147, 152, 159–66, 169, 171–72, 174–75, 177–80, 182
  as infallible teacher, 162
Jesus Christ, 74–77, 93, 102
John the Apostle, St., 175
John of Thessalonica, 205–6
Josephus Flavius, 227
Joshua, 213, 221–22, 228
Judaism, 15, 69, 73, 75, 80–81, 87, 94, 132, 172, 217, 222
  hatred of, 75
judgment
  based on false principles, 119
  faculty of, 115, 118–19

failure of, 122
false object of, 122
impeded by ignorance, 121
and opinion of learned men, 121, 138
of submission to the Church, 147
principles of, 120
uncertainty of, 151
justification, 199
Justin Martyr, St., 172

Karlstadt, Andreas, 150
Kempis, Thomas à, 4
knowledge, 130
certainty of, 118
dangerous forms of, 53
deception by others, 114
of divine nature, 119
illuminating the mind, 59
of the infinite, 119
limitations of, 58
means of, 114
of probabilities, 118
scrutiny of authorities, 119
of self, 110
senses and, 111
of true religion, 61

Lactantius, 58, 126
Lateran Council IV, 203
learning
and the good, 57
Leclerc, Jean, 11–13, 16, 18–19, 28–31, 35, 37, 42–46, 49, 87, 90, 92, 94–95, 98, 101, 105, 154–58, 160, 162–65, 184
liberalism, 2, 9
limits of church authority. *See* authority
liturgy, 7, 9
loci theologici, 173
Louis XIV, king, 13, 41
love, 116
love of the good innate, 54
innate desire, 53
Luke, evangelist, 215, 217
lust, 30, 53, 55, 117
Lutheranism, 11, 19, 135, 157, 159
Luther, Martin, 150, 152–53, 168, 169

Manichaeans, 88–89, 92, 96, 101, 105–6, 110
Marcion, 200
martyrs, 83

Mary, Mother of God, 7
Immaculate Conception, 8, 22
mathematics, 212
Matthew, evangelist, 141
Maurists, 2
mercy, 141
method, theological, 154
Milan, 2
mind, 135
affections and, 115, 117
authority of the, 186
Catholic, the, 188
creative, 199
excitement of as source of error, 116
images in the, 115
imagination, 114–16
lack of moderation, 191
limitations of, 118
memory, 114, 116
narrowness of, 119
philosophical bias, 116
proud, 183
restraining the, 110, 183
sharpness of, 111, 118, 119, 121
slavish, 184
temptations for the, 116
undecided, 136
weakness of, 114
miracles, 31, 75–77, 82, 93, 99, 158, 160–61, 164
Modena, 2, 10, 13, 26, 28, 35, 50
moderation, 1, 4, 55, 193
of the mind, 110
Mohammed, 76–77
Monothelitism, 135
monsters, 124
Moses, 76–77
motiva credibiliatis, 12, 16, 83, 90–94, 98, 110, 133, 135, 139, 151
murder, 122

natural laws, 66
natural rights, 66–67
Nestorianism, 135
Netherlands, 42
Nicholas of Lyra, 221
notes, theological, 27, 184
novelty. *See* innovation

obedience, 185
obiter dicta, 202
Oecolampadius, 150
Olympus, 219
opinions
    delirious, 152
    on doctrine, 136, 138
    foolish, 112
    preconceived, 149
    about Scripture, 138
    theological, 188, 201
    of theological schools, 188
    tolerated, 202
Origen, 102

paganism, 73, 87, 94, 106, 163–64
parents, 95–97
passions, 16, 195
    of the soul, 144
Paul, St., 126, 137, 180, 217
Pelagianism, 29–30
Pelagius, 105
Peripatetics, 54
persecution, 178
Persians, 125
Pétau, Denis, 181
Petronius, 215
Phereponus, 86, 90, 92, 94–101, 103–7
    and Leclerc, Jean, 169, 181
Phoenicians, 125
physics, 118–19, 123, 212
Plato, 16, 116
Plutarch, 213
Polycarp, St., 165, 179
pope, office of, 9, 22
    limitations, 22
    primacy, 22
popes, 174
Preadamites, 151
predestination, 101, 104–5
prejudice, 3, 65, 128, 149
pride, 128
principia per se nota, 14, 67
prophecies, 75, 76
prophecy, 108
Protestantism, 145–46
    rule of faith, 145
    sola scriptura, 145

prudence, 137
    moderator of doubt, 67
    in theology, 21
Ptolemy, 214, 228–29
public good, 122
Puritanism, 151
Pyrrhus, 58

Quakerism, 145, 151

rashness, 21
reason
    and authority, 131
    dictates of, 18
    faculties of, 12, 14, 16, 71
    first principles of, 130
    foolish, 75
    grace and, 17, 101, 104, 106
    harmony with authority, 158
    harmony with faith, 133, 137, 148–49, 158, 172, 228
    illuminating faith, 89, 92, 108
    immoderate praise of, 169
    impeded by memory and imagination, 115
    limitations of, 16–17, 88, 110, 118, 168
    moderation of, 127, 183
    pleasure and, 52
    presumptuous, 182
    rights of, 147
    rule of, 116
    as sole interpreter of Scripture, 154, 158, 169
    supremacy of, 169
    unfit judge of doctrine, 152
    universal claim to, 142
    weakness of, 88, 110–11, 113, 126–27, 129, 132, 136–38, 144, 146, 148, 157, 168, 182
reasons
    extrinsic, 17, 83, 88, 91, 93, 96, 99, 110, 139, 177, 186
    intrinsic, 17, 19, 88, 91–92, 103, 118, 130, 139, 182
recta ratio, 149, 184–85, 190–91
religion
    choice of, 69–70
    contradictory to reason, 73, 76
    deceiving, 94

harmony of authority and reason, 16, 71, 82
inquiry about its divine origin, 72
knowledge of true, 61
moral teachings of, 77
search for true, 79
spread through the power of truth, 74
spread through violence, 74, 77
Republic of Letters, 116
research, moderation in, 55
revelation, 135, 136, 169, 171, 177, 182, 184
    certainty of, 137
    communication to humans, 88
    direct, 129
    language of, 214–15, 217
    reason and, 82
    secrecy, 129
    transmission channels, 182
    truthfulness of, 140
    understandability of, 132
Riccioli, Giovanni, 220, 224
right to investigate the truth, 80
Rimini, synod of, 176
Roman Army, 227
Romans, 125

Sacred Heart, 217
saints, 93
    veneration of, 31
salvation, 7, 19, 23, 30, 139, 157, 159, 177, 182, 185, 192, 215
    outside the church, 19
Salvian, 72
scholasticism, 3, 29, 182, 188, 201
school opinions, 7. *See* opinions, theological science and church authority, 25
Scotus, Duns, 8
Scripture, 70, 75, 77, 89, 101, 103, 108–9, 117, 136–42, 144–51, 153, 174, 181, 187–91, 196–99, 201–3, 205, 207, 209–10, 212–14, 216, 218–20, 222, 224, 226–28
    absurd interpretation of, 223
    accommodation of, 172, 214, 222–23
    authority of Church Fathers for interpretation, 225
    canon of, 138
    church's authority over interpretation, 215
    distorted interpretation of, 172
    divine guidance of interpretation, 145
    divine origin of, 137
    figurative literal meaning, 226
    figurative meaning, 224
    inerrancy of, 199
    interpretation of, 154, 172, 177
    interpretation of figurative speech, 214–15, 219
    literal meaning, 224
    literal meaning, integrity of, 227
    literal reading, 221–22
    meaning of, 104
    mystical meaning, 224
    obscurity of, 146, 225
    plurality of literal meanings, 225
    private interpretation, 148, 157, 158
    proper interpretation, 212, 214
    proper literal meaning, 226
    proper meaning, 224
    quarrels over interpretation, 146, 225
    reasonable interpretations, 228
    as rule of faith, 18–19, 144–45
    sola scriptura, 150
    translations of, 137
    uncertainty of interpretation, 139, 145–46, 153, 158, 161
    use of hyperbole, 227
Scythians, 125
Seleucia, synod of, 176
senses, 111, 115, 118
Septuagint, 107–8
sexual desires, 77
Simon, Richard, 12, 35, 39
skepticism, 5, 12, 14–15, 58, 102, 127, 152
slavery, 117
Smyrna, 165
Socinianism, 11, 19, 135, 153, 159, 168, 169, 172
Socrates, 63
sorcery, 56
soul, 127
Spinoza, Baruch de, 168
Stephen, pope, 210
succession, apostolic, 93, 166
superstition, 1, 8, 10, 14, 19, 21, 29, 84, 95, 101, 184, 193
syncretism, 151, 159

Tacitus, 43
taste, good, 3
teachers, legitimacy of, 159
temerity, 170, 179, 182, 186, 189, 195
Tertullian, 216
testimony. *See* trust: in testimony of others
theologians, 91
   clergy, 84
   defense of the faith, 85
   their prudence, 212
   witness to rational faith, 84, 102
theological notes *de fide*, 8
theology
   dogmatic, 181–82
   positive, 29
thinking, act of, 111
Thomas Aquinas, St., 191
Tiberius, Emperor, 53
toleration, 11, 27
tradition, 173, 175, 200, 210
   age of, 176, 179
   custodian of true doctrine, 180
   foolish rejection of, 179
   necessity of, 176
   oral transmission, 174
   sacred, 71
   unanimous, 177, 179–80
traditionalism, 65
Trent, Council of, 30, 175
Troy, 158
trust
   in clergy without reasons, 98
   foolish, 74, 76
   in the opinion of learned men, 67–68
   in the opinion of unlearned men, 118
   in testimony of church, 94, 171, 185–86
   in testimony of others, 71, 76, 83
   unreasonable, 95

truth
   distinction from error, 112
   enciting will to evil, 57
   illuminating the mind, 57
   mixed with errors, 112
   never evil, 55–56
   possession of, 53
   search for, 61, 136, 144
   virtue of, 51
truths
   hierarchy of, 19
   order of, 59
   supernatural, 82, 88–89, 92, 102, 118, 133
tyranny, 194

understanding as wisdom, 60
uneducated mass, 89

Vincent of Lérins,, 192, 196, 210

welfare, 61
will
   desire for glory, 117
   desire for innovation, 117
   desire for lust, 117
   hedonism, 117
   perversity of, 117
witnesses
   credibility of, 68, 171
   harmony of, 166
worship, 186

zeal
   exaggerated, 21, 27, 29
   imprudent, 193, 195
   unreasonable, 193
Zwinglians, 150

Also in the Early Modern Catholic Sources series

~~

Jansenism: An International Anthology
Edited by Shaun Blanchard and Richard T. Yoder

Discourses on the State and Grandeurs of Jesus:
The Ineffable Union of the Deity with Humanity
Pierre de Bérulle
Translated by Lisa Richmond

A Defense of the Catholic Religion:
The Necessity, Existence, and Limits of an Infallible Church
Beda Mayr, OSB
Translated by Ulrich L. Lehner

On Slavery and the Slave Trade: De Iustitia et Iure,
Book 1, Treatise 2, Disputations 32–40
Luis de Molina, SJ
Translated by Daniel Schwartz and
Jörg Alejandro Tellkamp

Metaphysical Disputations III and IV:
On Being's Passions in General and Its Principles
and On Transcendental Unity in General
Francisco Suárez
Translated and annotated, with corrected Latin text,
by Shane Duarte

*Metaphysical Disputation II:
On the Essential Concept or the Concept of Being*
Francisco Suárez
Translated and annotated, with corrected Latin text,
by Shane Duarte

The Predestination of Humans and Angels:
Augustinus, *Tome III, Book IX*
Cornelius Jansen
Translated by Guido Stucco

The Catholic Enlightenment: A Global Anthology
Edited by Ulrich L. Lehner and
Shaun Blanchard

*Metaphysical Disputation I: On the Nature of
First Philosophy or Metaphysics*
Francisco Suárez
Translated and annotated, with corrected
Latin text, by Shane Duarte

On the Motive of the Incarnation
The Salmanticenses (Discalced Carmelites of Salamanca)
Translated by Dylan Schrader